"You Know We Belong to the Land"

THE CENTENNIAL HISTORY OF OKLAHOMA

Paul F. Lambert and Bob L. Blackburn

SERIES EDITOR: GINI MOORE CAMPBELL
EDITORIAL ASSISTANT: KATHERINE MCLEMORE

Oklahoma Horizons Series

For Debbie and Beau
—Bob Blackburn

For Judy and Matthew
—Paul F. Lambert

And for all the people of Oklahoma.

"You Know We Belong to the Land"
The Centennial History of Oklahoma

Dr. Willis J. Wheat

Colonel Martin A.
"Marty" Hagerstrand

A Special Tribute

By J. Blake Wade

Throughout my career, I have had the privilege of working with many remarkable individuals. None of them have been more outstanding than Colonel Martin A. "Marty" Hagerstrand and Dr. Willis J. Wheat. Both of these men, now deceased, loved Oklahoma, gave great service to their state, and chaired the Oklahoma Centennial Commission. Hagerstrand was born in Chicago in 1911 while Wheat was born in Oklahoma City in 1926, but they were similar in many ways. Both men served their nation in the Pacific theater during World War II, and they were effective planners, dedicated volunteers, and inspirational leaders.

Col. Hagerstrand first visited Oklahoma in 1946 when he married Tahlequah native Marion Brown. She was an officer in the Women's Army Corp, and they met in New Guinea while both were serving their country. Hagerstrand continued his military career, eventually serving in Europe and the Pentagon before retiring in 1960. Marty and Marion moved to Tahlequah and he quickly became involved in preserving the heritage of the Cherokee people, founding the Cherokee National Historical Society and leading the establishment of the Cherokee Heritage Center in 1967, the creation of the Trail of Tears pageant at TSA-LA-GI theater, and building the Cherokee Nation Museum in 1975.

Hagerstrand also became active statewide, working with the zeal of a convert to preserve the history of his adopted state. To learn more about western Oklahoma, he took a 2,500 mile trip to learn about every county in that part of the state. In addition to serving as president of the Five Civilized Tribes Museum in Muskogee, he chaired the Oklahoma Arts Council, the Capital Preservation Commission, and the Capitol Dome Task Force. During the last 18 years of his life he was an active director of the Oklahoma Historical Society, serving as president of that organization from 1990 to 1992. He also accepted appointment as Chairman of the Oklahoma Centennial Commission at age 87. Tragically, he died in a traffic accident on July 6, 1999. Col. Hagerstrand was a tireless volunteer, an effective planner, and an inspirational leader.

Hagerstrand was succeeded as chair of the Oklahoma Centennial Commission by Dr. Willis J. Wheat. After serving in the United States Army during World War II in New Guinea and the Philippines, he earned bachelor's and master's degrees at Oklahoma State University. Four years later, in 1954 Wheat was named dean of what now is the Meinders School of Business at Oklahoma City University. During eight years of service, he established an MBA program, raised endowment funds to support the program, and earned a Doctorate degree in Public Administration from Pacific University.

Dr. Wheat then entered the banking business, serving as executive vice president for Banks of Mid-America from 1964 to 1987, pioneering the first Oklahoma bank-based credit card, directing a committee responsible for marketing the Visa credit card to banks worldwide, and introducing consumer certificates of deposit in Oklahoma. He also was an active trustee of Oklahoma City University and served as interim president of that institution in 1979 to see it through a severe financial crisis. He returned to OCU in 1987, serving five years as a professor of management and two years as dean of the business school. Working with university president Gerald Walker, Wheat established the first MBA programs in the Peoples Republic of China, Hong Kong, Malaysia, and Singapore. His appointment as chair of the Oklahoma Centennial Commission in 1999 was the culmination of decades of volunteer civic work. His outstanding work on behalf of Oklahoma continued until his death on June 10, 2006.

Oklahoma is indeed a better place because of the work of these talented and dedicated men.

J. Blake Wade

Oklahoma 1907-2007

By N. Scott Momaday

The Land

The first people to enter upon it
Must have given it a name, wind-borne and elemental,
Like summer rain.
The name must have given spirit to the land,
For so it is with names.
Before the first people there must have been
The profound isolation of night and day,
The blazing shield of the sun,
The darkness winnowed from the stars—
The holy havoc of myth and origin,
True and prophetic, and inexorable,
Like summer rain.

What was to become of the land?
What was the land to become?
What was there in the land to define
The falling of the rain and the turning of the seasons,
The far and forever silence of the universe?

A voice, a name,
Words echoing the whir of wings
Swelled among the clouds
And sounded on the red earth in the wake of creation.
A voice. A name.
Oklahoma.

Settlement

And there was the flow of migratory blood,
Rising from time and glacial mist
From the four directions,
Touching story and music to the Plains,
Red men dancing, chanting prayer:
    Give us the pounding hooves of horses and buffalo,
    Give us the plumage and paint of ceremony,
    Give us bravery, steadfastness, generosity, and virtue,
    Give us beauty. Give us the heart of hunting and roving.

Then came homesteaders in wagons,
Muledrivers with hammers and plows,
Cattlemen and sheepherders,
Pastors and schoolmarms,
Bankers and doctors and soldiers of fortune,
All bringing definition to the land,
All shaping a destiny, a geometry of camps within camps.
There came about a harvest of community,
An American story, a miracle play,
An enactment of civilization.
They came with the force and energy of driving rain.
Oklahoma.

Statehood

Along the old hunting trails
There sprang up towns and town squares,
The stark architecture of churches and cemeteries on the prairie,
The machinery of settlement and industry,
The stitching of railroads to the horizons.
All the rude and rustic monuments
That became the gleaming glass and metal of upstart cities,
And at last the immersion into a field of stars
On the unfurled flag of liberty and union.
The coalescence of hope and passage,
Of sacrifice and triumph,
A becoming as bold as thunder above a confluence of rivers,
Roaring between luminous banks of rain—
Oklahoma.

Foreword

By David L. Boren

No place is more American in its spirit and in its history than Oklahoma. Most nations are best described by what might be called tribal definitions. In general, a nation consists of a group of people who have for many centuries shared a common geographical area, a common language, a common religion, and a common culture. The United States eludes that definition. Americans have come from many parts of the globe. They are diverse and composed of people of different colors and races. This ethnically diverse group identifies with many different religions and has varied cultural perspectives.

Indeed, Americans are defined by the values and ideals which they share. Americans are committed to freedom in all of its forms— intellectual, religious, and economic. Americans believe in equal rights for all men and women and in the equal opportunity for all to develop the tools needed to live full lives.

It often has been said that the strength of a nation can be measured by the belief of its people in a better future. From the very beginning, Americans have worked to build a fuller life for the generations which would follow them. They have had the courage to dream and the perseverance to make those dreams come true.

As Oklahoma enters its second century of statehood, it has kept alive those values which define us as Americans. In fact, those who seek to revive the spirit and confidence of America need to look no further than Oklahoma to find that strength. Why is the example of Oklahoma so uniquely powerful? Perhaps it is the closeness of the state to its frontier heritage. Oklahomans alive today have heard the stories about the courage of those who confronted an undeveloped land from those who heard the firsthand memories of the pioneers themselves.

Perhaps the commitment to equal opportunity comes in part from the "land run" experiences. It was a questionably American experience. Men and women from all races and backgrounds lined up to wait for the signal that allowed all of them an equal chance to race to stake out farm lands or city lots where they would build new beginnings. Those who succeeded did so because of hard work and strength of character and not because of the social standing or wealth of their families from somewhere else.

In Oklahoma, ordinary men and women had a chance to make history. They came with little but their dreams and their tenacity. It was these strong men and women who would build a state where people still take care of each other. Rugged individualism and a spirit of community combined in a special way to build a state and create schools and universities as well as religions and charitable institutions of lasting importance. They built a state which nurtured leaders of national and international stature in the arts, sciences, and government.

Perhaps the commitment to respect the dignity of others and to conserve our environment comes from the state's Native American heritage. Conservation and environmentalism have their roots in the reverence which Native Americans have for the natural world. From the earliest days, they valued artistic expression and surrounded themselves with objects of beauty in items used in everyday life, from beaded clothing to decorated pottery and baskets.

The western tribes were pushed out of their hunting grounds by the pressure of settlements moving across America from the two coasts. Yet, they had the strength to endure in Oklahoma. The eastern tribes were pushed west in forced marches over the "Trail of Tears." Many died along the way, but once they settled in what is now Oklahoma, the survivors rebuilt their communities, schools, and political institutions. Today, tribal languages are preserved and taught in the state's educational institutions and important culture perspectives continue to flourish.

Long before statehood or the land runs in western Oklahoma, Native American tribal governments granted African Americans a wide range of political rights. Those who had recently been freed from slavery came to see Oklahoma as a place where they could build new lives for themselves. In Indian Territory they built communities of their own. The great writer, Ralph Ellison, described their aspirations in his essay "Going to the Territory."

The earliest Oklahomans of all races and backgrounds passed on enduring strength, mutual respect, and an undying sense of hope that were to be tested many times in the course of the state's first century. Terrible droughts and economic depression forced the migration of farmers and others to the west coast in the 1930s, though many would return to Oklahoma. Booms and busts in the oil and gas and other industries forced many businessmen and women to start over again more than once in the 1960s and 1980s. Natural disasters and a tragic bombing by domestic terrorists in the 1990s drew national attention to the speed with which Oklahomans reach out to help each other. Media commentators describing Oklahoma's spirit of community called Oklahoma "America's Heartland" just as they had once referred to Oklahoma's Will Rogers as "America's Conscience."

There is a statue of a pioneer nestled among tall buildings in the state's capitol city. At the base of it are words which describe the courage and future of pioneers who forged raging rivers and crossed limitless prairies without turning back. They speak of the schools and religious buildings, of the farms and fortresses the pioneers established, of the buildings they lifted into the sky, and the deep holes they drilled in oil-rich earth. The inscription ends by asking passersby, "Where else in a single life's span have men and women built so mightily?"

The question could be answered by saying that Oklahomans believe the best is yet to be. The greatness and strength of America continues to be measured by the nation's faith in its future. Its identity continues to rest upon its shared values and ideals.

It is indeed appropriate to conclude these words of introduction as they began. No place is more American in its spirit or in its history than Oklahoma.

David L. Boren

David L. Boren is the first person in state history to have served as a state legislator, Governor of Oklahoma, United States Senator from Oklahoma, and President of the University of Oklahoma.

Authors' Preface

When Blake Wade asked us to write the centennial history of our state, we had mixed emotions. On the one hand was the honor and privilege of contributing to a better understanding of what it means to be an Oklahoman. On the other hand was the challenge of how to accomplish that important task.

The first challenge was the story itself. If there is one word that describes Oklahoma history, it is diversity. We do not have a Plymouth Rock, an Alamo, or a Gold Rush to symbolize the beginning of a shared saga. Instead, we have a series of opening chapters, each overlapping the others, each adding an important line to the narrative but oftentimes running on parallel paths until converging in the distance. The result is a rich mixture that defies attempts to create a simple chronology or dominant story line.

The other challenge was how to distinguish this book from the excellent work of other historians such as Joseph B. Thoburn and E. E. Dale, Angie Debo and Muriel H. Wright, A. M. Gibson and Odie B. Faulk, or David Baird and Danney Goble. Through their skills of observation and synthesis, we have a deep reservoir of narrative histories that bridge the diversity of the story and offer an overview of the highs and lows that, taken together, make Oklahoma history so unique. One more narrative overview, we decided, would not add much to the understanding of our state.

As we considered our options, we noted the essential qualities needed in the book. To make the book accessible to the widest possible audience, we wanted the structure to revolve around stories, which, laid end on end, would paint a broader picture of the whole. To stand the test of time, we wanted to include not just the triumphs and stories of success, but also the challenges and human failings that have tested the fabric of our community. To capture the spirit of Oklahoma's youth, we wanted to emphasize the importance of individual action in America's last frontier where everyone came from someplace else and anyone could rise according to their own abilities and ambitions.

Our answer was a series of biographies, arranged in rough chronological order that would advance the story of Oklahoma through the lives of its people. That, of course, begged the question of which biographies to use. We decided we should not use a "who's who" list of the rich and famous, which would paint a false impression of ease and comfort. Instead, we labored over a list that we think represents the thematic, regional, and ethnic diversity of the state. Some stories will be familiar to many people; others will be new. Hopefully, all will add a piece to the puzzle that we call Oklahoma history.

The biographical structure, although strong on story, left us with gaps that needed to be bridged. We have attempted to fill in some of those gaps with sidebars, historical photographs, and historical sites that can be visited. Introductions by two of Oklahoma's most perceptive leaders, a foreword by University of Oklahoma President David Boren and a short essay by University of Tulsa professor James Ronda, set the stage for this work. Adding a spiritual element is a poem by one of Oklahoma's favorite sons, N. Scott Momaday. Still, some readers will not find their favorite stories or the people they admire the most. We hope they will understand the limits of this one work and the delicate balancing act in trying to cover the diversity of our story.

There have been many people who have contributed to this journey into Oklahoma history. We want to thank Blake Wade, director of the Centennial Commission, for trusting us with this responsibility. Others who have contributed to the task include Jim Argo, a gifted photo-journalist who opened his collections to us; Shannon Nance and Gini Campbell of the Oklahoma Heritage Association, who edited and published the book; and Sue Hale, Linda Lynn, and Mary Phillips of *The Oklahoman*, who made their archival collections accessible for research and photograph selection. We also want to recognize Betty Price and photographers Scott Cowen and John Jernigan of the Oklahoma Arts Council, who provided digital scans of art on display in the State Capitol, as did Senator Charles Ford, Pam Hodges, and photographers Stu Ostler and Travis Caperton. Mike Gonzales of the 45th Infantry Division Museum also provided valuable assistance. Many of the colorful images came from the Fred Wiemmer Collection at the State Historic Preservation Office. Finally, we want to thank our wives and families for giving up so many weekends and lost vacations as we worked on this labor of love. May the next 100 years be as momentous as the last.

Paul F. Lambert and Bob L. Blackburn

Finding Oklahoma

By James P. Ronda

In the blistering hot summer of 1990 my wife Jeanne and I moved from Ohio to Oklahoma. Our families had gone West once before–hers to Nebraska in 1877 and mine to Colorado in 1893. Their crossings had been hard. We thought ours would be easy. After all, in the highway atlas Oklahoma was just one page away from Ohio. Our first hint that things might not be quite what we expected came when an Ohio neighbor wondered how we would like Arizona. Tulsa/Tuscon—for him it was all just the Great American Desert. Isn't it really all the same in the vast American Outback, especially if you are looking from Youngstown, Ohio and the steel mills of the Mahoning Valley?

In the years since coming to Oklahoma I've struggled to make sense of my adopted state, my state of mind, and my own place on the southern Great Plains. I've read about it, taught it, and traveled over much of it. I came voluntarily and intend on staying indefinitely. This brief essay is a modest meditation on my search for Oklahoma and the sense of the plains. Someone once said that "the going is the goal." If I have not fully discovered the Oklahoma of my imagination, I treasure what I've encountered along the way. I've spent my professional life writing about the exploration of the American West. Now I was going to explore my piece of it. What I found is a simple truth. Oklahoma needs neither boosters nor bashers. This part of the Great Plains has had more than its share of that. It needs people who care about the place and can see it with fresh eyes. What follows is a deeply personal, on-the-road progress report from someone who loves this part of the world enough to have a lover's quarrel with it.

I grew up in suburban Chicago, in a place perfectly named Evergreen Park. This was the crabgrass frontier of the 1950s. Notice the color–green–and the dream of living in a park but working in the city. The names in my childhood geography were places like Ernest Hemingway's Oak Park and Al Capone's Cicero. My Mom came from a proper Oak Park doctor's family; my Dad grew to manhood on the mean streets of Cicero. But now in Oklahoma my world has names like Tahlequah, Oologah, and Tonkawa–all emblems of an enduring native presence on the plains. And because I'm interested in the way the potent mix of oil and cattle has shaped this end of the Great Plains, I've paid attention to towns like Slick, Seminole, Shidler, and Foraker. Those names–and the stories they tell–are a long way from Evergreen Park. And they are just as far from the fiery furnaces of the Mahoning Valley. On the highway atlas Oklahoma may be just a turned page from Ohio but a world away in so many other things.

As I soon learned, the contrasts between Ohio and Oklahoma are striking and instructive. They can teach you all about that elusive but very real sense of place, that sense of the plains. Once it was Ohio's big trees, now it is an ocean of grass. Once it was black soil, now it is red dirt. Once it was sky hemmed in by the horizon, now it is sky that reaches from horizon to horizon. Once it was the Great Lakes and the snow belt, now it is Great Plains weather and a weather-eye for super-cells that might become tornadoes.

Oklahoma looms large in my life; now it is the home place. But where is it on the American map? How much space does it occupy in our collective national memory? Calling it the Heartland doesn't change the reality that most folks on the two coasts think of the plains as fly-over country, the Big Empty. My guess is that until the Oklahoma City bombing in April, 1995, Oklahoma was nearly invisible, the most forgotten part of the forgotten plains. It was nowhere on the national evening news, and consistently overlooked even by the Weather Channel except in storm season. But I wanted to find that place, not the least of all because it had become home. Finding Oklahoma meant finding home. The search first led me to think about borders, the defining edges of our sense of place.

For Oklahoma's Great Plains experience perhaps the most important boundary has been the one we share with Texas. Of all our neighbors, Texas has been the most influential and perhaps the most troublesome. When I came to Oklahoma in 1990 the two states were still arguing about who would maintain a key highway bridge over the Red River. During the Civil War an army of Confederate Texans crossed the Red River and invaded Indian Territory. Some Oklahomans have been waiting for a chance to return the favor ever since. And searching for Oklahoma's border with Texas I quickly discovered the way traces of resentment can define a place. We resent Texas for its big, brash, boastful ways. Now and again we still envy Dallas for stealing a television show that should have been named Tulsa. And we might have a bit of anger over Houston for capturing all the oil companies that were once in Bartlesville and Tulsa. The Boomers and Sooners came from Kansas but in some way Oklahoma still defines itself in terms of is and is not Texas. You can't look at a map of Oklahoma counties without seeing Texas County in the Panhandle and recalling a time when this chunk of land was claimed by that other state. I quickly came to know that the joke about Texas as Baja Oklahoma was no joke at all! Long before coming to Oklahoma I learned that knowing places meant spending time there. You could begin in the library but at some point you needed to pull on a strong pair of boots and have what the Australians call a "walk-about." Lately I've been spending too much time at airports and on airplanes. In a Seattle hotel room or at that airport all travelers know as DFW you can lose track of the search for Oklahoma. So with the grass greening up in mid-April I thought it was time to take another look at my end of the plains. It was Jack Kerouac, Michael Wallis, and Willie Nelson who reminded me that being on the road was the best way to find the spirit of a place.

I wanted to travel the roads that branched off from William Least Heat-Moon's blue highways. I knew that Oklahoma could embrace Mozart and Shakespeare; I was looking for another kind of geography. So I headed north out of Tulsa into the Osage—the Big Open—the country of oil, cattle, Indians, ranchers, and lawyers. Tulsa calls itself Green Country but it is really the last gasp of the Ozark Plateau. On the Osage you know you are in the world of the plains. The trees give out and the grass takes over. Despite the Nature Conservancy's determination to call their part of the Osage the Tallgrass Prairie Preserve, this is mixed- grass country. The real tall grass prairies were in Abraham Lincoln's Illinois. The short grass—just beer can high—begins west of the I-35 line. The Osage is a landscape dotted with blackjack thickets, working oil wells, and, at least in the summer, countless head of cattle fattening for market. The rusting remains of half a dozen oil booms and busts litter the landscape, a reminder that this part of the plains had more roughnecks and pipe fitters than cowboys and cattle kings. Out of Pawhuska on a gravel road to Foraker I pulled over for a while, just looked around, and remembered what the poet Walt Whitman said long ago. Bound for Denver in 1879, Whitman said that the Great Plains was the most American of all our landscapes. With Whitman on my mind and in my mind's eye, what I saw on that lonely road were the plains fundamentals—earth, grass, and sky. The great dome of sky seemed to overwhelm the earth and make me feel properly small. Underfoot was dirt. We could politely call it soil but by any other name it was still dirt. And there was the sea of grass. Centuries of Great Plains adventurers talked about the ocean of grass that swept north from what is now Canada to the Red River and beyond. Now it exists only in memory and imagination. Except for some pieces of the

Osage and the Flint Hills we have transformed the waves of grass into squares of wheat and corn. Sky, earth, and grass: they are the holy trinity of the plains, the ground of our being. They built the stage for our dreams in dry places.

But those fundamentals I found on the Foraker road are only the stage. Alone or together they do not write the script or speak the lines or give meaning to it all. Oklahoma cannot be reduced to the sum of sky, earth, and grass. The words and meanings come to us in the stories we tell, the stories that live inside of us. The stories are beyond counting. They touch the strings of hope and plumb the depths of hatred and despair. They whisper promises of quick riches and weep over dispossession and death. But more than anything else, Oklahoma's plains experience has been shaped in the past century and a half by our journey stories. Whether we are natives or newcomers we have always been a people on the road. The Trail of Tears and the Interstate Highways are bookends to our history. The Chisholm Trail and I-40 are like the X that marks our spot. We talk about "Home, Sweet Home" but it is Route 66 and her sister roads that call us, lure us, and make us promises we know won't be kept but we go anyway. Oklahoma is the real crossroads, where a southbound highway splits a westbound road. Traveling the back roads you can trace all the passions and hopes of Chief John Ross and Geronimo, Satanta and Kicking Bird, Chitto Harjo, and Osage chief James Bigheart. And there is more to be seen and sensed out on the Foraker road. Here are all the churned up dreams and schemes of cowboys and cattle barons, tool pushers and oil gusher millionaires. Look around and every pump jack reminds you about how sudden, unpredictable oil wealth remade lives and sometimes shattered friendships. The names are legion and legend in the oil patch: J. Paul Getty, H. F. Sinclair, William G. Skelly, Frank Phillips, E. W. Marland, and James A. Chapman. Turn on the car radio and the air is filled with the voices of earnest evangelicals and fiery fundamentalists all giving directions to a life in glory land beyond the River Jordan. But in the here and now, Oklahoma is where southern Indians and their black slaves came as pioneers to a new country and built homes and towns with churches, schools, and the first printing press west of the Mississippi. And on Oklahoma prairies ex-slaves built towns like Langston, Red Bird, and Boley.

The view from the road reminded me that Oklahoma is a place of extremes. This is where the South meets the West with often explosive force. It is the boom and bust of oil, the violence of an F5 tornado, and some of the most spectacular, five-star political scandals in American history. From the road you could see the charred remains of Greenwood after the 1921 Tulsa Race Riot. You would not have to look far to see the wreckage of Osage lives shot, blown up, and poisoned by men eager to get their hands on black gold. And from the side of the road you might hear well-meaning talk about family and community but know that the state has an unenviable record for public health, education, and violence against women. It looks peaceful out here on the Foraker road, but don't be deceived. From Custer on the Washita to Tulsa 1921 and the Osage Murders this can be the dark and bloody ground. This always has been a rambunctious, violent, and uncertain place. Change is the one constant, the one unchanging thing. The house next door has neighbors one day and strangers the next. Quiet now, but on the southern Great Plains violence is just a thunderstorm or an angry word away.

Out on that road and under a lowering sky heavy with rain I began to find my sense of place, my sense of the plains. There is an invisible country here, a country sunk deep in memory. This is the landscape of half-remembered songs, snatches of stories, and bits of talk echoing in cafes and auction barns. If you have ears to hear this is what you can catch from Idabel to Boise City, from Bluejacket to Altus by way of Shawnee and Ponca City. It is a patchwork of names–family names, town names, pasture names, and names now slipping away. Out on the road this is the place where long forgotten voices still gather to sing and speak, to dance the dance of life on the stage we call Oklahoma.

James P. Ronda

James P. Ronda holds the H. G. Barnard Chair in Western American History at the University of Tulsa, is the author of numerous books and articles, and is a past president of the Western History Association.

"You Know We Belong to the Land"

The Centennial History of Oklahoma

Constructed as the Cherokee National Female Seminary in 1899, this building now is the centerpiece of the campus of Northeastern State University at Tahlequah. The change in ownership of this building in the early 1900s reflected the transitions taking place throughout the Indian Nations.

CHAPTER ONE

Twin Territories

America's Last Frontier

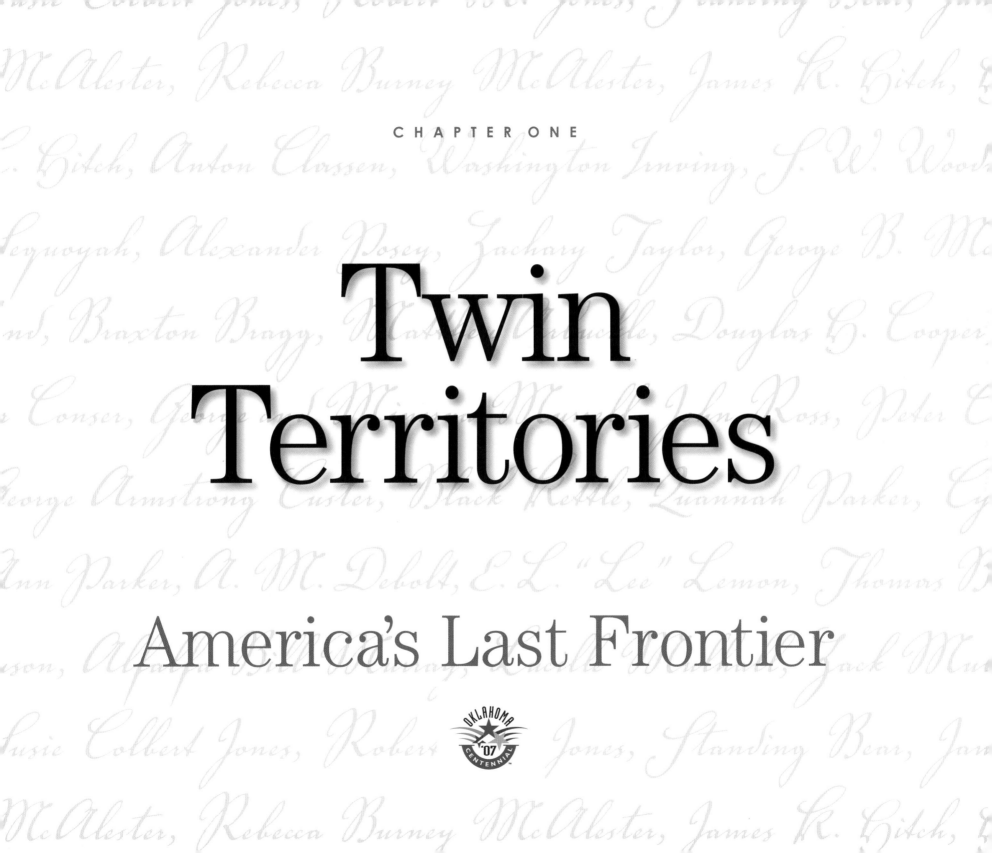

A Bridge to a New Land: Robert M. Jones

To President Thomas Jefferson, the Louisiana Purchase was an investment in the future, a vast territory of natural resources, trading partners, and precious land that someday would be needed for farms and towns. In the meantime, he predicted, the distant region would serve as a relocation zone for Indian tribes caught in the relentless march of American pioneers pushing through the Appalachian frontier.

In the American Southeast, this new policy forever changed the lives of the people cumulatively referred to as the Five Civilized Tribes—the Cherokee, Choctaw, Chickasaw, Creek, and Seminole—and set in motion the history of the State of Oklahoma as the "land of the Red Man."

The first of the so-called removal agreements was the Treaty of Doak's Stand, signed with a few Choctaw bands in 1820 to exchange ancestral lands for a new homeland stretching across southwestern Arkansas and southeastern Oklahoma. As part of the deal, the federal government funded the Choctaw Academy in Blue Springs, Kentucky, where Choctaw families could send their sons to learn the ways of the white man's world. One of the first students to enroll was a nineteen-year-old, mixed-blood Choctaw named Robert M. Jones.

The young, ambitious Choctaw graduated just as his homeland was under final siege. On September 28, 1830, 171 tribal leaders signed the Treaty of Dancing Rabbit Creek, selling more than 10 million acres of their land in Mississippi and agreeing to move west to what would become Oklahoma. With one foot in the traditional world of his tribal ancestors and the other foot in the world of Euro-American culture, Jones would help build a bridge to their future.

It took three harsh winters to complete the trek west, with groups ranging from 500 to 1,000 traveling on foot and on horseback through snow and ice. They suffered from exposure, disease, and sheer exhaustion, a "trail of tears" that did not improve much once they reached their new homes. Jones, who had secured a job as an assistant Indian agent, was put in charge of driving a herd of 1,000 horses west. More than half died on the way. In later years, Jones would recall that killing season as "the severest winter I ever saw."

Like his people, Jones started rebuilding his life in the new Choctaw Nation. By 1836 he

Robert M. and Susan Colbert Jones

was a partner in a trading post at Doaksville, a rough-cut community of log cabins and surrounding farms located less that a quarter mile from Fort Towson, the last federal outpost before crossing the Red River into the newly formed Republic of Texas. That same year, Jones married Susan Colbert, the daughter of a wealthy Choctaw planter and an ally in his quest to build a new life on the frontier.

Over the next twenty-five years, Jones prospered. He expanded his mercantile business until he owned twenty-eight stores. He imported the first cotton gin to the Indian Territory and bought two steamboats which plied the Red and Mississippi rivers as lifelines to cotton buyers and merchants in New Orleans. He eventually expanded his farming operations to six plantations, including a sugar plantation in Louisiana. In the Choctaw Nation, one farm had 10,000 acres under the plow. By 1860 he had more than 220 slaves and produced as much as 700 bales of cotton each year.

Jones and his wife, Susan, lived a Southern aristocratic life in their favorite home, Rose Hill, located about seven miles north of the Red River not far from the banks of the Kiamichi River. Each room of the two-story home featured a different exotic wood, and the library was lined with shelves filled with books. In the gallery, as in thousands of plantation homes throughout the South, hung portraits of United States presidents. Outside,

(Facing page) Susie Colbert Jones and Robert M. Jones were married in 1836, not long after their arrival in the new Choctaw Nation. For this formal portrait, they dressed elegantly in a style typical of southern planter aristocracy of the era. (Courtesy Oklahoma Historical Society)

The Robert M. Jones home at his Rose Hill plantation, located near the Kiamichi River about seven miles north of the Red River. The identity of the people in front of the home is unknown, but the quality of their clothing indicates that they likely were members of the extended Jones/Colbert families or prosperous neighbors. (Courtesy Oklahoma Historical Society)

Beginning with the Land Run of 1889, much of what would become the state of Oklahoma was opened to non-Indian settlement through a series of land runs and land lotteries. In 1901 lands formerly belonging to the Kiowa, Comanche, and Apache tribes were distributed in 13,000 tracts of 160 acres each by drawing lots. An estimated crowd of 4,500 gathered outside El Reno's Irving Schoolhouse in the July heat, each of them hoping to obtain homesteads. (Courtesy Oklahoma Publishing Company)

leading to the river landing, Jones planted two rows of cedar trees, some of which would still be standing 150 years later.

Although an exception in a land where most people lived as small self-subsistent farmers, the prosperity enjoyed by Robert and Susan Jones reflected the remarkable social and political recovery of the Choctaws after removal. They had their own government, established through a written constitution, with judicial, executive and legislative branches, and a school system that was the envy of people in surrounding states.

By 1842 the tribe maintained twelve neighborhood schools and eight boarding schools, supplemented by church-sponsored schools run by missionaries such as Cyrus Kingsbury, Alfred Wright, and Cyrus Byington. One visitor, passing through Doaksville on his way to fight for Texan independence, wrote a letter to his wife describing the beauty and prosperity of the "Choctaw country." After the fighting was done, he said, he wanted to return. That man, Davy Crockett, never got the chance.

While building his fortune and turning the wheels of economic development, Robert M. Jones found other ways to serve his fellow Choctaws. In 1838 tribal leaders sent him to Washington, D.C., to negotiate payment of the "net proceeds" for land sold to the United States and to press their claims for property lost during the disastrous removal. After years of negotiations, the Senate refused to pay for losses but did pledge $3 million to pay for the land. Payments were to begin in 1861.

Despite the promise of money long due to them, the Choctaws severed their ties with the United States that spring and signed treaties of alliance with the Confederate States of America. Once again, the Choctaws turned to Jones, a fiery secessionist who was elected as the largely honorary president of the "United Nations of the Indian Territory." While Jones negotiated with Confederate officials, the tribe raised a regiment to fight under the command of their former Indian agent Douglass Cooper. Two years later, Jones was given a seat in the Confederate Congress in Richmond, Virginia, as a delegate from the Indian nations.

At the end of the war, Jones was one of five Choctaws sent to negotiate a new treaty with the victorious Union government. Over Jones's objections, the final terms of the Reconstruction Treaty of 1866 allowed the first railroads to cross the Indian nations, confiscated the western half of the territory for the settlement of other tribes, and stipulated that the Choctaws would work toward allotment of land to individual tribal members and start the process of becoming a territory and ultimately a state.

With painful memories of removal, Jones

balked at the prospect of giving up tribal lands once again. In a letter, he offered a warning to his fellow Choctaws: if the Indians "lose their nationality by allotting lands…it is the first step toward admitting emigrants into their country…they would sell themselves out and be left without homes." In 1870, following the advice of their senior statesman, the Choctaws voted against the allotment process, a fate they would skillfully delay until 1898.

Robert M. Jones died from malaria in 1873. He lived long enough to restore his fortune, thanks in large part to the 4,500 bales of cotton he had stored during the Civil War. He also lived to see the first railroads built through his native land and the coal mines opened near J. J. McAlester's store. And he saw the devastating impact of non-Indian intruders who quickly outnumbered his fellow tribesmen. Still, Jones probably died with hope in his heart. He had seen his tribe forced from its ancestral lands. He had seen the devastation of Civil War. Each time, he had seen the spirit to recover, to adapt, to build upon the ruins of the past. Robert M. Jones, with one foot in the Indian world and one foot in the white man's world, had been a bridge to a new land.

The home of Peter Conser, captain in the Choctaw Light Horse police, is available to the public for visitation. Constructed in 1897, the home has been renovated by the Oklahoma Historical Society and features period furnishings. Restoration of the barn on the property is an Oklahoma Centennial project expected to be completed in 2007. The site is located four miles south of Heavener on U. S. Highway 59. (Courtesy Jim Argo)

The First Oklahomans

Sophisticated works of art, such as this disk, were produced by artisans working at Spiro from 800 A.D. to 1300 A.D. (Courtesy Oklahoma Historical Society)

For thousands of years, the land that is now Oklahoma has been a good place to live. The soils are rich, especially on the Great Plains and in the many valleys that have been cut by rivers winding their way from west to east. A rich diversity of plants and wild life abound in an environmental zone that varies from the timbered lowlands in the southeast to the arid table lands surrounding Black Mesa in the far northwest.

The first people, entering the region sometime between 10,000 and 30,000 years ago, were hunters and gatherers. Those nomads roamed the landscape, drawn by the seasonal ripening of wild grapes, sand plums, berries, and the maturing of edible greens. At first armed with spears and later with bows and arrows, they tracked big game such as mammoths and ancient buffalo and smaller game such as deer and bear. Evidence of their habitation has been uncovered by archaeologists in the caves of the Ozarks, Winding Stairs, and volcanic mesas of the Panhandle. Even more common are the camp sites dotted along the river valleys of the Washita, Canadian, Red, and Arkansas rivers.

About 2,000 years ago, the people of the region learned how to grow corn, beans, squash, and pumpkins. With a more stable supply of food, they settled in larger villages, learned to trade with distant tribes, and adapted new skills such as pottery, basketry, and metal work. Every fall, after the harvest, they followed ancient hunting trails to intercept migrating herds of buffalo and elk. In the spring, they returned to their villages and fields to plant the next crop.

To deal with the seasonal floods that could wash away their prized possessions, they built homes and communal structures on mounds. By 800 A.D., the mound builders of the region were part of the Southern Mississippian Culture that extended east to the hills of Georgia, north to Kahokia near the present-day city of East St. Louis, Missouri, and west to the spiritual and ceremonial capital of the empire, a place we now call Spiro Mounds. There, surrounded by rich fields and the homes of commoners, the elite of the empire built a carefully designed complex of temples that tracked the sun, moon, and stars throughout the year.

For some reason, it was at this site, the gateway to the high plains, that the Southern Mississippians buried their most important leaders, accompanied to the afterlife by the greatest pre-Columbian art produced north of the Valley of Mexico.

By 1300, following what was most likely a combination of environmental change and cultural decline, this far-flung empire unraveled as people fled the large cities to live in scattered villages once again. In the land that would become Oklahoma, three linguistic groups continued to harvest the bounty of the land for the next 200 years. The dominant group was Caddoan, known today as the Wichita, Caddo, and Pawnee tribes. To their east and north were the Siouan speaking groups known today as the Quapaw and Osage. To the west were the Plains Apache, part of the Athapascan linguistic group. Much as their ancestors had done, they lived a semi-nomadic life, hunting and processing hides and meat during the fall and winter, followed by life in their villages from planting to harvest.

The European quest for empire added a new chapter to this unfolding history of the first Oklahomans. Most influential were the French, who fanned out from their bases at New Orleans, Louisiana, and St. Louis to trade guns, knives, and trinkets for furs, slaves, and horses. From the early 1700s to the 1760s, the Wichita grew strong as mercantile middlemen between the French traders and tribes to the west, especially their allies and recent migrants to the region, the horse-mounted Comanche, known as the Lords of the Southern Plains. Also growing in strength were the Osage, a fierce and powerful tribe that grew stronger armed with French weapons. By 1803 and the Louisiana Purchase, the Osage dominated a large area bounded on the south by the Arkansas River valley, while the Wichita tenuously held their last fortified town, San Bernardo, located on the north bank of the Red River in present-day Jefferson County.

Armed with rich cultures and experienced in the ways of politics, trade, and war, the first Oklahomans were about to enter a new era of change.

The Mound Builders constructed mounds to elevate homes and communal structures above the flood plains of nearby streams. Some of the mounds were constructed over wood-frame structures and thus were hollow while others were solid. Mounds such as this one may be seen at Spiro Mounds Archaeological Park in LeFlore County. (Courtesy Oklahoma Historical Society)

Chief Standing Bear: "I Am a Man."

When the American Civil War erupted, most of the Chickasaws and Choctaws proclaimed their allegiance to the Confederacy. The Seminoles, Creeks, and Cherokees were split, with some fighting for the Union. Nonetheless, following the war all were required to negotiate treaties redefining their relationships with the United States. These Reconstruction Treaties of 1866 stripped away their western lands, making them available for reassignment to other tribes. Soon after, the federal government assembled representatives of the Apache, Arapaho, Cheyenne, Comanche, and Kiowa tribes for a major conference at Medicine Lodge, Kansas. Three separate treaties were signed in which the tribes agreed to accept reservations in what is now western Oklahoma. Not all members of these tribes agreed with the treaties and warfare on the Southern Plains ensued, especially with the Kiowa and Comanche, who were not defeated militarily until 1875.

The federal government moved other large tribes, such as the Osage, into the Indian Territory as well as numerous smaller tribes such as the Otoe, Kaw, Iowa, and Sac and Fox. Most of these tribes experienced their own "Trail of Tears." The Ponca, led by Chief Standing Bear, suffered greatly, but their leader was destined to strike a blow for the civil rights for all American Indians.

In 1875 the Ponca's agent, A. J. Carrier, traveled to Washington, D. C., to visit with President Ulysses S. Grant to recommend that the Ponca be removed from their small reservation in Nebraska to Indian Territory. Grant agreed to the move if the Ponca were willing to leave Nebraska. Carrier returned to the reservation and began discussions on the subject with Standing Bear and other tribal leaders. Standing Bear and Ponca leaders signed a document in which they agreed to move to Indian Territory. Standing Bear, however, later claimed that he thought he had agreed to move to the Omaha Reservation in Nebraska. The Omaha, while considered to be a distinct tribe, were allies who spoke virtually the same language as the Ponca.

Nevertheless, Indian Inspector Edward C. Kemble was ordered to meet with the Ponca and make arrangements for them to visit the Indian Territory to select a site for their new reservation. Standing Bear told Kemble, "We do not wish to sell our land, and we think no

Chief Standing Bear

man has a right to take it from us. Here we will live, and here we will die." Despite his initial reluctance, Standing Bear finally agreed to travel by train with nine other tribesmen and Kemble to the Indian Territory.

The trip to "the Warm Lands" did not go well and several of the Ponca fell ill. Standing Bear informed Kemble that he and the others would not lead their people to this place to die and that they were ready to go home. Characterizing the Indians' actions and attitudes as "insubordination," the furious Kemble simply abandoned Standing Bear and his party with no money and no means of transportation in a land where no one spoke their language. Standing Bear and his party began the long, 500-mile trek home on February 21, 1877.

Some nights they were able to sleep in haystacks; others were spent on the open prairie. The nights were cold and they had only their blankets to combat the frigid conditions. Standing Bear later recalled that, "We hardly lived until morning, it was so cold." They had little food and resorted to scavenging "ears of corn that had dried in the fields," eating it raw. The soles of their moccasins wore out, causing them to leave bloody footprints in the snow. They were "nearly dead" when they reached the Otoe Reservation in Nebraska fifty days later. There they remained for ten days to regain their strength. The Otoes provided a pony for each Ponca. They arrived at their reservation on April 2.

Standing Bear found that Kemble already was there, and he had orders to move the Ponca to Indian Territory regardless of their wishes, using force if necessary. Some of the Ponca were willing to leave and departed with Kemble for Indian Territory on April 16. Standing Bear, his brother Big Snake, and others refused to go. As a result, they were imprisoned for ten days. When released, they found that their possessions had been stolen. Finally, on May 21, the army forced the Indians to begin the trek "toward the heat," traveling in carts and on foot. The journey was disastrous for Standing Bear and his people. They endured bad weather almost from the start and by the end of the trip were enduring sultry summer heat plagued by insects. By July 9, when Standing Bear's party arrived at their new home, which had been carved out of the Quapaw Reservation in present Kay County, at least nine had died, including Standing Bear's daughter, Prairie Flower, and his wife, Shines White. Both of them had succumbed to "consumption."

The Ponca quickly discovered that the government had not made provision for their support as had been promised. By the end of 1878, pneumonia and malaria had claimed the lives of 158 of the 730 Ponca who had survived their "Trail of Tears." In January, 1879, Standing Bear's son, Bear Shield, fell ill. As he lay dying, Bear Shield asked his father to take his body back to the Ponca homelands in Nebraska for burial. This the grieving Standing Bear vowed to do. When the boy died, Standing Bear departed one night in January with 29 followers and his son's body to return once again to his home. During the ten-week trip, the travelers endured winter storms but finally arrived at the Omaha Reservation where they were offered homes by the Omaha. In the eyes of the United States Government, however, Standing Bear and his party were renegades. They were arrested by troopers under the command of General George Crook and brought to Fort Omaha for detention, with the understanding that they were to be escorted back to Indian Territory as soon as possible. The post commander, Colonel John H. King, reported that many of the Indians were ill, their horses were weakened, and thus it would be impossible to return the Ponca to Indian Territory for some time.

Referring to his orders to return Standing Bear and the other Ponca to Indian Territory, Crook reportedly remarked, "I've been forced many times by orders from Washington to do most inhuman things in dealing with the Indians, but now I'm ordered to do a more cruel thing than ever before." Determined to help Standing Bear, Crook contacted Thomas Henry Tibbles, assistant editor of

(Facing page) This 22-foot bronze statue of Ponca Chief Standing Bear by sculptor Oreland C. Joe is located in a beautiful 63-acre park in Ponca City, Oklahoma. The Standing Bear Memorial Park was designed to honor all Native Americans, with special emphasis on tribes located in the immediate area, including the Osage, Pawnee, Otoe-Missouria, Kaw, Tonkawa, and Ponca. (Courtesy Jim Argo)

The southern Poncas retained much of their cultural heritage after their removal to Indian Territory from their homes in Nebraska, while their kinsmen, who were allowed to move back to Nebraska due to the efforts of Standing Bear, did not. These Poncas in traditional regalia posed for a photographer near Ponca City in 1912. (Courtesy Scotty Howard and Carl Graham Collection, Oklahoma Historical Society)

the *Omaha Daily Herald*, who was known to be in sympathy with the plight of American Indians, and informed him of Standing Bear's situation.

Crook could not execute the order until the Indians were fit to travel. Tibbles, most likely at Crook's urging, moved quickly to spread the word of Standing Bear's plight. He telegraphed the story to newspapers in the East and he penned a powerful editorial that was published in the *Omaha Daily Herald* on April 1. He also enlisted the support of ministers in the region and telegraphed Carl Schurz, secretary of the interior, imploring him to reverse his removal order. Tibbles quickly roughed out a possible legal case based on the recent Fourteenth Amendment to the Federal Constitution, which in part provides that no state shall "deprive any person of life, liberty, or property, without due process of law; nor deny to any person within its jurisdiction the equal protection of the law." Tibbles contacted John L. Webster, a young lawyer friend, and A. J. Poppleton, the chief attorney for the Union Pacific Railroad, and both men agreed to represent Standing Bear free of charge.

The attorneys petitioned Judge Elmer S. Dundy of the United States District Court to issue a writ of habeas corpus to force General Crook to justify his detainment of Standing Bear. Dundy issued the writ and ordered the opposing parties to appear before him on April 30. G. M. Lambertson represented Crook and the United States Government. He argued that Standing Bear and his followers could not bring any sort of legal action against the government because they were neither persons nor citizens within the meaning of the law. Standing Bear's lawyers countered that the Ponca had made great advances in assimilation, were engaged in farming, and were entitled to be treated like other people under the provisions of the Fourteenth Amendment. They also argued that the government did not have the right to take their land and force them to move to Indian Territory.

After the attorneys' final arguments, Standing Bear was allowed to speak. His words were interpreted by Susette "Bright Eyes" LaFlesche, a highly educated Omaha Indian woman. As Standing Bear rose, he extended his hand toward the Judge and said, "That hand is not the color of yours, but if I pierce it, I shall feel pain. If you pierce your hand, you also feel pain. The blood that will flow from mine will be the same color as yours. I am a man. God made us both." After a brief two-day trial, Judge Dundy ruled, "That an Indian is a person within the meaning of the laws of the United States." Consequently, the judge held that Standing Bear and his followers were being held illegally and were to be released. He also ruled that "no rightful authority exists for removing by force" the Ponca to Indian Territory. Standing Bear was thus free to return to the Niobrara River to bury his son.

In 1881 Congress finally decided that a great wrong had been done to the Ponca. They were compensated monetarily and later that year the Sioux gave up their claims to the Ponca lands on the Niobrara. In 1890 the Ponca were given their choice of accepting individual allotments of land either in Indian Territory or in Nebraska. Conditions had improved in Indian Territory and two-thirds of them chose to stay while the others, including Standing Bear, chose to live in Nebraska. Although Indians did not become citizens of the United States until 1924, the plight of Standing Bear and his people, and the resulting court case, helped change attitudes of whites toward Native Americans. But in Indian Territory, the Indians were not secure in their reservations for long. With the coming of railroads and cattle trails, the isolation of the region began to erode. Intruders entered the Indian Nations in ever increasing numbers and pressure began to build to end the Indian tribes' control over their lands in the name of progress and economic development. By 1900 Native Americans were a minority in Indian Territory and the national policy of assimilation was in full bloom.

Among those who recorded their impressions of the Indian Nations was naturalist and surgeon S. W. Woodhouse, who accompanied a company of surveyors in 1849. In this painting titled *Woodhouse at Lost City* by Wayne Cooper, Woodhouse is camped on the banks of the Arkansas River near present-day Sand Springs. The limestone boulders in the background resembled a village when viewed from a distance. Hence the area was known as "Lost City." It was during this expedition that Woodhouse observed a Scissortail Flycatcher, which eventually would become the state bird. He also recorded his impressions of life and land in the Indian Nations. This painting hangs in the State Capitol. (Courtesy Oklahoma State Senate Historical Preservation Fund)

Frontier Adventurers

From 1541 to the 1830s, the land now called Oklahoma became a battlefield for empire. It was not a conventional battle, neither defended by walls nor occupied by invaders. Instead, it was a contest for access to resources, especially furs and Indian allies, that pitted explorers and frontiersmen against one another in a constantly changing effort to establish control, encourage trade, and gather information that would benefit the mother country.

The first explorers to penetrate the borders of the future state were the Spanish. In 1539, flush with wealth plundered from the Aztecs in Mexico and the Incas in Peru, Spanish officials mounted an expedition into the northern frontier in search of gold and silver rumored to be available for the taking. Two years later, Francisco Vasquez de Coronado led a column of soldiers, friars, and Indian allies as far north as the Arkansas River in central Kansas. On the way, they passed through the future Panhandle of Oklahoma. To their disappointment, all they found were tribes living in grass huts, bison-hide teepees, and mud-covered earth lodges. There was no gold and silver.

For the next 180 years, the Indians of the region lived in virtual isolation from the constant bickering of the European powers. All of that changed in 1718 when the French founded a new town on the lower Mississippi River. From that bastion of empire, called New Orleans, French explorers and traders rapidly moved north and west along rivers and creeks in the search for Indian allies who could provide furs in exchange for guns and trade goods. In 1719 Bernard de la Harpe ascended the Arkansas and Canadian rivers and brought back to his fellow Frenchmen tales of rich lands, plentiful game, and friendly Indians. The rush was on.

Unlike the latter-day mountain men who trapped their own fur-bearing animals, the Frenchmen were merchants who transported trade goods by canoe and flat boat up the rivers, set up seasonal camps for the rituals of exchange, and fled the wilderness each year to cash in their profits with the trading houses in New Orleans. Evidence of their success can be found in place names such as the Poteau, Canadian, and Verdigris rivers, and extended families such as the Chouteaus.

By the time the Americans entered the battle for empire, the prize extended beyond furs to control of land and the acquisition of information about their new frontier. In 1806 two expeditions were mounted to help define the borders of the Louisiana Territory. One, under the banner of Captain Richard Sparks, ascended the Red River until it was turned back by Spanish soldiers. The other, a small exploration party led by Lieutenant James Wilkinson, barely survived ice flows, cold weather, and near starvation as it explored the Arkansas River.

While a series of military expeditions continued this constant assault on the edges of the frontier, a few explorers came for something other than trade or control. They came for information. In 1819 English naturalist Thomas Nuttall tested his survival skills to gather data on plants and animals on two tours, one up the Red River and an ascent of the Kiamichi valley, the other a trek up the Arkansas River valley for a tour of the Three Forks Region, a strategic spot where the Arkansas, Grand, and Verdigri rivers converged.

An even more dramatic tour of the new country was undertaken by three curious explorers. One was the most famous American author of his age, Washington Irving, best known for his frontier tales such as *The Legend of Sleepy Hollow*. With him were the English naturalist, Charles Latrobe, and a Swiss nobleman, Count Albert de Pourtales. This affable group left Fort Gibson in the spring of 1832, traveled as far west as present-day Oklahoma County, and experienced a series of frontier adventures that ranged from a horse-mounted buffalo hunt to a "ringing of the wild horses." The expedition produced three books, including Irvings' celebrated classic, *A Tour on the Prairies*.

Irving's tour, offering a view of the new land to a world-wide reading audience, was a fitting conclusion to the age of exploration in Oklahoma. In 1541, when the first Spaniards arrived to conquer the northern frontier, maps of the time showed only a far country of unknown features and mythical legends. By the time the Five Civilized Tribes arrived in the territory, maps of the region were filled with details about rivers, salt plains, mountains, and tribal communities. The frontier was drawing to a close.

Washington Irving Meeting the Osage, by Wayne Cooper, is exhibited in the State Capitol. It depicts the meeting between author/explorer Washington Irving and Osage Indians on the banks of the Arkansas River near present Tulsa in 1832. He later described the Osages as being "the finest looking Indians" he had ever seen in the West. Irving's subsequent book, *A Tour of the Prairies*, provided fascinating descriptions of the region that would become Oklahoma as it appeared in the 1830s. (Courtesy Oklahoma State Senate Historical Preservation Fund)

J. J. McAlester: Tracks to the Future

Between the end of the Civil War in 1865 and 1900, Indians became a minority within the Indian Territory. The intrusion of cattlemen and cowboys was followed by traders and farmers who wished to exploit the resources of the region such as coal and oil. Railroads were built into the Indian Nations with the support of some Indians, usually mixed bloods, and against the opposition of others. Full-blood leaders, such as Chief Coleman Cole of the Choctaw, knew that tribal customs and control of their lands were enhanced by their isolation, which the railroads would effectively end. Other tribal citizens, often mixed blood or non-Indians who had married into the tribe, viewed the coming of railroads and development of resources as desirable because they would spur economic development and enhance economic opportunity for themselves and others. One such individual, James Jackson McAlester, would become known to some as the "Father of eastern Oklahoma" in recognition of his prominent role in the economic development and non-Indian settlement of the Choctaw Nation.

Born in Arkansas, McAlester was 18 when the opening shots of the Civil War were fired. McAlester took up arms on behalf of the Confederacy in the Indian Territory under the command of Brigadier General Albert Pike, but his most significant action was at the Battle of Pea Ridge on March 7 and 8, 1862, in northwest Arkansas near Bentonville. The battle resulted in a resounding victory for the Union forces and solidified federal control over Missouri. During the course of the war it appears that McAlester rose to the rank of captain, although in later years he often was referred to as "Colonel McAlester."

After the war, McAlester decided to attend school as he had not been a dedicated student prior to the war. He became friends with a man who had surveyed the Choctaw Nation, and this individual told McAlester that he had seen outcroppings of high-quality coal in the region. He drew maps to indicate where these outcroppings were located and encouraged McAlester to take possession of these areas as soon as possible. "School didn't interest me much after that," McAlester later recalled.

James J. and Rebecca Burney McAlester

McAlester secured a job with a freighting company and transported materials needed to build a saw mill from Fort Smith, Arkansas, to Fort Sill. A new army post was being established in southwestern Indian Territory on Cache Creek near the Wichita Mountains. The material was transported in wagons pulled by teams of oxen. There were no bridges between the two installations, so streams had to be forded. On many occasions the heavily loaded wagons would bog down and McAlester and his fellow teamsters would have to hitch as many as ten teams of oxen to free the wagons from mud and sand.

McAlester later worked for Harlan & Rooks, a firm of Indian traders that established trading posts at Tupelo and Stonewall. Among McAlester's tasks was the clearing of trees and brush for the post building at Stonewall. He still had his map showing the location of the coal outcrops in his pocket, and with that location in mind obtained a position in 1869 with another trading company, Reynolds & Hannaford. He managed to convince his new bosses to establish a trading post a short distance from the coal outcrops, which he had previously managed to locate using his map. McAlester was assigned the task of hauling the materials needed to construct the post building via wagon from Poteau to Bucklucksy, where the post was to be constructed. He brought some trade goods

along with the building materials and had $19 in sales on the day he arrived at the construction site. A year later, McAlester bought Reynolds' interest in the company.

McAlester's coal outcropping continued to beckon, but he knew that for the coal to have real value, there must be a means of transporting it to market. The logical solution at this time was a railroad. In the various reconstruction treaties negotiated with the Five Civilized Tribes after the Civil War, provisions were included to allow the construction of railroads across Indian Territory. Congress, in 1866, extended land-grant subsidies for a north-south railroad across the region. These subsidies would give railroads alternate sections of land in a strip five miles wide on each side of the right-of-way. Three different railroads announced plans to build from north to south through Indian Territory, but under the terms of the reconstruction treaties, only one would be approved. The legislation that provided the land-grant incentives also stipulated that the subsidies would be awarded to the first company that completed construction to the Kansas-Indian Territory border near the Neosho or Grand River.

McAlester saw an opportunity to encourage one of the railroad companies not only to build its line through Indian Territory, but also to establish its route to pass near Bucklucksy. This would benefit his trading

post and provide both a customer for his projected coal production and a means of transporting the coal to market. McAlester loaded a wagon of coal and headed to Parsons, Kansas, to show it to officials of the Missouri, Kansas, and Texas Railroad, which quickly came to be known as the "Katy." It was a difficult journey through territory where rivers had to be forded because of the absence of bridges. He eventually arrived at Parsons and presented the coal to Katy officials. They in turn sent a sample of the coal by train to Sedalia, Missouri, where it was determined that the coal was of high quality, the "best steam coal west of Pennsylvania." The coal

(Facing Page) James J. McAlester as he appeared in 1910. By this time, he was a highly successful entrepreneur and was serving as a member of the Oklahoma Corporation Commission. He would serve as lieutenant governor of Oklahoma from 1911 to 1915. (Courtesy Oklahoma Historical Society)

(Above) Rebecca Burney McAlester was of Chickasaw and Choctaw lineage. Her marriage to J. J. McAlester in 1872 enabled McAlester to obtain the rights of citizenship in the Choctaw Nation, thereby making possible the development of his extensive business interests in the area. Their marriage endured for 48 years, and Mrs. McAlester remained a prominent citizen of McAlester until her death in 1919. (Courtesy Oklahoma Historical Society)

would be ideal for use in steam locomotives and other purposes.

The Katy ultimately won the race when it reached the border on June 6, 1870, just north of Vinita in the Cherokee Nation. The Katy began building into Indian Territory, essentially following the route of the famed Texas Road. The route ran adjacent to McAlester's store at Bucklucksy, reaching the store in 1872. McAlester believed that he had some influence in motivating the Katy to win the race and to select the route through his community, which the railroad renamed McAlester in his honor. Soon thereafter, McAlester married Rebecca Burney, a woman of Choctaw and Chickasaw lineage, thus obtaining the rights of citizenship in the Choctaw Nation. When he purchased Hannaford's interest in the company and became sole owner in 1972, McAlester was positioned as an intermarried citizen of the Choctaw Nation to begin developing his economic interests in earnest.

When the Katy arrived, McAlester and some partners opened a coal mine near Krebs, a short distance from McAlester. Coal from the mine was hauled by wagon to the nearby railroad for shipment. At this point, McAlester got caught in the middle of Choctaw politics between the "progressives" who favored economic development of the region and the "conservatives" who feared that the railroads and exploitation

Fort Gibson was established by Colonel Matthew Arbuckle in 1824 to keep the peace between Cherokee settlers in western Arkansas and Osage Indians in present northeastern Oklahoma. It was located at the Neosho River about three miles north of where it joins the Arkansas River. By 1830 the military considered it to be Headquarters of the Southwestern Frontier. It was there that many members of the Five Civilized Tribes who were removed from their homes in the Southeast by water disembarked in the Indian Territory. Abandoned in 1857, the fort was reactivated during the Civil War and was the primary Union outpost in the Indian Territory. After the Civil War troops from the garrison constructed Forts Arbuckle and Sill. Fort Gibson later played a role in protecting against intrusions into the Indian Nations and was abandoned permanently in 1890. Now a property of the Oklahoma Historical Society, the fort has been extensively restored. (Courtesy Jim Argo)

of resources would lead to the downfall of the Choctaw Nation. McAlester had obtained a mining permit and officials of the Katy decided to build a switch from the main line to the mine to facilitate the more rapid development of the mining operation. Choctaw Governor Coleman Cole heard about the plans to build the switch, was determined to halt it, and, if possible, shut down the mining operation. Before the Choctaw Council could meet, however, the Katy built its switch, an action which further angered Cole.

Taking advantage of a statute that called for the death penalty for any tribal member who "sold any part of the land," Cole interpreted the sale of coal as being illegal and thus sent Captain Olasechubbee, captain of the Choctaw Light Horse, to arrest McAlester and several of his colleagues. He was successful in arresting McAlester and two others, but a third, Tandy Walker, escaped. According to McAlester, Olasechubbee told him that he and his partners were to be shot and then left them on their own recognizance while he departed to pursue Walker. Other accounts give varying reasons why McAlester and the others were left unguarded. At any rate, McAlester determined that he "wasn't ready to be shot" and did not wait for the Light Horse to return.

McAlester and his colleagues walked

The Creek Council House Museum at Okmulgee originally was constructed in 1878 to serve as the capitol of the Creek Nation. It housed the executive and judicial branches of the Nation's government. It has been renovated in recent years and houses a museum highlighting the history of the Creek people. (Courtesy Jim Argo)

north on the Katy until they came to the first section house where they talked the man in charge into letting them use a hand car and "two big Irishmen" to help them pump it. The escapees piled on the hand car and all of them began to pump vigorously. "I reckon we were too anxious," McAlester later recalled, "for we went so fast the car jumped the track and spilled us on the right-of-way."

Fortunately, there were no serious injuries, and they put the hand car back on the track and pumped it up the tracks north to Eufaula in the Creek Nation. While McAlester remained in Eufaula, his friends put together a band of fifty men who called on Cole to encourage him to change his position. Other friends of McAlester, some of whom had reputations for "doing what they said they

would do," according to McAlester, told Cole that if McAlester were harmed they would "hang [Cole's] hide on the fence." McAlester subsequently went to see Cole, showed him his mining permit, and agreed to share revenues from the coal with the Choctaw government. The issue was resolved.

Coal mining developed into a major industry in the region, playing a significant role in the economy until the 1930s. Many immigrants from the mining regions of the United States and Europe came to the area to work in the mines. McAlester soon controlled hundred of acres of ranch land, which supported large herds of cattle, and his merchandizing business flourished. A new community, South McAlester, sprang into existence when another railroad built through the area from east to west. McAlester quickly invested in land and property. In time, South McAlester and North McAlester would merge into one community. McAlester became a prominent banker, was active in Democrat Party politics, and in the 1890s served four years as a United States marshal. By the time of statehood in 1907, he had built a large mansion in McAlester and was ready to serve his state as one of the first corporation commissioners and as the second lieutenant governor. His wife Rebecca died in 1919 and he passed away in 1920, still acclaimed by some as the "Father of Eastern Oklahoma."

Located halfway between Madill and Durant on State Highway 199, Fort Washita was founded in 1841 by General Zachary Taylor with the goal of protecting the Choctaw and Chickasaw Indians from the Plains Indians. Taylor later would achieve fame as a general in the Mexican War and as president of the United States. Numerous other important figures served at Fort Washita, including George B. McClelland and Braxton Bragg, later prominent generals for the Union and Confederate armies during the Civil War. Used extensively by Confederate forces during the Civil War, the fort was abandoned by the military in 1870. In 1962 the fort came into the possession of the Oklahoma Historical Society. (Courtesy Jim Argo)

The guard house building at historic Fort Supply was constructed in 1892 and has been restored by the Oklahoma Historical Society, along with four other historic structures on the site. It is located just northwest of Woodward. Established in 1868 as "camp of supply" for a winter military campaign against the southern plains Indians, the fort was an active military installation until 1894. From there Lieutenant Colonel George Armstrong Custer and his 7th Cavalry launched their winter campaign in 1868 which resulted in the infamous Battle of the Washita during which Custer attacked the camp of a peaceful band of Cheyenne Indians led by Chief Black Kettle. Custer's troops killed men, women, and children indiscriminately. The site was occupied by Oklahoma's first insane asylum, Western State Psychiatric Center, in 1908, and the Fort Supply Historic District and the William S. Key correctional facility were established there in 1988. (Courtesy Jim Argo)

From Here to There

Oklahoma is a big land with wide open spaces and resources scattered over vast distances. To make a living, or even to survive, has always required mobility and the ability to get from here to there.

The first Oklahomans covered distance by walking. Even with dogs to drag travois, they were severely restricted in their ability to chase herds of migrating buffalo, move to the next valley in the never ending search for food, or find neighboring tribes with which to trade for scarce commodities. All of that changed when the Spanish brought a strange new animal to the North American continent—the horse. For American Indians, the world grew smaller almost overnight.

Even with horses, overland trade was inefficient and expensive. The most cost effective means of moving goods and people prior to the 1870s was by water. The Spiroans used dug-out canoes, some of which

were fifty to sixty feet long, to transport food surpluses and trade goods throughout the empire from their city on the Arkansas River. The French followed those same free flowing waterways to move furs and trade goods by canoes and flat boats.

The real revolution in hauling goods and people came with the application of steam power to river craft. By 1824 riverboats were ascending the Arkansas River as far as the Three Forks, making that community the fertile crescent of economic activity in the Indian Territory. In 1838, when the Red River was cleared of a massive log jam near Shreveport, Louisiana, riverboats every spring and summer started plying the waters as far west as the mouth of the Kiamichi River. One of the first boats making that journey, the *Heroine*, hit a snag just a few miles short of its destination and sank. Today, remnants of the wreck and its cargo can be seen in the museum exhibits of the Oklahoma History Center in Oklahoma City.

Overland transportation, although less efficient than river steamboats, advanced nonetheless, due in large part to the limited range and seasonal vagaries of navigable waters outside of eastern Oklahoma. Many of the major routes later used by horses and wagons started as hunting and war trails. The Osages, from their ancestral homelands north of the Ozarks, followed a natural trail south to the Three Forks area near modern Muskogee, then turned west to hunt buffalo and plunder nomadic tribes. In 1821, when legal trade with Mexico opened for the first time, traders from St. Louis followed this "Osage Trace" south to the Three Forks, then continued south-southwest toward settlements south of the Red River. This new trade route became known as the Texas Road.

The first improved roads were established by the United States Army as military posts moved farther west onto the frontier. From Fort Smith, established in 1819, roads were built first to Forts Gibson and Towson in 1824, followed by an entire network that spanned the territory to Forts Supply, Sill, and Reno in the 1860s and 1870s. Intersecting the east-to-west roads were the famous cattle trails, the Shawnee, the Chisholm, and the Great Western, all providing a low cost method of moving cattle from the hills of Texas to the railheads in Kansas.

The conquest of vast distances took another revolutionary step when steel rails pierced the borders of Indian Territory in 1871. The first iron horse to enter the future state was the Missouri, Kansas & Texas, better known as the Katy. It connected settled Kansas with settled Texas, while providing a new link with the outside world for people living in the Cherokee, Creek,

Traders on the Santa Fe Trail as depicted by artist Wayne Cooper. This scene is in present-day Cimarron County and the painting may be viewed in the Oklahoma Capitol. (Courtesy Oklahoma State Senate Historical Preservation Fund)

and Choctaw nations. With this opportunity came store keepers, coal mine operators, hotels, and towns such as Vinita, Wagoner, Muskogee, Eufaula, Atoka, and Durant, all built on the new rail lines. Over the next two decades the Katy was followed by the Santa Fe, the Frisco, and the Rock Island as tracks spread in all directions.

By the time of statehood in 1907, Oklahoma was still a big country with widely scattered resources, but the ability to cover vast distances and take advantage of resources from coal and cotton to wheat and oil was made possible by improved transportation. The world was getting smaller all the time.

Mike Wimmer's, *Ceremonial Transfer of the Louisiana Purchase in New Orleans – 1803*, illustrated the official transfer of the Louisiana Territory from France to the United States. With the exception of the Panhandle, the future state of Oklahoma thus became American territory. The 6' by 10' canvas may be viewed in the State Capitol. (Courtesy Oklahoma State Senate Historical Preservation Fund)

James K. Hitch: No-Man's Land Pioneer

While J. J. McAlester and his fellow pioneers were transforming the economy of the old Indian Territory, cattlemen were establishing large ranching operations in the area known as the Neutral Strip or No-Man's Land, so called because from 1850 to 1890 the area was not a part of any state or territory. No-Man's Land was attached to Oklahoma Territory in 1890 and would become known as the Oklahoma Panhandle. Agriculture dominated the economy of the Panhandle at the time of statehood and, 100 years later, agriculture, along with oil and natural gas, would continue to drive the economy of the state's most prosperous region on a per capita basis.

The range cattle industry began in earnest prior to the Civil War, when Texans began driving herds of Longhorn cattle through the Indian Nations over the Shawnee Trail to southwestern Missouri where the bovines could be shipped by rail to a large, growing market in the North and Midwest. This activity was disrupted by the Civil War. Allowed to multiply unmolested throughout the war years, vast herds of Longhorns greeted Texans when they returned home from the conflict. All enterprising cattlemen needed to do to realize fabulous profits was to get the longhorns to shipping points on railroads laying track west through Kansas. In 1866 an estimated 260,000 Longhorns were driven overland from Texas through Indian Territory to Kansas, and the tide of cattle moving north was just beginning. From 1866 through 1885 more than 5.7 million longhorns were moved through the lands that would become Oklahoma. Cowboy culture bloomed as cattle were driven north along the West Shawnee, the Chisholm, the Great Western, and the Jones and Plummer trails.

To increase the weight and market value of their cattle, cattlemen preferred to graze their animals while on the drive, often just before reaching Kansas. Some cattlemen then began making arrangements with various Indian tribes to lease pasture land. This allowed cattle herds being kept there on a long-term basis to benefit from the grass and a shorter trip to market. While the eastern portion of the Cherokee Outlet had been used to provide

James K. Hitch

reservations for the Osage and other, smaller tribes, the central and western areas of the Outlet were available for lease. In 1883, the Cherokee Strip Livestock Association, an organization of cattlemen with leases in the area, leased the entire Outlet from the Cherokee Nation and divided the land into allotments for its members.

Another haven for cattlemen, where they initially did not have to purchase or lease the land, was the Neutral Strip. By the 1870s, replacing Mexican sheep herders who had entered the area from the west, cattlemen were establishing ranches restricted in size only by how much land they could use. Into this region in 1884, determined to establish his own ranching operation, came James K. Hitch.

A native of Tennessee, Hitch had left home at age 20 to make his own way in the world. At Springfield, Missouri, he found work with farmer Henry Westmoreland. Jim Hitch was a slender young man with coal black hair, piercing blue eyes, and a mustache, and he caught the eye of Westmoreland's daughter. For several weeks Jim would speak to Mary Frances Westmoreland only when spoken to, but he eventually overcame his shyness, fell in love, and the young couple married. In 1876, when Westmoreland decided to go into the cattle business in southwestern Kansas, Hitch borrowed money to purchase 200

head and joined his father-in-law and other family members in the cattle business. Hitch prospered, enjoying the favorable market conditions and weather in the late 1870s and early 1880s, while Mary Frances learned how to be a homemaker in a small sod house.

By 1884 Hitch had discovered some excellent ranching land in the Neutral Strip and was running cattle there as well as in southwest Kansas when disaster struck. A

severe drought beginning in 1885 caused the usually lush grasses to be sparse, resulting in little hay to be harvested and stored for the winter. When a three-day blizzard struck the plains and plunged the temperature to 20 degrees below zero, half the cattle in the region perished. Many cattlemen went out of business, but Hitch was determined to continue, skinning 500 animals and selling their hides to provide some revenue. Shortly

(Facing page) James K. Hitch founded the family business that would become Hitch Enterprises, a diversified agri-business with operations in the Oklahoma and Texas Panhandles, as well as in Kansas. (Courtesy Hitch Enterprises)

Henry C. Hitch, left, with his son, Henry C. "Ladd" Hitch, Jr., in 1960. James Hitch is between the two men. Ladd Hitch continued the Hitch Family operations, eventually passing the leadership of the enterprise to his son, Paul W. Hitch. (Courtesy Oklahoma Historical Society)

The home of George and Minerva Murrell, located at Park Hill near Tahlequah, was constructed in 1845. George was a Virginian and Minerva was a niece of Cherokee Chief John Ross. Fortunately the home survived the general devastation of the Cherokee Nation that took place during the Civil War and today is a historical site accessible to the general public. Shown here is a lawn social recently reenacted on the grounds of the Murrell home. (Courtesy Jim Argo)

thereafter he moved his entire operation to the valley of Coldwater Creek, not far from present-day Guymon, where he was joined by his wife's relatives as well as some of his own.

By now Jim and Mary Frances had three children, two girls and a boy. Hitch and his men constructed a 24' x 40' sod house for his family. Numerous other sod structures were built for hired hands and family members. When a second son was born in 1887, Jim constructed an 18' x 24' limestone addition to the "soddy." He also built a limestone barn and a corral and had success harvesting good hay crops. When another severe blizzard struck in February 1897, he had plenty of hay available and his losses were minimal. By 1893 he had an orchard of 150 fruit trees. Mary Frances played a predominant role in the establishment of the first church in the area, and the Hitches joined the Westmorelands and other families to organize a school in 1890. In that same year, the Neutral Strip was added to Oklahoma Territory.

Tragedy struck in 1891 when Mary Frances died. Several lonely years followed for Hitch, who worked hard to expand his ranching operations and to care for his children. During this time, he demolished the sod portion of his house and replaced it with a two-story limestone structure, which attached to the original limestone addition.

By the late 1890s, through hard work and sound business practices, Hitch's operations had grown to the point that he had nearly 5,000 mother cows and was grazing them in both the Texas and Oklahoma Panhandles. In November of 1899, Hitch married Josephine Brown, the daughter of an area cattleman, and over the next six years they had two boys and a girl. By 1900 the Hitches and the Westmorelands owned at least 10,000 head of cattle grazing on 40,000 to 50,000 acres.

At this time Hitch turned day-to-day management of his ranch operations over to his son Henry, constructed a new home in Guymon, and moved there to enjoy time with his wife. He continued to reinvest profits from his operations into obtaining more land in the Panhandle, Texas, and Kansas, and by the time of his death in 1921 had acquired 30,223 acres in three states. The Hitch family enterprises in the Panhandle continued to be enlarged and diversified into the twenty-first century in turn by Henry C. Hitch, Sr., Henry C. "Ladd" Hitch, Jr., and Paul Hitch. Characterized by massive cattle feed lots, wheat production, hog farming, meat processing, and commodities futures trading, the Hitch family continued to be innovators in agribusiness, helping to bring prosperity to the Panhandle.

This family proudly posed in front of their sod house in northwestern Oklahoma. The structure has been improved with a wood shingle roof. The absence of trees on the Great Plains made the use of sod necessary for the construction of houses, providing reasonable insulation against heat and cold but also offering an inviting home to insects and snakes. (Courtesy Oklahoma Historical Society)

William H. "Alfalfa Bill" Murray and his family in front of their residence at Tishomingo in 1905 for what perhaps was a "campaign" photo. His wife was Mary Alice Hearrell, a niece of Chickasaw Governor Douglas H. Johnston. While Murray always liked to run for office as one of the "folks," he was capable of dressing and speaking with sophistication when the occasion demanded it. By the time he presided over the Oklahoma Constitution Convention, he had studied every written constitution in existence. (Courtesy Oklahoma Historical Society)

The home of Thompson B. Ferguson, Governor of Oklahoma Territory from 1901 to 1905, is located at Watonga, where Ferguson founded the *Watonga Republican* newspaper. A staunch Republican, he was appointed Territorial Governor by President Theodore Roosevelt. The Ferguson Home, owned and maintained by the Oklahoma Historical Society, is open for touring. (Courtesy Jim Argo)

Czech Hall was constructed when two Czech lodges joined together in 1901 to build a place where Czech people could meet and socialize. The building has been in continuous use since it was opened. A polka dance has been held in the hall every Saturday night since 1930. Built on land donated by Czech immigrants, the venerable structure, located on Czech Hall Road in Yukon, is listed on the National Register of Historic Places. (Courtesy State Historic Preservation Office, Oklahoma Historical Society)

Shaping a State: Oklahoma's Borders

Located in the south-central part of the United States, Oklahoma was formed by the combining of Indian Territory, Oklahoma Territory, No-Man's Land, and Old Greer County into one state in 1907. The lands that became Oklahoma either were left over from the formation of other states or territories, land that other states did not want, or land that had been set aside to provide "forever a home for the Indians." This process resulted in a state that is the "meeting ground between the North and the South, the East and the West in natural, cultural, and economic characteristics and appearance."

Although evidence now exists that American Indians lived in present Oklahoma as long as 30,000 years ago and that Spiro was an important cultural center for North America between 850 and 1450 A.D., Spain was the first European nation to lay claim on the land that now is Oklahoma. In 1541, Francisco Vasques de Coronado claimed the region for Spain and in 1688 Robert Cavelier sieur de LaSalle claimed it for France. From that point on, Spain, France, and England sought dominion over the region, with control changing periodically until the United States purchased the Louisiana Territory from France in 1803.

The southern and western boundaries of the Louisiana Territory were vague until approval of the Adams-Onis Treaty of 1819. By this agreement, Spain and the United States agreed that the "south-cut bank" of the Red River to the 100th meridian was the southern boundary of the Louisiana Territory and the 100th meridian from the Red River north to the Arkansas River became the western boundary of this portion of the Louisiana Territory. The present Panhandle of Oklahoma was determined to be Spanish Territory with its eastern boundary established at the 100th meridian. Thus, the southern and western borders of Oklahoma, up to the southern boundary of the Panhandle, were established in 1819.

In his painting *Creek Council Oak Tree*, displayed in the State Capitol, Mike Larsen illustrated a gathering of Creek Indians who had just completed their difficult trek from their homes in Alabama to their new home in the Indian Territory. It was there that the Lochapoka clan of the Creeks made their new home. The magnificent post oak is located between Seventeenth and Eighteenth Street and Cheyenne and Denver Avenues in present Tulsa. (Courtesy Oklahoma State Senate Historical Preservation Fund)

With *Fort Smith Conference – 1865*, on display in the State Capitol, Mike Wimmer illustrated one session of the council that was called by the federal government to renegotiate treaties between the government and the tribes who aligned with the Confederacy during the Civil War. Twelve tribes were represented, including those which had only a faction of the tribe fight for the South. The conference was the precursor to a series of treaties negotiated later in Washington, D. C., which reduced the land holdings of many of the tribes, paving the way for the removal of additional tribes to the region. (Courtesy Oklahoma State Senate Historical Preservation Fund)

The Choctaw Council House at Tuskahoma was constructed in 1833-1834 and remained the seat of government for the Choctaw Nation until Oklahoma statehood in 1907. With the rebirth of the Choctaw Nation in the 1970s, the Council House was restored and presently houses the Choctaw National Museum and the Choctaw Nation's Judicial Department Court System. (Courtesy Jim Argo)

The state's remaining boundaries were formed when other areas were organized as territories, Indian Nations, or states. The northeastern border with Missouri was established when that state joined the Union in 1820, while the border with Arkansas was defined when the Cherokee and Choctaw nations were carved out of the Arkansas Territory in 1825 and 1828. Texas by 1845 had evolved from being a Spanish colony to a province of Mexico to an independent republic. In that year, the Lone Star Republic joined the Union as a "slave state" and had to give up its claim to the present Oklahoma Panhandle because that land was north of the line where slavery was prohibited by the Missouri Compromise of 1820. Thus, the southern boundary of the Panhandle was established. When the territories of New Mexico, Colorado, and Kansas were formed in 1850, 1854, and 1860 respectively, the western boundary of the Panhandle and the northern boundaries of the Panhandle and of Oklahoma were established. The Panhandle was not attached to any territory or state until 1890 when it became part of Oklahoma Territory.

The process of establishing Oklahoma's borders was completed, with the exception of ongoing arguments over defining the "south-cut" bank of the Red River and the accuracy of surveys of the 100th meridian, in 1896. Texas had claimed that the North Fork of the Red River was the main channel of the river and claimed all of the land between the Prairie Dog Fork and the North Fork of the river. The region, known as Old Greer County, became part of Oklahoma Territory in 1896 when the Supreme Court of the United States ruled that the Prairie Dog Fork was the main channel of the Red River referred to in the Adams-Onis Treaty of 1819.

The shape of the future State of Oklahoma, which encompasses 69,956 square miles, was defined. In its centennial year of statehood, Oklahoma was the 18th largest state in the Union, larger than any state east of it except Minnesota. One-eighth the size of Alaska and 57 times the size of Rhode Island, Oklahoma is a land of tremendous geographical diversity. This circumstance, combined with the fact that it became a home for numerous Indian nations, caused it to develop considerable social and cultural diversity. Oklahoma indeed can be considered one of the most "American" of all the states because of its cultural and geographical richness.

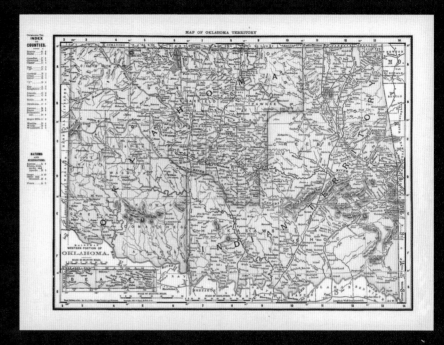

The boundaries of the Indian Territory and Oklahoma Territory as of 1895. (Courtesy Oklahoma Historical Society)

Anton H. Classen: The Spirit of '89

On April 22, 1889, the sun rose over a vast expanse of unclaimed land deep in the heart of the Indian Territory called the Unassigned Lands. It was an unfenced region of prairie and woods, well watered, with few marks of man save the steel tracks of the Santa Fe Railroad and a few buildings around the water stops. That evening, after the first land run in American history, every part and parcel would be claimed by 50,000 hardy pioneers. One of those '89ers was Anton Classen.

Classen's story reflects the American experience. His parents fled religious persecution in Germany when he was one year old. After his mother died on board the ship on the way the New World, the rest of the family landed in New Orleans and made their way to Illinois in 1862. Young Anton did well in school, eventually attending the University of Michigan Law School, where he graduated in 1887.

Casting about for his lot in life, the young attorney read an article about a new frontier soon to be opened to non-Indian settlers. It was called the Unassigned Lands because it had been taken from the Five Civilized Tribes after the Civil War, but had never been "assigned" to another tribe. Farmers suffering from an extended drought in the Midwest combined with railroad lobbyists to convince Congress to declare the land surplus and available for settlement under the terms of the Homestead Act.

Unfortunately, there were too many land seekers to use the tried and true methods of transferring the frontier to landowners along a gradually expanding line of settlement. It had to be done overnight. President Benjamin Harrison, true to his era's belief in Social Darwinism and a minimal role for government in daily life, decided the best way to settle the land was through a land run. In theory, only the smart and quick would get the land.

On the day of the run, Classen joined a small army that bought tickets on the many trains that would enter the Unassigned Lands no faster than a horse could run. Others lined up around the borders of the territory, prepared to make their way on horses, in wagons, and even on foot. At high noon, the signals sounded and the rush was on. By sundown almost half

Anton H. Classen

(Facing page) Anton H. Classen, ca. 1907. By this time he was one of the most prominent leaders in Oklahoma City. (Courtesy Oklahoma Historical Society)

The interior of Anton Classen's real estate office in June 1909. Classen is second from the right. (Courtesy Oklahoma Historical Society)

to build the first building. In August of 1891 the bond issue passed and Edmond became home to what would eventually become the University of Central Oklahoma.

Unfortunately for Classen and his fellow '89ers, the mid-1890s were lean years of drought, agricultural depression, and subsequent land openings that drew people and resources east to the former lands of the Sac and Fox/Pottawatomie, west to the former reservation of the Cheyenne/Arapaho, and north to the rich soil of the Cherokee Outlet. Classen, who had become active in politics, received an appointment as Receiver of Public Money at the United States Land Office in Oklahoma City.

As he had done in Edmond, Classen jumped into the swirl of his community's life. He helped reorganize the old Commercial Club, which emerged as the Oklahoma City Chamber of Commerce, and served as president for five years. He also organized the Classen Company and started buying land on the fringes of town. In June of 1898 he purchased 25 acres for $2,500 from E. W. Bourne, a farmer who had won title to the homestead between 10th and 16th streets and Broadway and Walker avenues. One year later, he purchased the adjoining 120 acres to the west for $10,000.

In 1900 the aspiring businessman subdivided part of his holdings as Classen's Highland Parked Addition, located between

of the '89ers had claimed 160-acre farms, while the other half, including Classen, had landed in towns along the Santa Fe tracks.

Classen started in Guthrie, which was destined to be the territorial capital and the city favored by the railroads. Within two weeks, however, he decided there was an oversupply of attorneys among the 10,000 settlers in Guthrie, so he moved south along the tracks and hung out his shingle in the little community of Edmond, where he quickly invested both his money and his energy. He purchased a quarter section of land northeast of what is now 2nd Street and

Broadway Avenue, became city attorney, helped start the first bank, and purchased the town's first newspaper, the *Edmond Sun*. He also helped build the town's first cotton gin, served as the first president of the town library, planted trees in Mitch Park, and earned the appointment of postmaster.

In 1890, as the territorial legislators in Guthrie contemplated the location for three institutions of higher education, Classen led an effort in Edmond to capture the teachers' college. He offered 40 acres of his homestead for the college, provided that the citizens of the town pass a $2,000 bond issue

The non-Indian settlers of northwestern Oklahoma generally came from the Mid-West and were attracted to the region for its agricultural potential, especially wheat with which they were familiar. Wheat quickly became the dominant crop of the area. Here the thrashing crew of E. L. "Lee" Lemon was harvesting the wheat crop near Nash in 1897. (Courtesy Oklahoma Historical Society)

13th and 16th and Broadway and Walker. He promoted the development in local newspapers. "Have you seen the Highlands? With its beautiful homes? Wide streets and handsome trees?" He even offered discounts. "Four lots in Highland Park, on 13th Street, among the Big Bugs. A bargain at $1,500!" Still, the lots did not sell well. They were too far from downtown in an era before automobiles.

The solution was public transportation. Joining forces with other real estate developers such as Charlie Colcord and Henry Overholser, Classen convinced the city council to grant them the city's first franchise for a streetcar system. Not surprisingly, the steel rails extended north and west to the unsold lots. For a nickel fare, homeowners could build in the suburbs, and get to work quickly and safely. A week after the streetcars started running, Classen announced his second suburban developoment, Classen's West Highland Addition. Just as it was beginning its reign as the "fastest growing city in the nation," Oklahoma City suddenly was a suburban city stretching in all directions along the streetcar lines.

As he had done in Edmond, Classen turned his gift for deal making to good deeds. He helped start the German Methodist Church downtown, where a stained glass window still honors him, then he approached the Methodist Episcopal Church Conference with an idea for a church-affiliated institution of higher education in Oklahoma City. In 1902, with the streetcar system at his disposal, he made the church leaders an offer. If they would bring their school to his hometown, he would plat a new housing addition, give them half of the lots, and extend the streetcar to the school. They accepted. The effort resulted in the creation of Epworth College, later named Oklahoma City University, and the first Medical School, which would eventually serve as the cornerstone of the Health Sciences Center.

For the rest of his life, Anton Classen continued serving his community. He lobbied for single statehood, helped raise a bounty to attract the first packing plants, served as president of the Oklahoma Children's Home Society for five years, and served on the Building Committee for the Scottish Rite Temple in Guthrie. After his death in 1920, Classen would be memorialized in the naming of Classen Boulevard, Classen High School, and Northwest Classen High School in Oklahoma City.

But Classen's legacy went far beyond the naming rights left behind. Through his willingness to work with others for the common good, he helped give birth to the modern Chamber of Commerce. Through his willingness to take a chance, he built a business empire that created jobs and fueled the fires of expansion. And through his generosity, he improved the quality of life through churches, civic groups, and schools. In every way, Anton Classen embodied the "Spirit of '89."

While Oklahoma City grew rapidly after the Land Run of 1889, Tulsa remained a small village in the 1890s as shown by this view of the community's Main Street. (Courtesy Tulsa Historical Society)

The Sue Bland No. 1 was the discovery well of the Red Fork oil field near Tulsa. Red Fork did not prove to be a major find, but it stimulated oilmen to keep prospecting for oil in the area. Strikes would follow at Cleveland, in the Osage Nation, and southwest of Tulsa on the Ida Glenn farm. By statehood in 1907, Tulsa was on its way to becoming the "Oil Capital of the World." (Courtesy Beryl D. Ford Collection, Tulsa City County Library)

Prior to the discovery of oil in the Muskogee area, cotton was the staple of the local economy as seen in this view of a cotton gin in Muskogee, ca. 1900. (Courtesy Oklahoma Historical Society)

Newkirk, ca. 1900, was a busy community, especially on Saturdays when people from the surrounding countryside would come to town to sell eggs or produce, to shop, and to visit with friends. Note the sign on the pole in the right foreground announcing that "Gentry's Famous Dog and Pony Show" would soon be in town. (Courtesy Oklahoma Publishing Company)

Creative Oklahomans

Sequoyah's cabin near Sallisaw is preserved inside this modern structure designed and built by the Works Progress Administration (WPA). The pre-Civil War cabin may be viewed by the public. (Courtesy State Historic Preservation Office, Oklahoma Historical Society)

During the one hundred years that preceded Oklahoma statehood, numerous creative individuals lived in the area. Among the most renowned in this category was Sequoyah, who created a syllabary that enabled the Cherokee people to have a written language. Born in Tennessee in 1776, Sequoyah began toying with the idea of devising a writing system for his people in 1809. He began working on the project in earnest after fighting in the Cherokee Regiment with General Andrew Jackson's forces in the 1813 Battle of Horseshoe Bend.

Despite the ridicule of family and friends, some of whom believed he was insane, Sequoyah created a phonetic system, wherein each sound was represented by a symbol, 85 in all. Within several months, a large number of Cherokees could read and write using his system, which was formally adopted by the Cherokee government in 1821. He had joined the Western Cherokees in Arkansas in 1818, and he moved to the newly established Cherokee Nation in 1828, living not far from the present community of Sallisaw. Until his death in 1843, Sequoyah remained a respected leader who had given the gift of literacy to his people.

Language, a central theme in American Indian identity, was the art form chosen by Alexander Posey of the Creek Nation. Posey became one of the best known Native American literary figures in the United States. Born in 1873 near the present community of Eufaula, Posey learned Creek history and culture from his Creek mother and was forced to learn English by his Scots-Irish father. At Bacone Indian University, he began writing poetry and establishing a reputation as an orator.

Posey believed that the Creeks should accept change and favored individual ownership of land and economic development, differing with conservatives such as Chito Harjo. He pursued a brief career in politics, serving a term in the tribal Legislature, and then held several positions in education, including Superintendent of Public Instruction for the Creek Nation. By 1900 his poetry and some autobiographical works had begun to gain attention beyond Indian Territory. His most renowned work came when he purchased the *Indian Journal* newspaper, merged it with the *Eufaula Gazette*, and began writing a series of humorous letters from the fictional Fus Fixico, a supposed full-blood Creek who spoke English with a Creek dialect. He used the letters, 72 in all, to comment on social and political issues of the day. The letters gained national acclaim for their satirical wit that presaged the political humor of Will Rogers. Posey's blossoming literary career tragically was cut short in 1908 when he drowned in floodwaters while traveling from Muskogee to Eufaula.

Another expression of culture in Indian Territory was music. Two residents of the Choctaw Nation were destined to create music that would become internationally recognized. They were not the products of a formal education, for they were slaves on a cotton plantation near Doaksville owned by Brit Willis. Wallace and Minerva Willis, better known as Uncle Wallace and Aunt Minerva, did not write their songs but composed them orally and evolved them over time as they sang them. Among the most famous of their creations were "Swing Low Sweet Chariot," "Steal Away to Jesus," "Roll Jordon Roll," and "I'm a Rollin'."

Fortunately, Reverend Robert Reid, a missionary at the nearby Spencer Academy, heard them sing their songs and was impressed by them. He later passed on the lyrics and melodies by memory, with the help of his wife and sons, to Professor George L. White of Fisk University at Nashville, Tennessee, and helped the professor train the Fisk University Choir to sing them. The talented choir first performed the "spirituals" in public at a religious conference in Ohio in 1871. The choir began performing the inspirational music to great public acclaim, and several of the spirituals became popular internationally. In 1873 Queen Victoria of England was moved to tears by the Fisk University Jubilee Singers' rendition of "Steal Away to Jesus," noting that she had been more comforted by this music than anything since the death of her husband, Prince Albert. The musical creations by a slave couple in the Choctaw Nation have been widely recorded and remain popular more than a century and a half later.

Creek Indian journalist and literary figure Alexander Posey at age 18 in 1891. His satirical letters from the fictional Fus Fixico character received national attention. (Courtesy Alexander Posey Collection, Oklahoma Historical Society)

Ora Eddleman: At the Crossroads of History

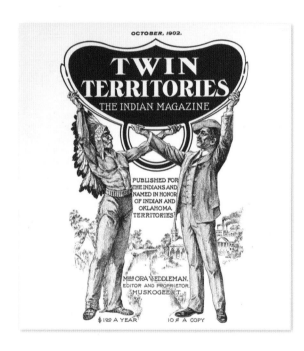

In 1898 the Indian Territory was a world of contradictions. Based on treaties and promises dating to the 1820s, the land belonged to the Five Civilized Tribes, but Indians were outnumbered almost four to one by white settlers. Full-blood Indians retained ancient traditions in their rural sanctuaries, while their mixed-blood leaders and white neighbors wore the latest fashions from New York and constructed two and three-story brick buildings in bustling towns such as Vinita, Muskogee, and Ardmore. While tribal members still elected their principal chiefs and council members, the federal government was taking control of the courts, allowing the platting of towns and putting barriers around the powers of the tribes.

Out of this world of contradictions came a fundamental question that would persist for the next 100 years. What did it mean to be an "Indian" in Oklahoma, the "land of the Red Man?" One person who tackled that perplexing dilemma in 1898 was a young, mixed-blood Cherokee woman named Ora Eddleman, editor of a remarkable periodical called *Twin Territories: The Indian Magazine.*

Eddleman was drawn to the issue of "Indian-ness" not only by curiosity and opportunity, but also by virtue of her heritage. Her father was David Eddleman, a Confederate veteran from Texas who had married Mary Daugherty, a one-quarter blood Cherokee whose grandparents had moved west in the 1820s as part of the Settlers Party. When she was born in 1880, her family lived in Denton, Texas, where David owned a ranch, invested in businesses, and served two terms as mayor. Fourteen years later, when Congress created the Dawes Commission to enroll tribal members for the allotment of lands, the Eddlemans moved to Muskogee.

During her impressionable teenage years, young Ora witnessed the accelerating changes transforming the lands of the Five Civilized Tribes. While Henry Dawes and his commissioners doggedly pursued the destruction of communally-owned tribal lands, Congress in 1898 passed the Curtis Act, which dissolved the tribal courts and extended

Ora Eddleman

American civil and criminal law to the territory. Towns were platted. Municipal bonds were sold. And the flood of non-Indian immigrants became a torrent. From 1897 to 1900, the leaders of the Five Civilized Tribes resigned themselves to the inevitable and concluded agreements to allot their lands to individuals.

Just as this transition was gaining speed, the Eddlemans purchased the *Muskogee Daily Times*, a newspaper where Eddleman split her time between attending school at Kendall College, the forerunner of the University of Tulsa, and working as a telegraph editor, proofreader, society editor, city editor, and, occasionally, press room printer. When her sister and brother-in-law started a new magazine, she eagerly joined them and became editor.

The first issue of *Twin Territories: The Indian Magazine* appeared in December of 1898 with a cover photograph of the historic cabin built by the great Cherokee innovator, Sequoyah. For ten cents an issue, or an annual subscription available for one dollar, readers found a mixture that perfectly reflected a sense of time and place. There were essays, poems, stories, serials, and illustrated articles as well as recurring departments focused on news pertaining to clubs, farmers, cattlemen, schools, and children. Dominating each issue, however, were articles by and about Indians.

(Facing page) The cover of *Twin Territories: The Indian Magazine* featured artwork that symbolized the changing world of the Indian Territory at the turn of the twentieth century. (Courtesy Oklahoma Historical Society)

Quannah Parker was the son of a Comanche chief and a white woman, Cynthia Ann Parker, who had been kidnapped as a child and raised as a Comanche. Parker led his people in their fight to remain free to roam the plains as they had for centuries. He eventually came to realize that the fight was hopeless and surrendered in 1875. Until his death in 1911 he led his people in their struggle to accommodate their society to the dominant white culture while preserving as much of their heritage as possible. He defended the use of peyote for religious purposes and he continued the traditional practice of having multiple wives in the face of strong pressure to abandon both customs. He is shown here (center) in traditional dress with two of his wives. (Courtesy Oklahoma Historical Society)

Most issues included historical pieces, ranging from narratives such as "About the Cherokees" and "A Tribe That is Almost Gone" to biographies of Indian leaders such as John Ross and Quanah Parker, the last of the Comanche chiefs who still was presiding over the welfare of his tribe from his home on the reservation near Fort Sill. This blurring of the line between historical perspective and contemporary news would be a recurring theme throughout the life of the magazine.

Eddleman welcomed sketches by the people who had witnessed the rapid changes in the territory. Among the autobiographical writers were the Baptist missionary Reverend Joseph Samuel Murrow and Alice Robertson, the daughter of missionaries who would become a pioneer businesswoman and eventual congresswoman from the state. Their memories, recorded while history was still unfolding, bridged the past and future. Even more importantly, Eddleman provided an outlet for aspiring Indian writers exploring their changing world. Political leaders such as Pleasant Porter, chief of the Creeks, used the pages of the magazine to express his views on allotment, sovereignty, and the possibilities of single statehood for the Indian nations. The noted Creek, Chinnubbie Harjo, better known as Alexander Posey, provided a constant stream of poems and short stories that captured the

unique structure and humor of American Indian language and culture.

Eddleman wrote many pieces herself. She started a series called "Types of Indian Girls," which featured photographs of young women, usually in fashionable white dresses, with text that emphasized the blending of two cultures and touted the sophistication of their lives deep in the Indian Territory. Turning to fiction, she wrote romantic serials that followed the adventures of young Indian girls as they experienced life, one chapter at a time.

In one series, titled "A Pair of Moccasins," a young Indian orphan is treated badly by a white girl at school until numerous acts of kindness and generosity melt away the racial prejudices. Other stories were titled "Lizonka, a Creek Girl," "Only an Indian Girl," and "Her Mother's Daughter," which left the last chapter of the serial open for a competition to see who could write the best ending. Harriet Bradley, a young blind woman, finished the story and won the prize.

In 1904, now twenty-four years old, Eddleman married Charles Reed, a reporter for the Associated Press, and left the staff of *Twin Territories*, which ceased publication in May. She still wrote, however, editing a section called the "Indian Department" in a new magazine called *Sturms*. In one of her early columns, she stated her goal as "the study of Indian history and literature…to

report the progress he has made and is making to the world of civilization."

Through both magazines, Eddleman followed the growing suspense over statehood and the essential question of whether Oklahoma would be admitted to the Union as one state or two. When representatives of the Five Civilized Tribes gathered to write the constitution for the State of Sequoyah, she gave them her hearty endorsement. When the advocates for single statehood carried the day in 1907, she lamented the lost opportunity to continue the experiment of Indian self rule.

Eddleman, like her neighbors in the former Indian Territory, went on with life despite the changed world around her. She raised a family, moved with her husband first to Wyoming and then back to Muskogee, and continued expressing her unique perspective on race and cultural survival. In the 1940s and 1950s, after a brief experiment at hosting a radio talk show called "The Sunshine Lady," she published several articles in *The Chronicles of Oklahoma*, yet another magazine dedicated to the unique blending of cultures. On June 19, 1968, Ora Eddleman died at her home in Tulsa.

The legacy of this mixed-blood Cherokee woman is clearly illustrated on the cover of the October 1902 issue of her beloved magazine. Set against a background showing a teepee, a river, a church, and a factory are two men, one bare-chested and dressed in buckskins and a feather headdress, the other wearing a business suit, tie, and vest. With arms crossed, they are holding aloft a banner with the words "Twin Territories: The Indian Magazine. Published for the Indians and Named in Honor of Indian and Oklahoma Territories." To Ora Eddleman, she was living at the crossroads of history, a time when the past was fusing with the future to create a new society, a new culture, a new place she was proud to call home.

A. M. DeBolt built this half-dugout on his claim near Oklahoma City. He later prospered as owner of DeBolt's Hardware Store. (Courtesy Oklahoma Historical Society)

One of the best known women in the territorial and early statehood period was Lucille Mulhull, a star of her father Zack Mulhall's wild west show as well as in Vaudeville. She was referred to as "America's Greatest Horsewoman" and "Queen of the Range." She competed effectively against men in riding and roping events, and Will Rogers considered her to be "the world's greatest rider." The town of Mulhall was named for her family, and the word "cowgirl" was coined to describe her when she played New York's Madison Square Garden in 1905. (Courtesy Oklahoma Publishing Company)

Although baseball was the most popular team sport in the Twin Territories prior to statehood, football was being played by some high schools and colleges. Town teams were formed, such as this Pauls Valley team in 1903. Considered to be one of the best town teams in the state that year, Pauls Valley defeated the University of Oklahoma "B" team as well as teams from Ardmore and Purcell. At this point helmets and shoulder pads were not used. (Courtesy Oklahoma Historical Society)

Another nationally known attraction along Route 66 in Oklahoma is the Round Barn at Arcadia, built in 1898. Over time the structure fell into a state of disrepair. Luther "Luke" Robison led a successful effort to restore the structure, which is owned and maintained by the Arcadia Historical Society.

CHAPTER TWO

The Forty-Sixth State

America's Melting Pot

Charles F. Colcord: The New Frontier

When Oklahoma became a state on November 16, 1907, the economy of the Twin Territories was still grounded squarely on agriculture, with farmers and ranchers pulling wealth out of the soil and merchants and professionals setting up market centers along the growing network of railroads. But just as the political winds were blowing from new directions, the forces of economic development were shifting to capital formation and added value. One of the most successful foot soldiers in the vanguard of this new frontier was Charles F. Colcord.

Colcord was born in Kentucky on the eve of the Civil War. His father, after serving in the defeated Confederate Army, sold his share in the family plantation to a brother and moved to Louisiana. When young Charlie came down with malaria, his parents sent the ten-year-old boy to live with an old friend who had started a ranch west of Corpus Christi, Texas. Two years later, to avoid returning to school, he ran away and found a job as a cowboy making $12 a month.

Colcord spent the next two decades on the back of a horse. He learned to ride, rope, shoot, and take care of himself under the worst of conditions. In 1875 he made his first trip to the Indian Territory, driving a herd of horses north along the Chisholm Trail. He joined his father to help form the Comanche Pool, a large open range cattle operation in western Kansas. He married, tried ranching in Arizona, and witnessed the meteoric rise and fall of the real estate boom in Wichita. Throughout each episode of this frontier saga, Colcord was learning the lessons of how to make money.

On April 22, 1889, Colcord made the land run into the Unassigned Lands. He claimed and quickly traded a quarter-section near Kingfisher for a team and wagon, then rode into Oklahoma City, a tent town of 10,000 immigrants where he traded the team and wagon for a lot and house next to the railroad tracks. In his pocket, he had a ten dollar bill and forty-five cents in change.

Through his connections as a native of Kentucky, Colcord was named the first chief of police, with his pay coming from the fines collected from those he arrested. He was elected

Charles F. Colcord

(Facing page) Charles Colcord was a cowboy, lawman, entrepreneur, civic leader, and philanthropist throughout his life in Oklahoma. (Courtesy Oklahoma Historical Society)

Colcord's financial success was reflected in his mansion on Northwest 13th Street, just north of downtown Oklahoma City. This magnificent home was demolished in the 1960s to make way for a business structure, an event that helped spur the historic preservation movement in Oklahoma City. (Courtesy Oklahoma Historical Society)

Oklahoma City's first police department was headed by Police Chief Charles Colcord, seated, who posed for this photograph with his officers in August 1890. (Courtesy Edna M. Couch Collection, Oklahoma Historical Society)

the first sheriff of Oklahoma County, bought and sold real estate, and became a deputy United States marshal. In 1893, when the government announced the opening of the Cherokee Outlet by run, he decided to try one more frontier.

Still a gifted rider at the age of 34, Colcord was one of the first to arrive in Perry, a promising new town on the Santa Fe tracks where he claimed a corner lot across from the town square and filed on a quarter-section just outside of town. With steady income from fees earned as a deputy

marshal, he farmed, raised cattle, and bought and sold property. By 1900, when he decided to leave Perry, he had $28,000 in cash and a like amount in notes. He decided to invest all of it in Oklahoma City.

Although Guthrie was the territorial capital and the city most favored by railroad officials, Colcord saw something he liked in Oklahoma City. He had connections there, linked to the community by the experience of the land run and his years as a lawman. He also recognized the potential impact of the Frisco Railroad, which had built into

town in 1897 and created an economic lifeline to St. Louis and cities beyond. He thought there was room to grow.

In March of 1900, Colcord met Bob Galbraith, a kindred spirit of the frontier who had started a real estate business in Oklahoma City. When Charlie told his new friend he wanted to buy some property, they looked at lots at Main Street and Broadway Avenue, a building north of 4th Street, and undeveloped farmland west of town. He bought it all. Within a year, Colcord had invested more than $50,000 of his nest egg in real estate. It was the right decision, in the right place, at the right time.

From 1900 to 1910 Oklahoma City was the fastest growing community in the country, exploding from a sleepy town of 10,000 people to a bustling city of 64,000. Unlike the Wichita real estate bubble that Charlie had witnessed in 1887, this boom had a solid foundation built on unprecedented agricultural prosperity and a decade of feverish railroad construction that connected Oklahoma City and its six trunk line railroads with hundreds of towns and villages filled with willing customers. Oklahoma City became a wholesale center with a mixture of manufacturing, milling, and services that created jobs and attracted investments. In on the ground floor, Charles Colcord made a fortune.

The former cowboy subdivided raw

Constructed in 1903, the mansion of Henry and Anna Ione Overholser was the first home built in the area that in the late 1960s would become the Heritage Hills neighborhood in Oklahoma City. Henry was a prominent business and civic leader in Oklahoma City from 1889 until his death in 1915, while Anna was the grand dame of Oklahoma City. The home is now the property of the Oklahoma Historical Society and is maintained for touring by the public. (Courtesy Jim Argo)

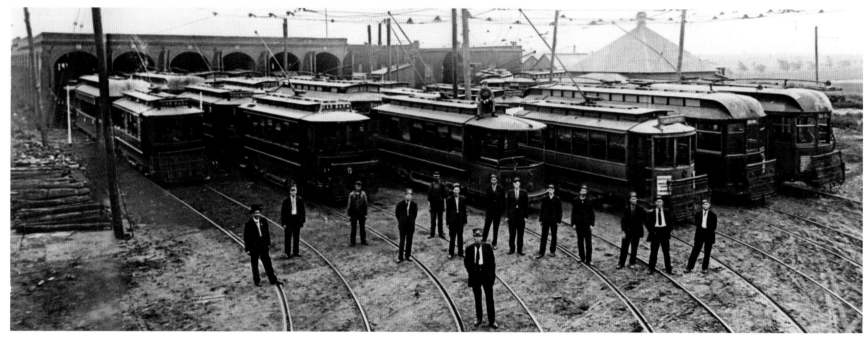

prairie into housing additions and built streetcar lines to carry homeowners to work and play. He constructed buildings on his land west of town for Delmar Gardens, an entertainment venue that included a beer garden, race track, and amusements. He provided the land and raised a bonus to build the city's first grand hotel, the Lee. To cap it all, in 1909 he built the Colcord Building at Grand and Broadway avenues, a twelve-story office building designed by William Wells, a student of the famed Chicago architect, Louis Sullivan. At the time, the white tower was the tallest building in town,

a symbol of promise and a source of pride.

In the spring of 1901, just as this real estate empire started producing a stream of revenue, Colcord and his partners bought several lots in Red Fork, a new town located on the Frisco tracks southwest of Tulsa. When a man drilling for water on one of these lots hit a shallow play of natural gas, Galbraith rushed to the community and started buying mineral rights from Creek families in the surrounding hills. The partners drilled, found both gas and oil, and started laying a pipeline to Tulsa. Before they completed the line, they sold

their holdings to Glenn Braden, who would organize Oklahoma Natural Gas Company five years later.

In 1905, while running a pack of hounds out of Colcord's camp at Red Fork, Galbraith lost a couple of dogs that were found on a nearby farm owned by Bob Glenn, a Creek Indian who had recently received title to his allotment. After a meal prepared by Glenn's wife, Ida, they were walking on the farm when one of the men struck a sandstone outcrop with a sledge hammer. Out of the stone came a few tablespoons of high-grade, green oil. Galbraith, acting on behalf of his

The advent of streetcars in Oklahoma City and other communities in the state was considered to be a great complement to city life. Neighborhoods that previously were too far from the central business district could be developed. The streetcar system in Oklahoma City was inaugurated in 1903 and was phased out by 1947. Here Oklahoma City streetcar drivers pose in front of their streetcars and barns. (Courtesy Oklahoma Historical Society)

partner Colcord, immediately secured leases in the surrounding vicinity.

The partners drilled a well and hit oil that flowed 140 barrels a day. They moved the rig a few hundred yards to the west and hit oil that flowed 600 barrels a day. Moving still farther, they hit a gusher that flowed 5,000 barrels a day. That first well, the Ida Glenn No. 1, had been on the eastern edge of the giant field. The result of that chance discovery was the fabulous Glenn Pool Field, the first giant field in Oklahoma history and the field that attracted the attention of "the greatest gamblers" from around the world. It also was the field that made Tulsa the "Oil Capital of the World."

Although Colcord never had an oil company named after him, his family did. His two daughters, Cadijah and Caroline,

married Walt Helmerich and John Wesley Bates respectively. Helmerich would partner with William T. Payne to create Helmerich and Payne, one of the most successful drilling firms in the world. Bates formed Reading and Bates, which eventually became one of the largest offshore drilling firms in the world. Both had their beginnings with Colcord capital.

Colcord, like many of his contemporaries, gave back to the community that provided him with opportunities. He helped organize the effort to move the capital from Guthrie to Oklahoma City in 1910, which was followed with service on the commission that chose the site for the Capitol Building northeast of the downtown business district at what is now Northeast 23rd Street and Lincoln Boulevard. When Governor Charles

Haskell demanded a cash bonus from the people of Oklahoma City to seal the site selection, Colcord helped raise the money.

Among the many organizations served by Colcord in his latter years was the Oklahoma Historical Society, organized in 1893 by the Oklahoma Territory Press Association to collect newspapers and other materials tracing the history of the region. Colcord was president of the society in 1930 when state officials dedicated the new Historical Building at Northeast 21st Street and Lincoln, the second building constructed in the State Capitol Complex. In 2005, two years before the centennial of statehood, that same organization would open the Oklahoma History Center, a 215,000-square-foot museum and research facility dedicated to collecting, preserving, and sharing stories such as that of Charles Colcord.

Colcord passed away in 1934. Before he died, he wrote his autobiography, one of the best memoirs ever written by an Oklahoman. Throughout the book are stories that evoke images of the frontier. He was a cowboy, a lawman, and an '89er. But it was the new frontier, the frontier of capital investments and taking chances, where Colcord achieved some of his greatest victories. By taking chances and gambling on the future, people like Charles Colcord helped shape the future of Oklahoma.

The heart of Oklahoma City's black community in the 1920s was "Deep Deuce," an area that encompassed several blocks near downtown on Northeast 2nd Street as well as several blocks to the north. Here black businesses and jazz musicians, including Jimmie Rushing and the Oklahoma City Blue Devils, flourished. After decades of neglect and decline, the area had been resurrected as a residential area adjacent to the Bricktown entertainment district. (Courtesy Oklahoma Historical Society)

After Guthrie lost the State Capital to Oklahoma City in 1910, the town went into a long period during which little was done to the Victorian-era business buildings and homes in the community. This "stagnation" came to be viewed as an asset as interest in the state's history and architectural heritage began to grow in the 1960s. Many buildings were restored and the entire downtown district of Guthrie was placed on the National Register of Historic Places. The city now is a popular destination for tourists and Oklahomans who enjoy the historic homes and business district as well as the many interesting museums in the community. (Courtesy Jim Argo)

The Fred Drummond home in Hominy was built in 1905 by Hominy's first mayor, who was a highly successful trader and rancher. The attractive home features a central square tower, a second floor balcony, and false dormers. The exterior combines native sandstone with light and dark green shingles. The beautifully furnished home, now is owned by the Oklahoma Historical Society and is open for visitation by the public. (Courtesy Jim Argo)

(Above right) The Mattie Beal home in Lawton is a popular historical attraction in that community. Beal won a 160 acre homestead in the land lottery of 1901. She was married to local lumberyard owner Charles Payne in 1902. Their home was a center of Lawton society for many years and today is owned by the Lawton Heritage Association, which maintains it for touring by the general public. (Courtesy Jim Argo)

(Lower right) Another home of prominence during the early statehood period was that of Chickasaw Governor Douglas H. Johnston, located at Emet in eastern Johnston County. Known as the "White House of the Chickasaws," the house was the home of Governor Johnston and his family from 1898 to 1971. Johnston, who served as Governor of the Chickasaw Nation for 33 years, died in 1939. It was at this home that William H. Murray married Johnston's niece, Mary Alice Hearrell, and prominent politicians and members of the Dawes Commissions often met. The home now is owned by the Chickasaw Nation, which is in the midst of carefully restoring it and developing an interpretive program in anticipation of opening the home to the public. (Courtesy State Historic Preservation Office, Oklahoma Historical Society)

Making a New State

On November 16, 1907, Oklahoma became the forty-sixth state in the Union. The road to that historic date was neither simple nor direct.

The first mention of statehood for some part of what would become Oklahoma appeared in the Reconstruction Treaties of 1866, which included a simple clause that the Five Civilized Tribes would start down the path of the state-making process. Skilled politicians, the leaders of the tribes used various tactics to delay the statehood process.

In 1887 Congress jump started the process by passing the General Allotment Act, which provided a framework for transferring land owner-ship from the tribes to individual members of the tribes. Finding a way to accomplish that task was assigned to the Dawes Commission, created in 1893. Again, the leaders of the Five Civilized Tribes put up a stout defense.

To the west, on the lands lost by the Five Civilized Tribes after the Civil War, pressure was mounting for statehood on a separate track that confused the issue even more. It began with the Land Run of 1889, which opened the Unassigned Lands to non-Indian settlement, and gained momentum with the creation of Oklahoma Territory in August of 1890. For the next eleven years, other sections of the old Indian Nations were opened and added to the formal territory governed under the provisions of the United States Constitution.

A central question arose. Would the Twin Territories be added to the Union as two states or as one? Many white leaders did not care which, as long as it happened quickly. As early as 1890, a bill for separate statehood was filed in Congress but no action was taken. Indian leaders, however, were adamant that the lands of the Five Civilized Tribes should be formed into one distinct state, an opinion that gained ground after 1898 when Congress passed the Curtis Act, abolishing all tribal courts and tribal laws. According to that act, tribal governments would cease to exist in eight years.

In July of 1905, with the deadline approaching, Indian leaders convened a statehood convention in Muskogee and called their proposed state Sequoyah. On November 7, 1905, the people of the Indian Territory overwhelmingly approved the constitution. The State of Sequoyah was not to be, however, because Congress, which was strongly Republican at the time, did not want two states that most likely would send Democratic senators to Washington. If there was to be a new state, there would be only one. On June 16, 1906, Congress passed the Enabling Act, which set the final stage for the state-making process.

Under the terms of the law, the people of Oklahoma Territory elected 55 delegates from districts created by the territorial Legislature. The people of the Indian Territory also elected 55 delegates. The Osages, the last of the tribes to accept allotment, elected two delegates. On November 20, 1906, the delegates gathered in Guthrie to organize the Constitutional Convention. William H. "Alfalfa Bill" Murray was elected president of the convention.

The document they produced was the longest state constitution ever written. It organized the proposed government at the state, county, and municipal levels, defined the boundaries and seats of counties, and dealt with issues such as child labor laws, mandatory education, and regulation of corporations. On September 17, 1907, the people of the Twin Territories approved the constitution and elected a slate of state officials. President Theodore Roosevelt signed the final document on November 16, 1907. With the stroke of that eagle quill pen, Oklahoma became the forty-sixth state in the Union.

Oklahoma statehood became official on November 16, 1907. A massive crowd gathered in front of Guthrie's Carnegie Library for the swearing in of Charles N. Haskell as Oklahoma's first Governor. (Courtesy Oklahoma Publishing Company)

The delegates to the Oklahoma Constitutional Convention convened in Guthrie in November 1906 and met into early 1907 to craft a constitution for the proposed State of Oklahoma. Democrats dominated the convention with 99 of the 112 delegates. The delegates took a break from their deliberations to pose for an official photograph. (Courtesy Oklahoma Historical Society)

Augusta I. Metcalfe: Oklahoma's Sagebrush Artist

While Anton H. Classen and Charles Colcord fostered commerce, industry, and urban development in the new state, other pioneers established farms and ranches in rural Oklahoma. One such couple was Edward G. and Mary Ann Davidson Corson, whose daughter would become nationally known for documenting the pioneer experience through her art. That sagebrush artist was Augusta Metcalfe.

Edward was a ship's carpenter in Philadelphia, Pennsylvania, and Mary Ann was a school teacher. Headed west, they settled near Vermillion in northeastern Kansas, near the Nebraska border. There Augusta was born in 1881. Mary Ann was artistic—she made wax fruit and human-hair flowers—and realized that little "Gustie" had talent when, at age four, she drew her first horse. Observing her daughter's continued interest in drawing, Mary Ann determined to "do all in my power to see that the spark is fanned into flame." In 1886 the family moved from Kansas to No-Man's Land, which would become the Oklahoma Panhandle.

By the time she was eight, Gustie was herding cattle for her parents. Before long she was herding cattle for her neighbors, as many as 300 head, at a rate of 17 cents per head per month, contributing significantly to the family income. While doing this chore, she would take time to scratch the various cattle brands into an abandoned white stone house. By the time the family departed the Panhandle in 1893, she had memorized more than 100 cattle brands. During these years she also practiced drawing cattle, horses, and dogs.

At age 12, Augusta moved to the place where she was destined to remain for 77 years. Her father moved the family to a homestead in the recently opened Cheyenne and Arapaho Reservation. Settling close to the Antelope Hills and the Washita River near Cheyenne, Oklahoma Territory, the Corson family worked hard to establish their farming operation. Augusta's new home stimulated her artistic sensibilities, as she was enthralled with the rugged, red hills, the nearby Washita River, and the trees that seemed to sing as the wind whistled through them. She also loved the hardy, pioneer people who lived in the area. Augusta viewed her dramatic environment and the scenes of everyday life through the eyes of

Augusta I. Metcalfe

an artist, and she began to execute sketches and pen and ink drawings of what she saw.

Augusta's art work usually would have to wait until evenings. As she recalled years later, "My Pa taught me to get my work done first and then play." And there was plenty of work to be done on the farm. Augusta worked hard, performing tasks such as roping and branding cattle that any boy her age would have been expected to do, as well as performing household chores. At the end of the day's work, however, she would record the day's activities by drawing pictures. She literally would sketch "anything and everything she saw," such as dogs, horses, calves being born, and cattle being rounded up. Some evenings she would join her mother, who played mandolin, in making music with her fiddle.

Leonard Clay, a local boy, remembered Augusta as a "slender like girl" who was "always laughing." He recalled seeing her for the first time when he and his family rode to the Corson place in their wagon to get acquainted: "Augusta came riding up on a bay stallion they called Kaiser and rode along with us a piece. She was a graceful rider and made quite a sight!" Augusta did not receive formal public education but had the benefit of learning from her well-educated mother. She continued to live at home, working and developing as an artist, until at age 25 she married Jim Metcalfe.

The marriage did not last long, but Metcalfe gave her a son, Howard. After three years he departed, leaving Augusta to care for a toddler, and, with her mother, a farm. Her father by this time was deceased. Augusta branded cattle, rode herd, fixed fence, and attended to sick cattle. She had little time to draw or paint, but she developed the habit of adding sketches and miniature paintings to letters that she sent to friends and relatives. These documents would become prized possessions. She did paint whenever she could make some time, and her work was noticed by T. C. Moore, who was County Superintendent of Schools for Roger Mills County. Moore encouraged Augusta to enter some of her work in the State Fair in Oklahoma City. She did so and won a blue ribbon in 1911.

As Howard grew older, he was able to do more work on the farm, giving Augusta more time to paint and care for her mother, who died in 1920. She labored in relative obscurity, however, through the teens, 20s, 30s, and much of the 40s. She held the farm together during the difficult years of the

(Facing page) Augusta Metcalfe combined her life experiences with her artistic talent to preserve images of pioneer life in western Oklahoma for future generations. (Courtesy Break O'Day Farm and Metcalfe Museum)

Metcalfe painted *Please Ma* in 1951. Along with many other works by Metcalfe, this painting may be viewed at the Metcalfe Museum, located on farm where she lived. Also on the property are the Metcalfe home and other buildings, all of which are available for touring. (Courtesy Break O'Day Farm and Metcalfe Museum)

Great Depression through hard work and frugality. During World War II, Howard fought for his country, leaving Augusta to run the farm. She milked 16 cows per day in addition to all the other work she had to do. Her art work was limited to the scenes she used to illustrate her letters to Howard. At the war's end, Howard returned, was married, and took over the bulk of the work on the farm. Augusta began painting in earnest, and she soon emerged from obscurity.

Roy P. Stewart, a widely read columnist for *The Daily Oklahoman* newspaper saw Augusta riding a horse in a parade during an Old Settlers' Reunion in Cheyenne in 1949. He met her, saw her art, and wrote about her in one of his "Country Boy" columns, titling the piece "The Sagebrush Artist." Nan Sheets, director of the Oklahoma City Art Center and an outstanding artist, read Stewart's column and soon traveled to Roger Mills County to visit Augusta. Sheets understood that Augusta had no formal art training but nonetheless proclaimed that she "wouldn't change her. She is developing a style all her own. She copies no one." Sheets also observed that Augusta had "no interest in painting anything other than scenes and incidents, as she remembers them, from her life in the early days among the ranchers and cowboys of Western Oklahoma."

Sheets returned home and quickly arranged a one-artist show for Metcalfe at Oklahoma City's Municipal Auditorium. An article by Stewart in the July 17, 1950, issue of *Life Magazine*, with photographs of some of her best work, drew national attention. Augusta quickly became nationally known. Her reputation was enhanced in 1958 when she began exhibiting her work in the Grand Central Art Galleries in New York City, where much of her work was sold. In the opinion of one of the New York art authorities at the time, she was "the only one living who has lived this life and can put it on canvas." She returned to Oklahoma City for a solo show at the Oklahoma Art Center in Oklahoma City in 1967, where patrons were charmed by paintings such as *Country*

Doctor, Fighting a Prairie Fire, Star Route from Hamburg to Durham, Oklahoma, 1912, Going to a Dance, Camp Meeting, and many more. Late in life, she was inducted into the Oklahoma Hall of Fame and the National Cowgirl Hall of Fame.

Augusta continued to live and work on her family's homestead until she died at age 89 in 1971. She was given many titles, including "The Sagebrush Artist," and "The Prairie Painter"—and she deserved them all and more, for she lived the pioneer life most of her years, and she documented for future generations the love, beauty, danger, and hardships experienced by those pioneers.

Men and women gathered for a quilting bee at the Ferdinand Engel farm, two miles east of Corn, a predominantly Mennonite community in northeastern Washita County, on July 10, 1908. The women would gather once a week at different homes to make quilts, comforts, and dresses. While the women worked and visited, the men gathered for a Bible discussion. Each year at Thanksgiving, all of the items that had been made were sold at auction at the local Mennonite Brethren church. Annual proceeds usually totaled about $800 and were donated to support mission work overseas. (Courtesy Oklahoma Publishing Company)

Thomas B. Slick: King of the Wildcatters

By 1907 the petroleum industry already had made its mark on Oklahoma, which was located in the middle of the huge Mid-Continent Oil Region that stretched from central Texas to eastern Kansas. For the next century, oil and natural gas exploration, production, and refining played a dominant role in the state's economy, while oilmen provided civic and sometimes political leadership as well as philanthropic generosity. The industry also produced colorful characters, such as Josh Cosden, Tulsa's "Prince of Petroleum," and Ponca City's E. W. Marland, the future governor of the state. But of all the men who were called wildcatters—those who leased and drilled for oil in areas that boasted no previous production—none were more colorful or important than Thomas B. Slick, the "King of the Wildcatters."

Oklahoma's first oil well was drilled in 1859, 55 years prior to Slick's arrival in the area. This was the same year that Colonel Edwin Drake launched the "Age of Petroleum" by drilling the discovery well at Titusville, Pennsylvania. Lewis Ross, brother of Cherokee Chief John Ross, was drilling a well, seeking salt water for his salt works near present Salina when he struck oil. For a variety of reasons, including difficulties of dealing with the Bureau of Indian Affairs in obtaining leases, the lack of significant local markets, and inadequate transportation available to ship crude oil, the industry did not blossom in Indian Territory until 1899. Bartlesville, connected by rail to a refinery in Kansas, became the territory's first oil boom town. This stimulated interest among oilmen from other producing areas who began combing the area for other potential oil fields. Among those was Tom Slick.

Slick was born in 1883 at Shippenville, Pennsylvania, approximately 30 miles south of Drake's discovery well at Titusville. At the age of 16, he went with his father to work in the oil fields of West Virginia. Two years later, in 1901, he moved to Illinois where he leased his first property for oil exploration. This process involved executing legal agreements with individuals who owned the mineral rights for a particular piece of property where an oilman or company wanted to drill. The lease generally involved payment of a specific amount per

Thomas B. Slick

acre, a percentage royalty on any production that might result, and a time limit for how long the lease would be in effect. The specific lease terms were subject to negotiation. Generally, leases in areas where production had been proven were more expensive than leases in areas where there had been no production.

In 1904 Slick moved to Kansas, where he went to work for Alexander Massey, who already had employed Slick's father and brother. Slick soon convinced Massey to let him buy some leases in Indian Territory. Massey had an office at Tryon, a small community located about 12 miles southwest of Cushing. Slick was to receive 25 percent of the leases he secured. After leasing about 27,000 acres, Slick began drilling a well near Tryon, but after reaching a depth of 2,800 feet he determined that it was a "duster" and abandoned it. Slick had no way of knowing that if he had continued to 4,000 feet he likely would have found significant production, as other operators in the area would prove years later.

This dry hole was the first of many that Slick drilled over the next eight years as he worked in conjunction with Massey, C. B. Shaffer of Illinois, and with other partners. He became known as "Dry Hole Slick" and as "Mad Tom Slick," but he refused to give up his dream, which was fueled by major strikes at various places in Osage County

and at Red Fork, Cleveland, and Glenn Pool. In 1912, to drill one more well, he turned to his former partner, Shaffer, who agreed to advance $8,000 in exchange for an interest in some of Slick's leases. Slick used this cash to begin drilling on the farm of Frank Wheeler, about 12 miles east of Cushing, where he later claimed "the smell of oil sands was perfume to his nostrils."

Slick found oil at 1,400 feet but decided to drill deeper to see if he could find a more productive sand. At four in the morning on March 17, 1912, his well blew in and he knew he had made a major strike. He temporarily set casing to stop the flow of the well and spread fresh dirt over the crude that had "gushed" over the top of the derrick. Still the news spread quickly. One competing lease hound, eager to start obtaining leases in the area, reported to his boss that he went to a livery stable in Cushing and "damned if Slick hadn't already been there and hired every rig." He finally managed to obtain use of a farm wagon and horse after walking three miles into the country to obtain it, returned to Cushing to get a notary to go with him to notarize leases, and "damned if Slick hadn't hired every notary in town, too. . . ." Slick's tactics gave him several days to get as much additional land under lease as possible.

Slick's Wheeler No. 1 proved to be the discovery well of what would become the greater Cushing-Drumright Field. The town

of Drumright was created by the boom, as was Shamrock, a colorful, Irish-flavored town which featured green buildings, a newspaper called the *Shamrock Brogue*, and a blarney stone. Cushing also boomed with the construction of numerous refineries. The field was at the height of its production during World War I, and Cushing crude played a vital role in the Allied war effort. By the end of 1919, Cushing was producing 17 percent of all oil marketed in the United States and about 3 percent of the world's production. The crude was the highest grade found west of the Mississippi River to that time, and because of the massive refinery and storage facilities built there, Cushing became one of the major pipeline connecting points in the United States. Prices for "light, sweet" crude still were being set at Cushing as the state began its second 100 years.

Slick made millions from his Cushing operations, sold them, and continued to wildcat other fields, playing a prominent role in the development of the Tonkawa, Seminole, Slick, and Oklahoma City fields, as well as fields in Kansas and Texas. The Creek County boom town of Slick was named in his honor after it sprang up in 1919 near his well which found the Slick Pool. By 1929 Slick was reputed to be the largest independent oil operator in the United States, producing 30,000 to 35,000 barrels of oil per day. By 1930 Slick had 45 wells being

(Previous page) A typical street scene in Drumright, a town that sprang into existence with the development of the Cushing-Drumright oil field. Tom Slick drilled the well that ignited the rush of oilmen to the area. (Courtesy Oklahoma Historical Society)

THE BIG OIL FIRE AT DRUMRIGHT AUG. 28.14
ELECTRIC STUDIO.

drilled and more than 30 wells completed in the prolific Oklahoma City Field.

Slick died in 1930 at the age of 47. Soon thereafter, one of the wells he had started in the Oklahoma City Field came in producing 43,200 barrels of oil per day. It proved to be his largest. Slick's remarkable career had been cut short, but his reputation as "King of the Wildcatters" was forever established. Men like Slick, whom one historian called "The Greatest Gamblers," played a vital role in developing the oil and natural gas resources of Oklahoma. They indeed were gamblers. For every oilman who struck it rich, there were hundreds who failed. The oil entrepreneurs, and their employees, transformed Oklahoma's economy and culture, and the state's energy companies remained vitally important to the state's future as it entered its centennial year of statehood in 2007.

The Cushing-Drumright Field which Tom Slick discovered grew into an internationally renowned oil field. The town of Cushing boomed and new communities were created, such as Drumright. In August of 1914 a thunderstorm spawned lightening strikes that ignited a number of 55,000-barrel oil storage tanks. The resulting conflagration became known as "The August Hell." This is a view of that event as seen from a hilltop in Drumright. Unlike its siblings Justright, Allright, and Dropright, Drumright survived the end of the boom. (CourtesyOklahoma Historical Society)

Progress also came rapidly to Bartlesville, Oklahoma's first oil boomtown. Here street car tracks are being constructed, ca. 1908. (Courtesy Oklahoma Historical Society)

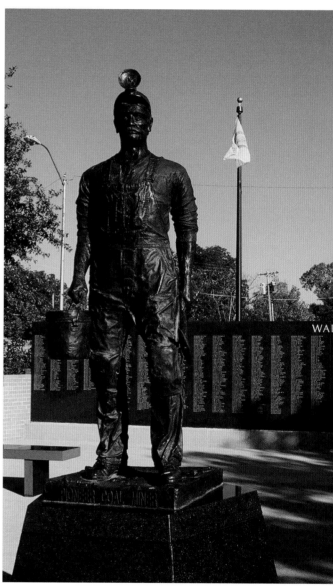

Coal mining was a major economic activity in much of eastern Oklahoma from the 1870s through the 1960s. The industry employed thousands of men, many of who migrated to the region from other mining states or from overseas. Communities such as Krebs have retained Italian identities while Hartshorne has the only Russian Orthodox Church in Oklahoma. Mining in this period was a dangerous occupation.>

The coal mining heritage of the McAlester area was recognized by the construction of a Coal Miner Memorial in a city park. Inspired and funded by Clark and Wanda Bass of the First National Bank of McAlester, the memorial included a statue of a pioneer miner and a black granite wall containing the names of more than 1,700 miners who were killed in mining accidents in the McAlester area. (Courtesy Jim Argo)

Progress in the form of telephone poles and lines came to McAlester in 1910. Note the workers sitting on top of the pole in front of the Palace Drug Store. (Courtesy Oklahoma Historical Society)

Frontier Politics, 1907-1932

Oklahoma's turbulent politics during the first 25 years of statehood reflected the frontier status of the state as well as its diverse population. Adding spice to this mixture were the national populist and progressive movements, racism, and the struggle for power between the state's executive and legislative branches. Eastern Oklahoma, with more political experience and a larger population, dominated the early politics of the state. Because that area had been settled primarily by people from the South, the Democrat Party dominated the region and thus the state as

well. The first governor was Democrat Charles Haskell of Muskogee, and his party swept all statewide offices and both houses of the Legislature. The Republican Party remained sufficiently strong to provide serious competition for the Democrats until the political realignment that would occur nationally during the Great Depression of the 1930s.

Perhaps the most significant accomplishment of the Haskell administration was establishing Oklahoma City as the permanent capital of the state, sending Guthrie, the former capital viewed by Democrats as

(Above left) An attorney and railroad promoter from Muskogee, Charles N. Haskell hoped to make Muskogee the "Queen City of the Southwest." He was a prominent member of the Sequoyah and Oklahoma constitutional conventions and was elected governor as a Democrat strongly urging voters to ratify the proposed constitution. He was elected governor in September of 1907 and took office on November 16. (Courtesy Oklahoma Heritage Association)

"a nest of Republicans," into decades of stagnation. Democratic Party squabbles between its various constituencies, such as farmers and labor, also caused some to turn to alternatives, such as the Socialist Party. The Democrats, however, united to pass laws that discriminated against blacks, who largely voted Republican. These "Jim Crow" laws ultimately provided for segregation of virtually all public facilities and greatly reduced the number of blacks who could vote. Decades of effort on the part of civil rights leaders would be required to address the damage caused by these laws.

Women did not achieve the right to vote until ratification of the Nineteenth Amendment to the United States Constitution in 1920. Yet, Kate Barnard was elected Oklahoma Commissioner of Charities and Corrections in 1910. Alice M. Robertson of Muskogee was elected to Congress in 1921. Nonetheless, few Oklahoma women would hold significant political positions over the ensuing six decades.

The Socialist Party managed to elect candidates to the Legislature, and by 1914 the party routinely received about 20 percent of the vote in Oklahoma. During World War I, however, a rag-tag band of Socialist farmers took up arms and attempted to march on Washington to demand America's withdrawal from the war. The effort was put down quickly by local law enforcement officers and the National Guard, but all Socialists in the state were branded as disloyal. Party newspapers shut down and state party leaders were jailed.

Democrats Lee Cruce and Robert L. Williams held the governor's office until 1919. Cruce believed strongly in enforcement of "blue laws" that required businesses to close on Sundays and declared gambling, prize fighting, bootlegging, and horse racing illegal. Cruce used the National Guard on numerous occasions to enforce blue laws. Guardsmen halted one horse race by firing a volley over the heads of the jockeys. Unhappy with Cruce over various issues, the House of Representatives failed by one vote to bring impeachment charges against him. In addition to serving as Oklahoma's World War I governor, Williams oversaw the completion of the State Capitol in 1917.

Many former Socialists blamed the Democrats for their party's downfall and voted Republican in 1920, carrying the GOP to power in the Oklahoma House of Representatives. The Republicans won a United States Senate seat, and five of the eight Oklahoma seats in the lower house. Added to this mix was the rise of the Ku Klux Klan as a political force in Oklahoma. Early in the twentieth century throughout much of the nation, the Klan enjoyed a revival. In addition to keeping blacks "in their place," the Klan disliked Catholics and Jews and operated as a vigilante force to punish various "undesirables," such as husbands who abused their wives and children. With their identities hidden behind pointed hoods, the ranks of local Klaverns included businessmen, ministers, and lawmen. The Klan also became heavily involved in state and local politics.

Republicans joined by some Democrats almost removed Lieutenant Governor Martin Trapp and Governor J. B. A. Robertson from office, but fell short. Democratic fortunes seemed to improve when the party nominated John C. "Jack" Walton, mayor of Oklahoma City, to run for governor. Walton was supported by the Socialists as well, and he was elected Governor easily in 1922. A great orator, Walton was a poor administrator who failed to pass legislation favored by the Socialists. He dispensed political patronage jobs with reckless abandon, and then, to regain public favor, declared war on the Klan in 1923. This, coupled with his earlier actions, led to a political fight that resulted in Walton's being impeached by the House of Representatives and convicted on eleven counts by the State Senate and removed from office. During his effort to prevent his impeachment, Walton used the state militia on several occasions in an attempt to keep the Legislature from meeting. His term was completed by Martin E. Trapp.

With the Republicans benefiting nationally from a strong economy and in Oklahoma from the reaction against Walton's regime, the GOP gained effective control of the Legislature and made life miserable for Democrat Henry S. Johnston, eventually removing him from office by impeachment for "general incompetence" in 1929. His term was completed by William J. Holloway. The Great Depression that began in October 1929, however, soon would change the nation's politics dramatically. By 1931 the state would have a powerful Democrat in the governor's office and the state would enter an era of Democrat Party dominance.

(Facing page, middle) Albert C. Hamlin was elected to the Oklahoma House of Representatives in 1908 and was the state's first and only black legislator until 1964. He was defeated for re-election in 1910 largely because newly passed "Jim Crow" laws dramatically reduced the number of blacks allowed to vote. While in office, Hamlin was an active legislator. This portrait of Hamlin by Simmie Knox may be viewed in the State Capitol. (Courtesy Oklahoma Arts Council)

(Facing page, right) This painting of Representative Bessie S. McColgin by Mike Wimmer is displayed in the State Capitol in honor of the first woman to be elected to the Oklahoma House of Representatives. McColgin, a Republican from Rankin in Roger Mills County, was elected in 1920 and served two years. She was considered to be a "superior orator" and was elected to the Oklahoma Women's Hall of Fame in 2005. (Courtesy Oklahoma State Senate Historical Preservation Fund)

Buck Colbert Franklin: Standing Strong

For many people, statehood meant a new beginning, a magical turning point full of hope and promise. To others, especially those who helplessly watched the first State Legislature pass bills segregating the races and then denying them the vote based on the color of their skin, it meant an era of strife and struggle for the basic rights of a free citizen. One of those who saw both promise and struggle was Buck Colbert Franklin.

Franklin was born in 1879 in Pickens County, Chickasaw Nation. His father was the son of a Chickasaw freedman who had moved west with the tribe in the 1850s before serving with the Union Army during the Civil War. His mother was one-quarter blood Choctaw and a member of the prominent Colbert family, which brought with it access to tribal schools and legal status as a member of the tribe.

The family carved two ranches out of tribal lands west of the Arbuckle Mountains where a number of black families had settled after the war. Buck, growing up as the seventh child in a family of 10 children, learned from his father both the skills of a cowboy and the values of hard work and character. He attended local one-room schools, excelled at the nearby Dawes Academy for African-American students, and left the Indian Nations to attend college in Tennessee and Georgia.

Franklin returned to the Chickasaw Nation in 1903 just as the allotment process was changing forever the lives of Indians and the African Americans who had lived among them for more than a century. He secured his rights to an allotment, married his sweetheart from college, and found a job teaching at a school for African-American students near Wewoka. Meanwhile, he studied law.

In 1907 Buck was admitted to the bar. He joined four other African-American attorneys in Ardmore, a boomtown served by three railroads and located between Tishomingo, the Chickasaw capital, and Healdton, center of a soon-to-be-discovered oil field. Then came statehood and new laws telling African Americans that they could neither ride coaches nor

Buck Colbert Franklin

72

attend schools with white people or Indians. Even more devastating was passage of the Grandfather Clause, which denied black people the right to vote and eroded their protection before the eyes of the law. Raised in a culture where the races mixed freely and every citizen of the Indian nations had protection under tribal and federal law, Buck Franklin suddenly found himself and his potential clients on the outside looking in.

The ambitious young attorney looked for fleeting opportunity in the all-black town of Rentiesville, located about four miles north of Checotah in the old Creek Nation. When Buck moved his family there in 1912, it was home to almost 1,000 African Americans who had been drawn to the economic activity generated by the hundreds of black families that had received allotments along Elk Creek and the Missouri, Kansas, and Texas Railroad. The town had a brick school with 500 students, a cotton gin, a general store, one doctor, and a drug store. The nearest black attorney was in Eufaula, the county seat almost fifteen miles to the south.

The Franklins quickly jumped into the stream of community development. Buck opened law offices in both Rentiesville and Eufaula, bought and operated an 80-acre farm, and started a newspaper, the *Rentiesville News*. He became the local postmaster, earned an appointment as justice of the peace, and helped organize a

county free fair that was dedicated to scientific farming and economic development.

Franklin also became the farm demonstration agent in the county, with responsibilities for supervising industrial

education in 32 rural, all-black schools. As he would recall years later, he tried to pass on his father's belief that "the values of industry, economics, and business is a foundation on which to build a life for

(Facing page) Buck Franklin returned to Rentiesville to visit friends. Here he posed with his former residence in the background. (Courtesy John Hope Franklin)

Attorney Buck Franklin at work in his office. Franklin endured racial discrimination with dignity and determination to build a better life for himself and his family. His son, John Hope Franklin, became recognized as the twentieth century's outstanding historian of the black experience in the United States. (Courtesy John Hope Franklin)

a people, a nation, and a government." That same sense of pride and optimism was passed onto his own son, John Hope Franklin, who in 1921 at the age of six was asked by a white judge what he wanted to be when he grew up. "I intend to be the first Negro President of the United States," he quickly responded.

In 1921, looking for even greater opportunity, Buck moved his legal practice to Tulsa, which was rapidly earning the title as the "Oil Capital of the World." Like all Oklahoma cities, Tulsa was rigidly segregated, with the black community north of the tracks in a section called Greenwood. Despite the limitations imposed by law, the community was prosperous and growing with a newspaper, a movie theater, hotels, restaurants, churches, and new homes. Booker T. Washington, when he saw the community, called it the "Black Wall Street."

Four months later, with his family still in Rentiesville, Franklin witnessed the bloodiest race riot in American history. It began when a young black man was accused of assaulting a white woman on an elevator. When a white mob gathered in front of the courthouse demanding the accused man be turned over for a lynching, a band of black men crossed the tracks and offered to help defend the courthouse. A gun was fired, bodies hit the ground, and open warfare erupted.

After a bloody night of fighting, the white mob stormed the Greenwood neighborhood looting and burning. By the time the National Guard arrived the next morning, all that was left of the formerly prosperous district was ruins. The black population, including Buck Franklin, was escorted to detention facilities, presumably for their own protection. When he was released, Buck found his law offices burned and his rented quarters in ashes.

Franklin did not flee the scene. He set up a tent and reached out to help his neighbors fight for justice. He filed an injunction for one client who objected to the city council's attempt to rezone the destroyed area so black people could not rebuild. He filed suits on behalf of home owners who were told that their insurance policies did not cover loss from "civil riots." Most importantly, he stood his ground in the midst of violence and intimidation. He had chosen Tulsa for his new home and he was going to stay.

Four years later, in an effort to heal the wounds of the Tulsa Race Riot, the Franklins and other black leaders joined hands with the white community of Tulsa to recruit and host the national meeting of the National Negro Business League. Governor Martin Trapp welcomed the convention, which was attended by leading black businessmen from around the country. As Franklin would recall years later, the joint effort fostered a sense of economic interdependence and goodwill.

Buck Franklin, after several more decades of seeking justice for his clients, suffered a paralyzing stroke in 1956. Still, he did not give up. He painstakingly wrote his autobiography on an old manual typewriter, using only the index finger on his left hand. In that gripping tale, he recounted his own personal journey from his cowboy days on the open range to the struggles against racism, greed, and intolerance. He recalled his pride in family and friends, especially his son, John Hope, who graduated from Fisk University, earned the Ph.D. in History from Harvard, and wrote *From Slavery to Freedom*, which quickly became the standard textbook for the story of African Americans.

Like his gifted son, Buck Franklin was a student of history. He had grown up on the frontier, a cowboy on the open range where the horizon seemed endless. From his father and mother, he had learned the values of education, hard work, and integrity. And during his career, he had witnessed the evil consequences of justice denied to a group of people because of the color of their skin. Throughout each chapter of that life, he had never given up, never lost hope in the future. To him, the future looked bright as long as good people were willing to stand up for what was right.

From 1878 to 1921 a number of race riots erupted in cities across the nation. One of them occurred in Tulsa in 1921. On May 20 a white female elevator operator claimed that Dick Rowland, a black man, had grabbed her arm as she fled in panic. Rumors about the incident spread rapidly, with the story becoming increasingly exaggerated. Rowland was arrested the next day and rumors that he would be seized and lynched began to spread among the black citizenry. An inflammatory editorial in the *Tulsa Tribune* on May 31 fueled a confrontation between armed mobs of blacks and whites. Shots were fired and the blacks, outnumbered, retreated to the Greenwood Avenue business district, often called the "Black Wall Street." Early in the morning on June 1, the Greenwood district was looted and burned by white rioters. A measure of the devastation can be seen in this photo. Within 24 hours, 35 city blocks lay in ruins, 800 people were treated for injuries, and the death toll was placed at 36. Recent investigations of the riot indicate that the number of fatalities may have been as high as 300. (Courtesy Oklahoma Historical Society)

Old Central on the campus of Oklahoma State University, constructed in 1894, was the University's first permanent building. It was used for classes until 1969. Beautifully restored, the building has served as a museum of higher education in Oklahoma and remains an important campus landmark. (Courtesy Jim Argo)

Constructed in 1909, the Old Science Building remains a prominent building on the campus of Southwestern Oklahoma State University at Weatherford. The building has been in continuous use and in 2006 underwent a major renovation. It was placed on the National Register of Historic Places in 1984. (Courtesy State Historic Preservation Office, Oklahoma Historical Society)

The Washita County Courthouse at Cordell was designed by noted architect Solomon Andrew Layton and was completed in 1911. The impressive structure has been called the "Grandfather of Oklahoma Courthouses" and is listed on the National Register of Historic Places. (Courtesy Jim Argo)

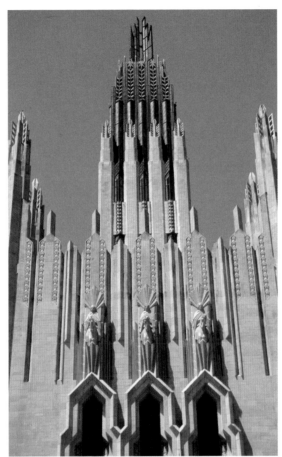

Tulsa's Mayo Hotel was opened for business in 1925. The opulent, 18-story structure contained all the modern features of the times and was elegantly furnished. The hotel became one of the symbols of Tulsa's oil-driven prosperity and was the meeting and resting place for oilmen such as J. Paul Getty and William G. Skelly and for celebrities such as Charles Lindbergh and Amelia Earhardt. Eventually the Mayo declined and fell into disuse, and a succession of owners were not able to revitalize it. In recent years major progress has been made in renovating the building. Used for special events, it appears that the Mayo Hotel will occupy a place of prominence in Tulsa's business and cultural life well into the future. (Courtesy, State Historic Preservation Office, Oklahoma Historical Society)

The oil prosperity of the 1920s in Tulsa made possible the construction of many remarkable buildings, including the magnificent Boston Avenue Methodist Church. Built at a cost of $1.5 million and completed in 1929, the basic style of the building was suggested by Miss Adah Robinson, an art instructor at the University of Tulsa. Church offices were added in 1963, and the Children's Building was added in 1965. The building has been carefully maintained and remains one of Tulsa's architectural gems. (Courtesy State Historic Preservation Office, Oklahoma Historical Society)

Bizzell Memorial Library on the campus of the University of Oklahoma was built in 1929 and later was named for university president William Bennett Bizzell. The ornate structure remains one of the signature structures of the institution. (Courtesy State Historic Preservation Office, Oklahoma Historical Society)

Creative Oklahomans

In 1907 the new State of Oklahoma featured a cultural diversity that was reflected in music and art. Among the talented individuals drawn to the opportunities the young state represented was Richard Francis Xavier Gerrer, who would found a remarkable art museum and become Oklahoma's best known artist during the state's formative years.

Gerrer came to the United States as a young boy with his family from the French province of Alsace. In 1891, at the age of 24, he decided to enter the Benedictine community at Sacred Heart, near the community of Asher. After his ordination as a priest in 1900, he was sent to Rome to study art and the restoration of paintings. While there, he painted a portrait of Pope Pius X that subsequently was shown in the St. Louis World Fair of 1904. The Vatican requested the portrait's return after the fair, but Gregory, his religious name, painted a copy and sent that to the Pope. He established a studio in Shawnee in 1905, continued to paint and teach art, and collected paintings, sculpture, and artifacts from the Middle Ages to the early twentieth century. This would be the basis for a museum he founded in 1915, now the magnificent Mabee-Gerrer Museum at St. Gregory's University in Shawnee. An outstanding artist, he brought priceless cultural treasures to the Sooner State.

While Gerrer was producing and collecting fine art, Otto Gray was popularizing rural western music in a manner that would lead to the commercialization of cowboy music and major changes in the music industry. In 1925 rancher Billy McGinty sponsored the performance of a cowboy string band on radio station KFRU in Bristow in what proved to be America's first radio broadcast of such a band. The band consisted of working cowboys who happened to be good musicians. They played songs such as "Ride 'em Cowboy" and "Who Stuck the Gum in Grandpa's Whiskers." The performance was well received and other broadcasts and performances followed. McGinty was not inclined to manage the band, however, and asked Stillwater businessman Otto Gray to assume that role.

Gray aggressively marketed the band, arranging radio and stage appearances in Oklahoma and surrounding states and refining the professionalism of the band's performances and appearance. They gave what is believed to have been the first commercial performance in 1926 over KVOO Radio in Tulsa. Gray became a popular announcer. By 1928 Otto Gray's Cowboy Band was traveling in a Cadillac bus with a massive set of longhorns for a hood ornament. Gray and his son also performed rope tricks during performances, and Gray's wife, known as "Mommie," was the female vocalist.

Father Gregory Gerrer as he appeared in February, 1928. (Courtesy Oklahoma Historical Society)

By 1931 the band was touring the United States in nine vehicles, all uniquely designed to attract attention. They also recorded for a variety of labels and performed live on numerous radio stations. They were the first western band to appear on the cover of *Billboard Magazine* in 1931. Gray was shown on the cover again in 1934. Gray retired from the music business in 1936 and the group disbanded. But Gray and his band had blazed the trail for subsequent singing cowboys, including Gene Autry who also performed on Tulsa's KVOO Radio before taking cowboy music to Hollywood.

While Otto Gray was promoting cowboy music on a national basis, another Oklahoman, Joseph Horace Benton, was making his operatic debut in Italy. Born in Kansas City, Missouri, Benton moved with his family to Sayre in 1901 when he was three years old. After earning degrees in vocal music and language at the University of Oklahoma, he traveled to France in 1923 and then to Italy in 1925 to continue his vocal training.

Performing as Guiseppe Bentonelli, by 1934 he was one of the most popular tenors in Europe. He made 512 appearances in 51 operas throughout Europe and North Africa and performed before many of the crowned heads of Europe. He grew homesick, however, and returned to the United States to perform as the leading tenor with the Chicago Opera Company. In 1936 he became the first Oklahoman to perform with the Metropolitan Opera Company in New York.

Benton returned to the University of Oklahoma in 1940, earned a master's degree in modern languages, and followed with additional work at Yale University. He then came home to OU as a professor of music. He became chairman of the Department of Voice in 1944, and his lifetime of achievement was recognized by his induction into the Oklahoma Hall of Fame in 1951. Benton, Gray, and Gerrer illustrate the cultural richness of Oklahoma that would generate an impressive array of creative talent in the remaining decades of the state's first 100 years.

Bob Wills and the Texas Playboys were photographed onstage at the Cains Academy of Dancing, preparing for their noon show to be broadcast over KVOO radio. Wills is third from the left. Wills combined cowboy music with jazz thereby creating western swing. Playing on KVOO helped Wills and his band to become widely known. KVOO also would play a major role in launching the careers of Gene Autry and Patti Page. (Courtesy Beryl Ford Collection, Tulsa City County Library)

Alice M. Robertson: Reluctant Pioneer

The accepted role of women in society in the decades following Oklahoma statehood was in a state of flux. Rapid industrialization and urban growth brought increasing numbers of women into the workforce, and, while the economy grew dramatically, the changes also were accompanied by increasing poverty, prostitution, epidemics, and other social ills. Some women tried to preserve the traditional social order by becoming active in a variety of causes, such as the temperance movement to eliminate the evils of alcohol or the women's suffrage movement to gain the right to vote.

Many suffragists believed that only by voting and exerting their influence in government could they protect the traditional role of women. They believed that women should leave business, the professions, and political office holding to men. To them, women were best suited to remain at home, creating a wholesome home environment for their husbands and children. The home was to be safe from the stress and corruption of the environment in which men were expected to function in order to support their families. By obtaining the vote, they asserted, women could encourage policies that would enable women to remain in the traditional "women's sphere" in the home as the defenders of "piety, morality, affection, and self-sacrifice."

Anti-suffragists such as Alice M. Robertson also wished to preserve the traditional role of women. They feared that extending the right to vote would soon pull women increasingly into the world of politics and other traditional male pursuits, damaging the family structure and reducing the collective role of women as the moral and social conscience of society.

Alice M. Robertson

Robertson was a traditional nineteenth century woman who believed strongly that the traditional role of women must be preserved. The realities of her life were such, however, that she never married and never relied on a man to provide income or shelter. She was the first woman in the United States to serve as postmaster of a post office the size of the one at Muskogee, Oklahoma, and the second woman in the nation to be elected to the United States House of Representatives.

Alice Mary Robertson was born into a distinguished missionary family in 1854 at Tullahassee Mission on the north bank of the Arkansas River near Muskogee. Her grandfather Samuel A. Worcester was a famed missionary to the Cherokees. Her mother, Eliza Ann Worcester Robertson, and her father, Reverend W. S. Robertson, taught Creek Indian children at the Tullahassee Mission. Alice's early life was one of sacrifice and hard work, but she and her siblings were infused with Christian piety and a desire to help others. Alice was impressed by her mother's ability to make the home a happy, nurturing environment even when the Civil War forced her family to leave the Creek Nation for five years.

At age 17, in 1871, Alice enrolled at Elmira College in New York. Two years later she was employed in the Indian Department in Washington, D. C., where she learned

shorthand and took lessons in Domestic Science. She had met President Ulysses S. Grant during a school trip to the nation's capital, and in her new position she managed to meet former president Rutherford B. Hayes and future president James G. Garfield. In 1880 she moved to the Indian Training School at Carlisle, Pennsylvania, where she served as secretary to the superintendent. She returned to Indian Territory upon the death of her father in 1882 to care for her mother and to teach at

(Facing page) Mike Wimmer painted this portrait of Alice M. Robertson in 2003 who had a remarkable career as a sort of anti-feminist feminist. The painting hangs in the State Capitol. (Courtesy Oklahoma State Senate Historical Preservation Fund)

Alice Robertson, only the second woman in the United States to be elected to the United States Congress, was a popular and respected figure in the House of Representatives. Here she posed for a photograph in the house chambers with Representative and former Speaker of the House Joseph G. Cannon of Illinois. (Courtesy Oklahoma Historical Society)

Tullahassee. In 1884 the two women raised money from friends in the East to build the Minerva Boarding School for girls at Nuyaka Mission near Okmulgee to provide income and meaningful activity for her and her mother. In 1894 the Presbyterian Board of Home Missions took over the school, operating it as Henry Kendall College. The school later was moved to Tulsa where in 1929 it became the University of Tulsa.

By 1884 at age 30, Miss Alice had resigned herself to being an "old maid." She believed she could not leave her mother, and she was poor, struggling to make ends meet. She had received "many offers … but the kind of man who would want a woman like me would not be the kind of man I would be interested in." In the late 1880s Alice and her mother began to take in boarders to supplement their income, but she struggled with her finances throughout the 1890s. Then, in 1891, a life-changing event happened when she met Theodore Roosevelt while attending a conference in New York to make an address on the education of children in the Five Civilized Tribes. This meeting began a long friendship that benefited Alice significantly in the future. They enjoyed a political affinity, in part, because Alice and the future president both were staunch Republicans. Alice had inherited her grandparents' dislike of President Andrew Jackson, a Democrat, for

his treatment of the Five Civilized Tribes in forcing them to move to Indian Territory during the 1830s and in subsequent decades.

She helped recruit volunteers to fight with Roosevelt in the Spanish-American War in 1898, and when Roosevelt became president in 1901, he appointed her United States Supervisor of Creek Schools. In 1904 Roosevelt appointed Miss Alice postmaster at Muskogee, with a salary of $3,400 per year. She held the post until 1913. By 1910 she felt sufficiently prosperous to build a handsome home of native stone on Agency Hill in Muskogee. She called it Sawokla, Creek for "gathering place." There she had a comfortable home for herself and her aged mother and a prosperous farm.

With the election of Democrat Woodrow Wilson as president, Miss Alice's job as postmaster ended. She opened Sawokla Cafeteria in Muskogee, with much of the food being produced on her farm, and it was highly successful. During World War I, she was among the first in the nation to provide food and refreshment for troops, as she met every troop train with sandwiches, pies, cookies, candy, cigarettes, post cards, and always a "big smoking can of hot coffee." At times she remained all night on the station platform. It is estimated that she fed at no charge thousands of soldiers and their families passing through Muskogee. Her mother had died in 1915 and she was free

of responsibility at home. Moreover, she appeared to enjoy the "motherly" role of caring for the "boys," even though she nearly bankrupted herself doing so.

Shortly after the ratification of the Nineteenth Amendment to the United States Constitution, which gave women the right to vote, Republican Party leaders asked Robertson to stand for election to the United States House of Representatives. Because she had been vice president of the state anti-suffrage league, her positive response stunned many observers. She still believed that the ideal role for women was in the home as wives and mothers, and she argued that she would go to Washington with the goal of protecting women's traditional role in society.

She campaigned primarily through classified advertisements in local newspapers, promoting both her cafeteria and her candidacy. She used the ads to explain her reasons for opposing women's suffrage and her position that women had a right to be supported by men. She indicated that she knew of only one woman who never asked for help, and she "was a bit of a freak." She also urged women to register and vote now that women's suffrage was a reality. They should endeavor to turn "the rotten politics of the men into good government." Moreover, she had known the burden of being the "provider," and that would enable her, she said, "to detect threats to family life."

Despite not making campaign speeches, which she viewed as unwomanly, she won a majority of votes in the Republican primary election, defeating four other candidates. She won the general election in a heavily Democratic district by 300 votes. Her election was part of a Republican national landslide, as war-weary voters swept Warren G. Harding into office and Oklahomans elected five Republican representatives and one Republican senator to Congress.

Miss Alice received national attention even before arriving in Washington, as political writers wondered how an avowed anti-suffragette could run and win such an election. She told one reporter that she represented the "good women who would rather cook a good meal than meddle with politics." She gave advice to women through the media on how they should handle their domestic responsibilities, noting that if a daughter wears clothes that make her look "like a prostitute," the mother is to blame. She refused to consider herself a pioneer in politics, referring to herself as "a warning, not an example."

In Congress, she was fiercely independent, and she took several positions that proved to be unpopular back home. Her strong belief in individualism led her to vote against the Sheppard-Towner Act, popularly called the "maternity bill." This bill would have had

the federal government finance a campaign to educate young women on the care of young children. Miss Alice opposed it on the grounds that it was an unnecessary expense and that it was "paternalistic and possibly Bolshevistic." She did not approve of what she saw as the beginnings of a welfare state and the intrusion of the government into a traditional realm of women.

Miss Alice also stunned her constituents by opposing legislation to provide a bonus payment to veterans of World War I as putting "a dollar sign on patriotism." Although she had helped obtain a veterans hospital for Muskogee, her opposition to the bonus bill cost her significant support in her district. She was defeated in her bid for reelection and returned to Oklahoma. She fell on hard times economically and accepted a job with the Oklahoma Historical Society in 1927 at $125 per month to write a history of the Creek Nation. She ended her days in relative poverty and alone, dying in 1931. Yet she accomplished much in her remarkable life, defending traditional values, but never limiting her potential when necessity called for her to expand her activities beyond the "women's sphere."

The Pioneer Woman Statue in Ponca City was a gift from oilman E. W. Marland to his city and state. Marland launched a design competition in 1926, and the completed monument was dedicated on April 22, 1930. The bronze statue weighs 12,000 pounds, is 17 feet tall, and rises to a height of forty feet on its pedestal. The monument was created "in appreciation of the heroic character of the women who braved the dangers and endured the hardships incident to the daily life of the pioneer and homesteader in this country." Near the statue today is the Pioneer Woman Museum. (Courtesy Jim Argo)

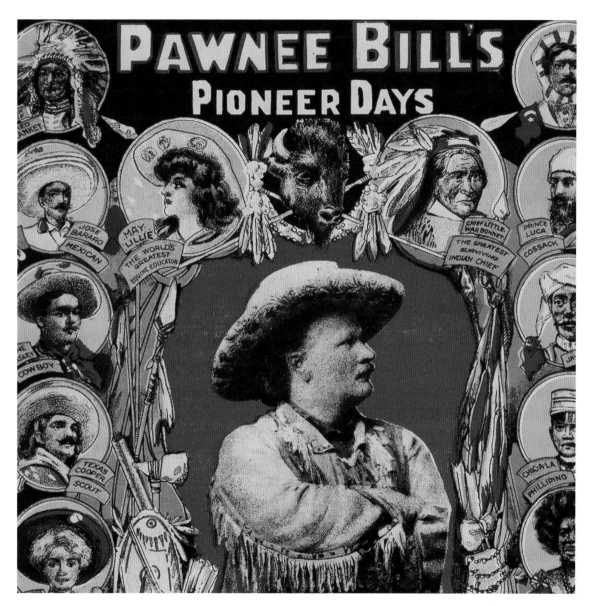

Gordon W. Lillie, better known as "Pawnee Bill," was a friend of the Pawnee Indians and lived on a ranch near the community of Pawnee. He was a successful rancher who operated a trading post at which he treated the Indians fairly. He was best known as the head of the Pawnee Bill Wild West Show, that operated from the 1890s to the 1930s in grand style. At its peak the show toured internationally with a cast and crew of 645 people, more than 400 head of horses and steers, and 20 buffalo. (Courtesy Jim Argo)

The discovery well of the Oklahoma City Oil Field was the Indian Territory Illuminating Oil Company (ITIO)—Foster Petroleum Corporation's Oklahoma City No.1 which blew in on December 4, 1928. The most famous well in the field, however, was ITIO's Sudek No. 1, shown here. Better known as the "Wild Mary Sudek," the well reflected the enormous natural gas pressure in the field. When the drill bit penetrated the Wilcox Sand on March 26, 1930, the well blew out and the crew was unable

to control it. Thousands of barrels of crude oil and two hundred million cubic feet of gas escaped daily from the well until it finally was capped on April 4. At times, wind carried a film of oil as far south as Norman, 11 miles away. Massive gushers and blowouts were common occurrences in the Oklahoma City Field, and the North Canadian River often carried large amount of crude oil, catching fire and burning spectacularly on at least one occasion. (Courtesy Oklahoma Publishing Company)

Oklahoma's first state flag was adopted in 1911. Its simple design with a white star containing the number 46 on a field of red became controversial to some after the Bolshevik Revolution in Russia. In 1924 a contest was held to encourage individuals to submit designs for a new state flag. Mr. George L. Fluke, Jr. of Oklahoma City won the competition, and her design was adopted by the Legislature in 1925. The flag featured a field of blue on which an Osage warrior's shield decorated with eagle feathers honors the Native American heritage of the state. Six white crosses or stars are said to represent high ideals, and the shield is overlain with an olive branch and a ceremonial peace pipe, European and Indian symbols of peace and unity. "Oklahoma" was added to the flag in 1941. Legislators acted again in 1988 to standardize the shade of blue used in the flag. (Courtesy Jim Argo)

Legendary Figures: Sports in Oklahoma

Baseball was the dominant sport in Oklahoma during the first fifty years of the twentieth century. Virtually every town of any size had at least a sandlot team, and many of them had a minor league baseball team. Other sports also were popular. Clearly Oklahomans were competitive, loved sports, and revered successful athletes. And they took pride in knowing that the state had produced one of the greatest athletes in American history—Jim Thorpe.

Born in 1887 near Prague, Indian Territory, Thorpe was a descendant of the legendary Sac and Fox Chief Black Hawk. His athletic prowess came to light at Carlisle Indian School in Pennsylvania, where he was a three-time All-American honoree in football. In 1912 at age 24, he participated in the Olympics at Stockholm, Sweden, where he won both the pentathlon and decathlon, setting records that would stand for decades. When the King of Sweden exclaimed to Thorpe, "Sir, you are the greatest athlete in the world!" Thorpe replied, "Thanks, King."

Thorpe was stripped of his medals when it was learned that he had played a few games of semi-pro baseball while at Carlisle. Thorpe was bitterly disappointed but soon moved on with his career, which included Major League Baseball for five years and professional football for 14 years. He retired in 1929. He was instrumental in forming the American Professional Football Association and eventually served as president of that organization, which eventually evolved into the National Football League. Thorpe died in 1953, but before his death he was named by the Associated Press as the most outstanding athlete of the twentieth century. His Olympic medals were restored to the family in 1982.

While Thorpe was Oklahoma's most prominent athlete of the early statehood period, there were many other remarkable performers. One of them was "Bullet" Joe Rogan, a black man born in Oklahoma City in 1889. After service in the military, Rogan joined the Kansas City Monarchs of the Negro National League at age 30 in 1920. He proved to be an amazing pitcher and hitter, but the segregated status of professional baseball prevented him from playing in the Major Leagues. His winning percentage as a pitcher was .721, and his lifetime batting average was .339. His talent was recognized when he was inducted into the Baseball Hall of Fame in 1998.

The football tradition at the University of Oklahoma had its beginnings much earlier than the Bud Wilkinson era. Legendary coach Benjamin G. "Bennie" Owen, for whom Owen Field is named, laid the groundwork for the subsequent success of Sooner football. Owen arrived at OU as

Andy Payne, winner of the amazing Transcontinental Foot Race of 1928, was a Cherokee Indian from Foyil. A natural athlete and runner, the unknown Payne defeated renowned runners from throughout the world to win the race from Los Angeles to New York City. The race, also known as the "Bunion Derby," took 83 days and covered 3,422.3 miles. Payne is shown here with his trainer, Tom Young. (Courtesy Alvin Rucker Collection, Oklahoma Historical Society)

the head football coach in 1905 after playing quarterback at Kansas University and coaching in Kansas and at Michigan University. At OU he established a "hurry-up offense" that had his quarterback calling signals for a play while the players were still lying on the ground from the previous play. His 1911 team was the first in OU history to go undefeated for a complete regular season. Owen's 1915 team, averaging more than 30 passes a game, also went undefeated. With a career record at OU of 155 wins, 60 losses, and 19 ties, Owen retired after the 1926 season but served as athletic director until 1936.

A native Kansan, Edward C. Gallagher was an outstanding football player and track athlete at Oklahoma A & M College (OAMC), where he established state record times in the 100-yard dash, the 220-yard dash, and the 220-yard high hurdles. He also ran for 99 yards in a football game against Kansas. But he won international recognition for his contribution to a sport in which he did not participate as an athlete—amateur wrestling.

Gallagher was hired to coach wrestling at OAMC in 1916. His engineering training helped him understand the importance of leverage in wrestling, and he taught this effectively to his wrestlers. He also developed more than 400 wrestling holds. The NCAA established wrestling as a championship sport in 1928, and the Aggies, under Gallagher's leadership, won 11 national championships between 1928 and 1940, the year Gallagher died of pneumonia. His university evolved into Oklahoma State University, which as of 2006 had won 34 national championships in wrestling.

Oklahomans in the late 1920s also were proud of a young Cherokee man named Andy Payne, who personified perseverance and pride by winning the 1928 Transcontinental Foot Race from Los Angeles, California, to New York City, a race that covered 3,422.3 miles spanning 84 days. Payne was not a professional runner—he ran track in high school at Foyil, Oklahoma—as were many who came from numerous continents to attempt to earn the $25,000 first-place prize. His natural ability, coupled with his determination to win, carried him to victory. When Payne collected his earnings, he paid off the mortgage on his parents' farm and built them a new home. He eventually was elected clerk of the Oklahoma State Supreme Court, earned a law degree in night school, acquired land over the years, and became wealthy from the discovery of oil, coal, and natural gas on his property. He continued to serve as clerk of the Supreme Court until his retirement in 1973. He died in 1977.

Jim Thorpe is shown here preparing to compete in a track and field event. Thorpe's athletic exploits earned him recognition as one of the greatest athletes of the twentieth century. (Courtesy Oklahoma Historical Society)

Cyrus Avery: Father of Route 66

When Oklahoma became a state, the world of transportation was ruled by the railroads. Location on the steel rails determined life or death for towns and cities, granted access to distant markets for farmers and ranchers, and made possible the exploitation of natural resources from coal and timber to oil and lead.

The reign of the railroads, however, was drawing to a close. Between World War I and World War II there would rise a new king—motorized vehicles—that would grant independence from corporate chieftains and offer freedom of the road. All that was needed was an efficient system of highways to open the way. One of the kingmakers who ushered in this transportation revolution was Cyrus Avery.

Like most Oklahomans of his era, Avery was raised on a farm. Born in Pennsylvania in 1871, he was 12 years old when his family moved to the Cherokee Nation to farm a plot of land along Spavinaw Creek, located northeast of the little community called Tulsey Town. The family subsequently moved to Missouri, where young Avery taught school and attended William Jewell College.

In 1898 he married and moved to Oklahoma City, which was just beginning its remarkable growth spurt that would make it the fastest growing city in the nation. Typical of his generation, Avery dabbled in a variety of businesses such as insurance, real estate, and loans. In 1907, after a short stint in Vinita and the discovery of the Glenn Pool Oil Field, he moved to Tulsa.

The young entrepreneur created a real estate development company, served as vice president of a coal company, and became secretary/treasurer of an oil company doing

Cyrus Avery

business in the Bartlesville and Bird Creek areas. His first love, however, remained farming, so he purchased a 1,400-acre spread northeast of Tulsa and quickly earned a reputation as an expert in low-maintenance pasture management and pure-bred livestock.

As an oilman, Avery recognized the importance of a flexible transportation system that could get crews and material into the oilfields and crude oil out. And as a farmer, he joined the ranks of those who had long believed that railroads sucked the profit from the production of cotton, grains, and livestock. Frustrated with the limitations of railroads, Avery saw cars and trucks as the keys to his own and his community's financial future.

From 1913 to 1924 Avery climbed the ladder of the Good Roads Movement, a loosely affiliated group of people and organizations across the country who advocated the construction and maintenance of highways. Elected to a three-year term as Tulsa county commissioner, he helped develop a low cost road maintenance system by paying farmers one dollar a mile to drag roads with a split-log rail after every rain. He also planted un-hulled sweet clover along rights-of-way to fight erosion and to improve the scenery. Clover would still be seen growing along those roads fifty years later.

In 1917, as a new member of the Tulsa

Chamber of Commerce Board of Directors, Avery helped organize the Albert Pike Highway Association to develop a scenic byway from Colorado Springs, Colorado, to Hot Springs, Arkansas. For nine years he served as president, which gave him the opportunity to meet other highway advocates from surrounding states. The result of his work became U.S. Highway 64, which naturally passed through Tulsa.

While working on the Albert Pike Highway, the ever popular Avery was elected president of the Associated Highways of America, a powerful lobbying group backed by 42 organized highway associations across the country. The timing was perfect for Tulsa and Oklahoma. That same year Congress passed the Federal Highway Act of 1921 that provided federal aid to the states for building an interconnected, interstate system of highways. The next year more than $75 million was appropriated to the states on a 50-50 matching basis.

While Avery was working his way into a position of power at the federal level, Oklahoma quickly fell behind other states in capturing its share of the matching funds. First, the problem was the rural dominance in the State Legislature, where county commissioners lobbied desperately to hold onto their control of the road building process. Then came the distraction of the brief but stormy administration of Governor

(Facing page) Cyrus Avery, one of the primary promoters of the building of the highway that became known as Route 66, worked hard to ensure that it would be built through Tulsa and Oklahoma City. He devoted his lifetime to the development of good roads and other important civic work to the benefit of Tulsa and the entire state. (Courtesy Tulsa Historical Society)

One of the many attractions that developed in Oklahoma along Route 66 was Ed Galloway's Totem Pole Park, located 3.5 miles east of the highway and the community of Foyil. Galloway spent 11 years constructing the "World's Largest Concrete Totem Pole." Completed in 1948, the totem pole is approximately 90 feet tall and consists of six tons of steel, 28 tons of cement, and 100 tons of rock and sand. The 30-foot-wide base rests on the back of a colorful turtle. The entire pole is covered with colorful Native American symbols, portraits, and animals. The park also featured an 11-sided "Fiddle House" supported by 25 concrete totem poles, which housed a collection of fiddles and handmade furniture and bas relief portraits of presidents of the United States up to John F. Kennedy. Galloway died in 1962 and much of the content of Fiddle House was stolen in 1970. The totem poles and buildings have been restored and now are the property of the Rogers County Historical Society and the Foyil Heritage Association. The Fiddle House now hosts a museum and gift shop. (Courtesy Jim Argo)

Jack Walton, who was impeached during his first year in office. By the end of 1923, the State of Oklahoma was providing a paltry $250,000 a year for the Oklahoma Highway Department. The only matching funds available came from the counties, and then only the counties with cities large enough to pass bond issues.

With Walton impeached, Lieutenant Governor Martin Trapp turned his attention to the Good Roads Movement. An oilman and former bond salesman who advocated internal improvements for business development, Trapp led the charge to overhaul the Oklahoma Highway Department and generate a stream of revenue to build roads. The Legislature responded by creating a three-person commission with broad powers to set standards and disburse funds. They also instituted a 2.5 cent tax on every gallon of gasoline and a $10 driving license fee. Sixty percent of the projected $4.2 million would go to the state, while 40 percent would go to the counties. To implement the plan, Governor Trapp turned to Cyrus Avery.

As chairman of the newly reorganized Oklahoma Highway Department, Avery led the effort to set standards, hire professional engineers, and designate more then 3,600 miles of roads eligible for the federal funds. Within six months there were 24 federal aid projects underway on 127 miles of concrete surface and 17 bridges. By May of 1926, more than $19 million had been invested in hard-surfaced roads.

In 1925, while he was organizing the state system, Avery was appointed consulting highway specialist with the United States Bureau of Roads, the federal agency tasked with the monumental job of selecting and numbering interstate highways. After more than a decade of experience in the Good Roads Movement, the Tulsa businessman and farmer found himself in a position to make history.

At the time, the major east-west transcontinental highway was the Old National Trail that crossed the Mississippi River at St. Louis, Missouri, and traversed the Great Plains through Kansas. Avery used his influence to pull together allies from Illinois, Missouri, Texas, and New Mexico to lobby for a different route. Under his plan, the new transcontinental highway would veer southwest from St. Louis, pass through Tulsa, and turn west in Oklahoma City. The new road, dubbed the Will Rogers Highway for promotional effect, became Route 66.

While Route 66 would eventually become his most famous legacy, Avery served the people of Tulsa and Oklahoma in a number of ways. From 1921 to 1923 he served on a committee to buy land and right-of-way for Spavinaw Lake and the pipeline that supplied Tulsa with a never-ending supply of water. In 1928 he was a member of the executive committee that built the Tulsa Municipal Airport. That same year he donated land for part of what would become Mohawk Park.

Other groups and leaders turned to Avery during the 1930s. Governor William J. Holloway appointed him to a special commission to study the state's educational system. The report was published. When the Great Depression cast its dark shadows over the state, Avery was asked to serve as the director of the 13-county northeast district of the Works Progress Administration. Within a year he had jobs for more than 18,000 desperate men and women. By the time his term ended, he had supervised an investment of more than $6 million in schools, armories, roads, dams, and parks. He also found time to serve as president of the Tulsa Chamber of Commerce, an organization he had supported since 1917.

Cyrus Avery retired in 1958 at the age of 87. When asked for his recipe for happiness, he answered: "Someone to love, something to do, and something to look forward to." Fittingly, his greatest achievement, Route 66, would offer a taste of that happiness to countless families looking for "something to do" and every bend of the road offering "something to look forward to."

Route 66 was an important factor in the prosperity of many communities in Oklahoma, including Miami in Ottawa County. This prosperity was reflected in Miami with the building of the Coleman Theater by lead and zinc entrepreneur George L. Coleman in 1929. Originally used to screen movies and stage vaudeville acts, the theater was donated by the Coleman family to the City of Miami in 1989 with the proviso that it be restored as a performing arts center for the community. This was accomplished, and the beautiful facility hosts numerous musical and theatrical programs on an ongoing basis. (Courtesy Jim Argo)

Radio Comes to Oklahoma

The "Information Age" often is said to have begun with the invention of the telegraph in 1837, which first made possible the transmission of information via Morse code over wires strung for that purpose. Instant communication via the human voice was made possible by the invention of the telephone. Both devices helped reduce the isolation previously imposed by distance and relatively slow means of travel.

In the twentieth century, the communications revolution accelerated with the invention of wireless telegraph, radio, television, wireless telephones, and the internet. For the citizens of the young State of Oklahoma, by the 1930s radio had transformed their lives, bringing news, information, and entertainment programs directly into their homes, often originating from distant locations.

By the time Oklahoma became a state in 1907, experimental radio broadcasts on the East Coast already were being undertaken. World War I interrupted the development of radio, but with the end of the war in 1918 efforts again turned toward developing radio as a means of military communication and as a potential medium for civilian communications. The first known radio station in Oklahoma was DM-6, established at Fort Sill near Lawton in 1919 to provide communications with Army Air Corp pilots who had wireless receivers built into their airplanes. DM-6 was followed closely by E. C. Hull and H. S. Richards of Oklahoma City, who managed to pull together sufficient parts and transmitter tubes to establish station 5XT in 1921. Their station was located in Hull's garage at 1011 West Ash in Oklahoma City. Other radio stations were being established around the nation, including the powerful KDKA in Pittsburgh, Pennsylvania.

On January 1, 1922, *The Daily Oklahoman* reported that there were 30 radio receivers in Oklahoma City. That number would grow rapidly statewide as radios became more readily available, often in attractive cabinets that allowed them to be welcome additions to homes. The Oklahoman's publisher, E. K. Gaylord, soon took an interest in the new technology and 5XT was referred to in the paper as "The Oklahoman's Radio Service." Soon music via phonograph records and live concerts were being broadcast. The radio craze was on as Oklahomans scrambled to acquire early production radios or obtain parts to build their own receivers.

In March 1922 the United States Department of Commerce began issuing liscences for radio stations. The first two issued for Oklahoma went to 5XT, which was assigned the call letters WKY, and to WEH in Tulsa, a station owned by W. G. Skelly's Midland Refining Company. It initially was

used for communications between company locations only, but within a few months began broadcasting to the general public. Programming on WKY continued to expand, including the use of local talent. One such performer was Miss Esther McRuer, "The Oklahoma Mockingbird," who whistled "The Glow Worm."

Over the next decade many new stations came on the air, but one of the most significant was KFRU at Bristow, founded by E. H. Rollestone, with a powerful signal heard throughout the United States. It was one of the first stations in the nation to begin broadcasting country music, often using local talent such as Jimmie Wilson's Catfish String Band. In 1926 the station became KVOO radio, "The Voice of Oklahoma," with studios in Bristow and Tulsa. It eventually was purchased by W. G. Skelly and became one of the best known stations in the United States, with programming

featuring Bob Wills and his Texas Playboys, Gene Autry, and Clara Ann Fowler of Claremore, who took the name Patti Page.

By 1932 Oklahoma had numerous radio stations in operation, and radios were found in most homes. In rural areas not yet blessed with electrical service, battery-powered radios were treasured possessions. Radio pioneers soon learned to use advertising to make money, and radio joined the print media as a major force driving consumerism in the nation. In the 1930s and in the decades to follow, radio became a primary source of news and entertainment. Politicians who learned how to use the new medium to communicate with voters prospered as well. Oklahoma's radio pioneers indeed played a major role in establishing radio as an important element of American culture.

(Facing page) The Anthony Avenue radio show ca. 1950 on WKY radio in Oklahoma City was sponsored by the C. R. Anthony chain of dry goods stores. The personnel included Julien Aikens, guitar; Secoy Evans, violin; Helen Webb, vocalist; Ben Morris, announcer; Joe Webster, vocalist; Al Good, vibes; Willie Watts, bass, and Al Tell, piano. (Courtesy Oklahoma Historical Society)

KVOO featured live big band music by 1927. Here announcer Glen Condon is getting ready to announce the Skelly Oil Company's first radio program. (Courtesy Tulsa Historical Society)

By the 1930s the former Chickasaw Capitol Building in Tishomingo was serving as the Johnston County Courthouse. Changing federal policy and court rulings brought a restoration of sovereignty rights in the 1970s for the Chickasaws and other tribes. The building now serves as a historical site with exhibits and as a meeting place for the Chickasaw Nation.

CHAPTER THREE

At the Crossroads of History

The Best Hard Times

Pearl Carter Scott: "Never Give Up!"

While Cyrus Avery and others were promoting roads and transportation by car and truck, 12-year-old Pearl Carter of Marlow, Oklahoma, owned her own airplane. At age 13, she was flying all over southwestern Oklahoma and making aviation history under the tutelage of her mentor, Wiley Post, who soon would be recognized as one of the world's greatest aviators.

Pearl would prove to be unique in many ways throughout her life. Her story could be described as a "riches to rags to riches" story, with the "riches" of her later years consisting of the love of her family and the overwhelming satisfaction she received from helping others. Her motto, "Never give up!" was inspired by Post and her remarkable, blind father, George Carter.

Pearl was born in 1915 to a half-Choctaw, half-Chickasaw mother, Lucy Gibson, and a white father, George, at Marlow. Her father, who had been blinded in an accident at age 16, was a talented and wealthy businessman. She enjoyed an idyllic early childhood during which time she learned the rewards of helping others.

One day in 1927, when Pearl was 11, an airplane flew over Marlow, circled the community several times, and then landed in a pasture belonging to George Carter on the edge of town. Airplanes were a rare sight in rural Oklahoma, so a large crowd of curious townspeople converged on the pasture to see the airplane and its pilot. The Carter family was among the throng, and like most of those present, Pearl saw an airplane up close for the first time.

As it happened, the pilot was the brother of one of the Carter's neighbors, Joe Post. Wiley Post had just completed his first solo flight and had flown to Marlow to visit Joe, who lived across the street from the Carters. Wiley introduced himself to George. Pearl was at George's

Pearl Carter Scott

96

side, as usual, and George introduced her to the fledgling aviator. Pearl did not realize it at that moment, but this would prove to be one of the most important days of her life.

Post had traveled a difficult road in life to arrive in Marlow that day as a full-fledged pilot. Born in 1898, Post during his youth had dreamed about being an aviator. Impoverished, possessing only a sixth-grade education, unemployed, and bored, he made a major mistake in 1921 when he began "hijacking" cars in Grady County. He eventually was caught, convicted of robbery, and sentenced to serve 10 years at the State Reformatory at Granite. Although a "model prisoner," Wiley suffered from what later would be recognized as clinical depression. He was said to be in a "melancholic" state that likely would only deepen. Fortunately for Wiley, he was paroled by Governor J. B. A. Robertson in 1922 after serving a little more than one year of his sentence.

Determined to acquire an airplane, Post began working on a drilling rig near Seminole, Oklahoma, hoping to save a sufficient amount of money to realize his dream. But the experience soon turned into a nightmare as a freak oilfield accident resulted in the eventual loss of his eye following a severe infection. Wiley spent several months training himself to have depth perception with just one eye and then used his insurance settlement to buy

an airplane. His face, with his trademark eye patch, was destined to become known internationally for two flights around the world, one of them solo, for discovering the jet stream, and for inventing the pressure suit for flying at high altitudes. Post's pressure suit was the forerunner of pressure suits that astronauts and cosmonauts would wear in space. But Wiley's remarkable accomplishments were in his future as the short, stocky, dark-haired, one-eyed aviator stood before George and Pearl Carter in 1927.

That afternoon, Wiley asked George if he would like to have the distinction of being the first person ever to fly with him. After Wiley and George landed, Pearl bombarded them with "a million questions . . . about the airplane and how he flew it." With George's

(Facing page) Pearl, left, and Lucy, ca. 1943. With her husband working away from home, Pearl put in long hours working outside the home, taking care of her children and managing the day-to-day tasks involved in keeping house. Yet, she found time to stay close to her mother. (Courtesy Pearl Scott Collection, Chickasaw Nation Archives)

Pearl Carter (center), her mother, Lucy, and her father, George, Sr., proudly posed in front of Pearl's Curtiss Robin airplane in the pasture that George had converted into an "airport," ca. 1931. (Courtesy Pearl Scott Collection, Chickasaw Nation Archives)

Around the World Solo Flight
7 days 18 hours 49 mins
Wiley Post
7/22/33

Wiley Post posed with the Winnie Mae shortly after his solo flight around the world in 1933. Shortly after this record-breaking achievement, Post allowed Pearl to fly his prized plane. Pearl was the only person other than Post and his chief mechanic who ever flew the *Winnie Mae*. (Courtesy Oklahoma Historical Society)

permission, Pearl became Wiley's next passenger. Wiley could see that Pearl was fearless and eager to learn. The plane had dual controls, so Wiley decided to give her a basic flying lesson. Pearl was enthralled. She knew immediately that she wanted to learn all about flying. Later that same day Wiley gave her another lesson. By the end of the day, she had extracted a promise from

Post that he would give her lessons again when he returned to Marlow. Post returned to Marlow frequently for a while to see Joe, visit with George, and to give "Shorty" her flying lessons.

During his visits to Marlow, Wiley liked to visit with George about aviation and about other "adult" topics. Unlike her siblings, Pearl preferred to stay in the house and

absorb the conversations between George and Wiley. She was especially fascinated when Wiley and George would talk about the future. She also was captivated by Wiley's discussion of an idea he had for a pressurized flying suit that would allow aviators to fly to unprecedented altitudes in the unpressurized airplanes of the day. The prediction that impressed Pearl the most, however, came from Wiley when he talked about the ultimate use of his pressure suit. Post said, "Shorty, one of these days, man is going to walk on the moon. It won't be in George's or my lifetime, and it may not be in your lifetime, but man is going to walk on that moon."

Pearl finally asked her father for an airplane, and with Post's enthusiastic endorsement of Pearl as a "born flyer," he agreed. He built an airport on some of his land and had Post select an appropriate airplane—a Curtiss Robin Monoplane. George also hired a pilot to fly him and to train Pearl. She learned quickly and at age 13 had soloed. For the next five years, she flew in air shows with spectators marveling at the exploits of the little girl. Post was especially proud of his protege. As he became world famous, he kept in touch with her, had her meet him whenever he flew into Oklahoma, and introduced her to the famed navigator Harold Gatty and to his friend Will Rogers. Meeting Rogers, a Cherokee Indian from Oklahoma who had become one of the most popular individuals in America for his movies, writings, and humor, was a special thrill for Pearl.

An even greater moment for Pearl came when Post let her fly his famed airplane, the *Winnie Mae*. Later in life, Pearl would realize that she and Post's chief mechanic were the only individuals other than Wiley to ever fly Post's beloved aircraft. Pearl's aviation career unfortunately was cut short at age 18. She had married at 16, had one child and another on the way, and realized that she was too much of a "daredevil." She just could not resist doing stunt flying and decided that she had to quit. The Great Depression and other circumstances, including a house fire, caused her to lose her wealth, but she had three loving children who she considered a blessing. After the last child graduated from high school, she divorced her husband and was at loose ends for several years.

She reconnected with her Chickasaw roots in 1972 when she began working for the tribe as a community health representative. Pearl worked long hours, traveling a multi-county area to help Indian people of all tribes. She was helping people with health, sanitation, diet, and accessing available services and enjoyed being in a position once again to help people. She retired from this job in 1980 at age 65, but three years

later she was asked to run for a seat in the Chickasaw Nation's Legislature. She was elected and served either as a legislator or as a community liaison for Chickasaw Governor Bill Anoatubby until she died in 2005. She had been inducted into the Chickasaw Nation Hall of Fame in 1995.

Pearl did get to fly a King Air airplane on her 80th birthday, and she was inducted into the Oklahoma Aviation and Space Hall of Fame in 1995. Her unique place in American aviation history had been recognized.

She reminisced that evening about what a joy flying was in those days when pilots "flew by the seat of their pants" with little instrumentation and few restrictions on when and where one could fly. It was a unique, and brief, period in aviation history when a one-eyed, convicted felon could teach a 12-year-old girl how to fly.

The elegant home of Phillips Petroleum Company co-founder Frank and Jane Phillips in Bartlesville was visited by Wiley Post on several occasions. Phillips Petroleum Company was an important sponsor for several of Post's aviation exploits. His use of Phillips' 77 aviation fuel provided valuable advertising for Phillips. The Phillips home was a center of business and social activity for decades. The house and grounds now are the property of the Oklahoma Historical Society and may be visited by the public. (Courtesy Jim Argo)

The Last Farewell of Will Rogers and Wiley Post by Mike Wimmer depicts Wiley Post and Will Rogers preparing to depart from Fairbanks, Alaska, on August 15, 1935, on their way to Point Barrow, Alaska, and Russia as part of an anticipated flight around the world. Later that day, Post landed his new airplane, equipped with pontoons, near an Eskimo village to seek directions to Point Barrow. He then "tinkered" with the airplane's engine and took off for the last time. About 50 feet off the ground, the engine shut down, and Post and Rogers were killed as the craft slammed into shallow water. Oklahoma and the world lost two of their most popular figures at the same instant. (Courtesy Oklahoma State Senate Historical Preservation Fund)

National Guardsmen carry the casket of Wiley Post into the State Capitol where it would be placed so thousands of grieving Oklahomans could pay their respects. His funeral, held at the First Baptist Church of Oklahoma City, was the largest in state history. Frank Phillips was chairman of 150 honorary pallbearers who included Oklahoma's two United States senators, Thomas Gore and Elmer Thomas, Governor E. W. Marland, former Governor Lee Cruce, United States Secretary of State Cordell Hull, and numerous other dignitaries. The church was filled to capacity, and as many as 40,000 were within a two-block radius of the church. The service was broadcast live on radio stations KOMA and WKY. Thousands more lined the route from the church to Memorial Park Cemetery, and another 10,000 waited at the cemetery. (Courtesy Oklahoma Publishing Company)

Will Rogers' funeral was held in California where he was residing at the time of his death. The Oklahoma Legislature appropriated $200,000 for the creation of a Will Rogers Memorial, and a beautiful facility, designed by Tulsa Architect John Forsythe, was opened in Claremore in 1938, expanded in 1982, and renovated extensively in the 1990s. This statue by Jo Davidson, a distinguished sculptor and friend of Rogers, was placed in the original entry. One of Rogers' most famous quotes is found on the base of the statue: "I never met a man I didn't like." The Memorial is visited by thousands annually who come to learn more about one of the most popular Americans of the twentieth century. (Courtesy Jim Argo)

One-Party Rule: Politics, 1932-1959

The Great Depression brought about a transformation in the politics of the nation and of Oklahoma. The Republican Party had dominated the presidency during the 1920s and had claimed and received more credit for the economic prosperity of the decade than it deserved. Consequently, Republicans received more of the blame for the Great Depression, a global economic disaster with many causes. Franklin D. Roosevelt, the Democratic candidate for president, was elected in a "landslide," and he put together a national political coalition of old-line Democrats, big city political machines, labor, farm groups, blacks, and other ethnic groups. Some of these groups, such as farmers and blacks, had traditionally voted Republican. Roosevelt's New Deal coalition not only shifted the balance of power to the Democrat Party nationally, but also altered the political landscape dramatically in Oklahoma for the next three decades.

William H. "Alfalfa Bill" Murray was elected Governor in 1931 and took office with strong Democratic majorities in both houses of the Legislature. Murray was a constitutional scholar, an experienced politician who had served two terms in Congress, and a staunch racist who professed to believe that as a group, blacks were best suited for manual labor. He used patronage power and political savvy to enhance the power of his office, which was constitutionally weak and had been debilitated further by the impeachment traumas of the 1920s. Faced with budget difficulties, he promoted a tax increase, cut state government spending, and asked the Legislature to establish the Oklahoma Tax Commission. Murray also was quick to use the National Guard for various reasons, including shutting down production in the Oklahoma City Oil Field to raise crude oil prices and take control over a toll bridge on the Red River in a dispute with the state of Texas. A bitter opponent of President Roosevelt, he did not cooperate fully with New Deal initiatives and made a failed attempt to run for the presidency in 1936.

William H. "Alfalfa Bill" Murray was a rural, populist Democrat who benefited politically from hard times. Murray demonstrated that politically shrewd governors in Oklahoma can wield considerable power despite the office's relatively diluted constitutional powers. (Courtesy Oklahoma Heritage Association)

Raymond D. Gary of Madill served as governor of Oklahoma from 1955 to 1959. Under Gary's leadership public schools in Oklahoma were integrated with little turmoil, as Gary made it clear that the law of the land as enunciated by the United States Supreme Court would be enforced in the state. (Courtesy Oklahoma Historical Society)

Oilman E. W. Marland, who had lost his oil company as a result of the depression and had served the previous two years in Congress, was elected governor in 1936. A staunch supporter of Roosevelt, he proposed a "Little New Deal" in Oklahoma, which the Legislature refused to approve, in part because of the $500 million price tag that came with it. Marland campaigned to create the Oklahoma Department of Public Safety and played a leading role in establishing the Interstate Oil Compact Commission with headquarters in Oklahoma City. He was succeeded in office by Leon C. "Red" Phillips, who benefited by the stimulation of the economy provided World War II. He successfully advocated a budget balancing amendment to the State Constitution that prevents the state from spending more money than it receives in revenue.

Belying the youth of the state, Oklahoma elected its first native-born governor in 1943, oilman Robert S. Kerr. During the course of his administration, the continued economic expansion filled state coffers and liquidated the state's debt. He skillfully cultivated relationships in Washington, D. C., enabling him to attract massive military spending to Oklahoma in the form of Army, Navy, and Army Air Corps bases and prisoner of war camps. After his term expired, he was elected to the United States Senate where he quickly accumulated sufficient power to be dubbed the "Uncrowned King of the Senate."

A feature of government in Oklahoma that had become pronounced by this time was rural domination of the Legislature. The State Constitution originally provided that each of the districts in the House represented approximately the same number of people, as did Senate districts. The districts were to be reapportioned after each census as needed to maintain equal representation. The Legislature had failed to do this, however, and the urban growth of the state had not been reflected in the Legislature. Governor Roy J. Turner proved to be an able administrator, but he did not confront the problem. The next governor, Johnston Murray, Alfalfa Bill's son, argued the need for change without success, and the issue was ignored by his successor, Raymond D. Gary. Gary did stand tall, however, when he announced that Oklahoma would follow the law of the land as enunciated in the *Brown v. Topeka Board of Education* ruling of the United States Supreme Court, which outlawed the segregation of public schools on the basis of race. When Arkansas Governor Orval Faubus used National Guard troops in an attempt to stop desegregation of the schools in Little Rock, Gary announced that if the state militia were to be used in Oklahoma, it would be to uphold the law.

As Gary's term as governor drew to a close in 1959, the state was on the threshold of a new era of politics in which Legislature would be reapportioned, prohibition of liquor would be repealed, and the Republican Party would be rejuvenated. A return to a two-party system was eminent.

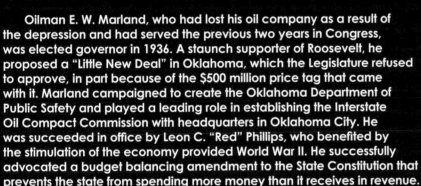

(Above) Oilman E. W. Marland constructed a fabulous home in Ponca City between 1925 and 1928. Marland and his wife had lived in the home only a short time when Marland lost his company due to financial reverses during the Great Depression. He and his wife lived in the chauffer's quarters as he could not afford to operate the huge mansion. He retained ownership, however, and used it for events, parties, and as his campaign headquarters when he ran for Congress and governor of Oklahoma. He sold the property six months before he died. Eventually the mansion, grounds, and out-buildings were acquired by the City of Ponca City for $1.4 million, one-half of which was donated by the Conoco Oil Company. The citizens of Ponca City approved a 1 cent city sales tax to fund the city's portion of the purchase price. Today the restored mansion is open for touring by the public. (Courtesy Jim Argo)

Thomas Gilcrease: Leaving a Track

The oil and gas industry has energized Oklahoma's economy through jobs, tax revenues, and the philanthropy of individual oilmen and companies. Oilmen have generously supported education, the arts, a wide range of charities, and the establishment and support of museums. While all parts of the state have been positively impacted, Tulsa, for decades known as "The Oil Capital of the World," has especially benefited from the generosity of oilmen and their families. The University of Tulsa's endowment was established primarily through petroleum-related philanthropy, and the nationally recognized Philbrook Museum of Art originally was Villa Philbrook before it was donated in 1938 by independent oilman Waite Phillips and his wife Genevieve to the City of Tulsa for an art museum. Tulsa's other nationally recognized art institution, Gilcrease Museum, was the result of oil wealth and the determination of Thomas Gilcrease to "leave some sort of track."

Gilcrease was born in 1890 at Robilene, Louisiana. He was the first of 14 children who eventually were born to his father, William, and his mother, Elizabeth, who was of Creek Indian ancestry. Soon after Thomas was born, the family moved to the Creek Nation where they were entitled to occupy land, provided they used it productively. They settled about 20 miles south of the village of Tulsa at a place now called Twin Mounds. There his father took Tom to the father of Creek poet Alexander Posey, who taught the youngster how to read and write. When that was accomplished, young Tom went to work helping his father on the farm.

"The time to begin plowing or picking cotton is when the sun rises and the time to stop is when it sets," his father informed him. Before sunrise Thomas was to feed the hogs, turn the cattle out to pasture, harness the horses, and start the cooking fire in the kitchen. After

Thomas Gilcrease

sunset, he had to feed the hogs again, milk cows, unharness the horses, and bring firewood in for the next day. After this was accomplished, he was free to read, which he did voraciously. When Tom was 12, he helped his father operate a flour and corn milling operation, and at age 14, he assisted his father in the operation of a general merchandise business.

In 1899 the lands of the Creek Nation were allotted to individual tribal members, and the family received 160 acres for Elizabeth and each of their children who were born at that point. That year a farmer showed Tom an oil seep on his land. The family used the crude for greasing harnesses and killing hog lice. In 1905 the discovery well of what would become the Glenn Pool, Oklahoma's first giant oil field, was drilled. As the field was expanded, Tom's land proved to overlay some of its most productive sands. After attending Bacone College for one year, he returned home briefly to farm and raise cattle before moving to Tulsa in 1908, where he dealt in oil leases. In 1910 he procured drilling tools and became an oilman. By 1917 he had 32 producing wells on his 160 acres.

Gilcrease's work ethic, good business sense, and good fortune enabled him to prosper in the oil business. In 1922 he organized the Gilcrease Oil Company, established headquarters in San Antonio,

(Facing page) Thomas Gilcrease as he appeared ca. 1952. The image is a black and white photograph of a formal portrait painting. (Courtesy Oklahoma Historical Society)

Here Gilcrease is viewing early American portraits in his extensive collection. As of 2006, the art collection housed in the Gilcrease Museum of the Americas included more than 10,000 paintings, drawings, prints, and sculptures.

Texas, and ultimately developed oil production in Oklahoma, Kansas, Texas, New Mexico, and Louisiana. That same year, he purchased his first oil painting.

By 1925 at age 35, Gilcrease had reached a crossroads in his life. He considered what he could do to "leave a track." His marriage to Belle Harlow, an Osage woman who bore him two sons, Thomas, Jr., and Barton, was drawing to a close. The couple divorced in 1926. Gilcrease decided to make a trip to Europe and ponder the future. There he realized that cultures are preserved in fine art, written records, and the work of artists and artisans. He also observed that Oklahoma had no museum dedicated to preserving the pre-Columbian civilizations of the Americas, the development of the American West, or the cultures of Native American people. Gilcrease determined that he would assemble a collection of art, documents, books, and objects that someday would be displayed in a museum in Tulsa. In 1928 he married Norma Smallwood of Tulsa, a part-Cherokee woman who had become Oklahoma's first Miss America in 1926. They had a daughter, Des Cygne, before they were divorced in 1933.

Gilcrease cautiously began to acquire items for his collection. He had the advantage of seeking art that was not yet in favor with major collectors on the East and West coasts; thus he was able to obtain art and artifacts at a reasonable price, seeking out single works as well as purchasing entire collections from dealers and collectors. He found much American Indian material in England. He formed the Thomas Gilcrease Foundation in 1942, and returned to Tulsa to live. Over the next several years, he hired renowned Pottawatomie artist Woody Crumbo to help assemble an outstanding American Indian art collection, and he also purchased many of Crumbo's own works for the collection. Gilcrease also hired Cherokee wood sculptor Willard Stone to be an artist in residence for three years, thereby acquiring a large number of Stone's unique sculptures.

Gilcrease placed part of his collection on public display in temporary quarters until the Thomas Gilcrease Museum opened in 1949. He had constructed it next to his home in northeast Tulsa, where he had a view of the Tulsa skyline and the Osage Hills. With 10 "ample" galleries, he had room to display only 4 percent of his collection. During the early 1950s, Gilcrease rapidly expanded his collection, but declining oil prices took a toll on his finances. In 1953 he found himself more than $2 million in debt.

Gilcrease was determined to keep his collection intact, so he let it be known that the entire collection was for sale. Rumors of potential purchasers abounded, and many believed that the collection was destined to leave Oklahoma. At that point, a group of Tulsa citizens, headed by oilman Alfred E. Aaronson, organized a "Keep the Gilcrease Museum in Tulsa" committee. The group proposed that the City of Tulsa float a bond issue in the amount of $2.25 million to pay the Gilcrease Foundation's debt. Gilcrease in turn would give the collection to the City of Tulsa, assign it a half interest in five Texas oil leases, and lease the building to the city for five years at $1 per year. The proposal was approved overwhelmingly by the citizens of Tulsa in a special election held on August 24, 1954.

The collection that had been saved for Tulsa truly was magnificent. It included more than 10,000 paintings, drawings, prints, and sculptures by approximately 400 artists who worked from colonial times to the present. Early American artists included Thomas Eakins, Charles Wilson Peale, John Singleton Copley, Winslow Homer, John James Audubon, and N. C. Wyeth. The collection also featured numerous outstanding Western and Indian artists, including Albert Bierstadt, George Catlin, Thomas Moran, Frederic Remington, Charles M. Russell, and J. H. Sharp. Featured among the collection, in addition to the works of Crumbo and Stone, was art by Oklahomans Acee Blue Eagle and Charles Banks Wilson. The collection also had some 65,000 books, letters, and manuscripts, including the only certified copies of the Articles of Confederation and the Declaration of Independence found outside the Library of Congress. Gilcrease had amassed a large anthropological collection of some 250,000 artifacts covering Native American, Hispanic, and Anglo-American cultures in North, Central, and South America.

Gilcrease started a new collection, and in 1958 donated the museum building and 13.5 acres to the city. When he died in 1962, the museum received all of the additional items he had collected. His remarkable contribution to the preservation of American culture in general and that of Native Americans and the American West in particular had been recognized by his induction into the Oklahoma Hall of Fame in 1952. In 1971 he was inducted posthumously into the Hall of Great Westerners at the National Cowboy and Western Heritage Museum in Oklahoma City. Thomas Gilcrease had indeed "left a track" that would benefit generations of Oklahomans and Americans, as well as foreign visitors, well into the future.

The Tulsa skyline as it appeared in 1947 looking east to west. The oil prosperity that fueled the city's growth also generated the wealth that enabled Thomas Gilcrease to build his remarkable collection of art, which eventually would provide the materials for an internationally renowned museum in Tulsa. Unlike Oklahoma City, Tulsa did not allow oil wells to be drilled within city limits, although the growth of the city eventually brought some existing wells within its boundaries. Located across the Arkansas River to the west of downtown was a large complex of refineries, an industry that remains important in Tulsa to the present. (Courtesy Tulsa Historical Society)

Creative Oklahomans

The rich culture of Oklahoma was reflected in the burst of creativity in all phases of the arts during the decades from 1930 to 1960. Oklahoma's famed Native American women ballerinas—Yvonne Chouteau (Shawnee/Cherokee), Rosella Hightower (Choctaw), Moscelyn Larkin (Shawnee/Peoria), and Marjorie and Maria Tallchief (Osage)—have been well recognized and honored, but the state's Native American women in music largely have been forgotten.

An exception was Te Ata Fisher, a Chickasaw born in 1895 who became internationally famous for her one-woman performances during which she combined her formidable skills in music and drama to entertain and teach about Native American cultures. Her cousin Mary Ataloa Stone McClendon, who was born in 1896, became known nationally as an artist, vocalist, educator, humanitarian, and philosopher. Tsianina Blackstone, a Creek/Cherokee, was born at Oktaha in 1892 and became

Woody Guthrie of Okemah was arguably the most influential folk musician of the twentieth century. Charles Banks Wilson's portrait of Guthrie is exhibited in the State Capitol. (Courtesy Oklahoma State Senate Historical Preservation Fund)

a renowned classical vocalist. And then there was Tessie Mobley. Born near Ardmore in 1906, Mobley was another talented Chickasaw who was given the name "Lushanya," or "Sweet Singing Bird" by the Cherokees. Mobley's rise to prominence began when she served as a soloist with the Hollywood Symphony Orchestra in the 1920s. She later toured many states performing in concerts and on radio before going to Europe to tour and to study in Germany. After several years of performances there, she made her debut at La Scala in Milan, Italy, becoming the first American to sing on that renowned stage. From there her operatic career skyrocketed. Soon she was performing before the crowned heads of state in Europe to rave reviews. She entertained United States troops during World War II and married Ramon Vinay, a star with the Metropolitan Opera. She retired to manage his career.

Three of the top female recording stars of the 1940s and 1950s were Oklahomans Kay Starr, Patti Page, and Wanda Jackson. All three of these women were highly popular and pursued successful careers well into the twenty-first century. Yet another remarkable performer, Lee Wiley, has not been so well remembered in Oklahoma.

Lee Wiley, part-Cherokee, was born in 1915 in Fort Gibson, Oklahoma. At age 17, she was singing with the Lee Riesman Orchestra in New York City. She was the first to record an album of songs by one composer, releasing a series of albums of the songs of Cole Porter, Irving Berlin, George Gershwin, and Rogers and Hart that are considered classics. She was described as "tall, strikingly attractive . . . with corn-colored hair and olive skin." She possessed a voice that critics described as "sultry," "magical," "genteel," and yet "devastating in its sex appeal." She retired in 1960 and died in 1975. Still a favorite of knowledgeable jazz buffs, a boxed CD set containing her recordings from 1935 to 1955 entitled *Legendary Lee Wiley* was released in 1998.

Another of the many outstanding jazz musicians Oklahoma has produced was Charles "Charlie" Christian. Christian was born in Texas but came to Oklahoma City with his family when he was five. He learned to play trumpet, piano, and other instruments, but he would become famous for his pioneering work on electric guitar. He was "discovered" by a talent scout for band leader Benny Goodman in 1939, and it was while playing in Goodman's orchestra that Christian revolutionized how guitars were used, turning them into lead instruments. He was an instant sensation, but his career was cut short when he died of tuberculosis in 1941. By that time he had pioneered modern jazz guitar, and subsequent electric guitarists n both rock and blues owed much to Christian's development of the instrument's role in music.

While Charlie Christian was one of the most influential instrumentalists of the twentieth century, Oklahoma's Woody Guthrie was one of the era's most prominent singers and songwriters. Born in Okemah, Oklahoma, in 1912, Guthrie and his family endured poverty and a tragic house fire in which Woody's sister Clara was killed. The family left Okemah in 1931 and headed for the Texas Panhandle. Woody soon hit the roads and rails, where he experienced the shameful treatment migrant workers received. This inspired much of the music he began to write and sing. By 1937 he was performing his Dust Bowl ballads on radio in Los Angeles. He later headed for New York where he continued to perform. In 1940 he made a series of recordings for the Library of Congress and for Folkways Records. By the 1950s he had become a folk music icon.

His political views, shaped by his experiences, were decidedly to the left, but he also was patriotic. During World War II, he served in the Merchant Marines and some of his songs, such as "Oklahoma Hills," "Bound for Glory," and "This Land is Your Land" continue to inspire unity and appreciation for his lyrical talents. He was diagnosed with

Huntington's Chorea, a degenerative disease, in 1954 and died in 1967.

His influence on folk and even rock music was profound. Performers such as Bob Dylan, Bruce Springsteen, and others have acknowledged his influence on their music. He was inducted into the Songwriters' Hall of Fame in 1971, The Rock and Roll Hall of Fame in 1988, and the Oklahoma Hall of Fame in 2006.

Opera star Tessie "Lushanya" Mobley as she appeared in 1964 upon her induction into the Oklahoma Hall of Fame. A Chickasaw Indian from Ardmore, Mobley was the first American to sing on the renowned stage at La Scala in Milan, Italy. (Courtesy Oklahoma Heritage Association)

Band leader Leslie Sheffield and his Rythmaites, playing a venue in Oklahoma City's Deep Deuce. To Sheffield's immediate left, with a guitar, was Charlie Christian, considered to be the first great soloist on the amplified guitar and one of the most influential musicians of the twentieth century. As a pioneer electric guitar player, Christian influenced subsequent jazz, blues, and rock guitarists. He was predominant in establishing the guitar as a lead instrument. Christian was "discovered" and recruited by band leader Benny Goodman and achieved major recognition before dying at age 25 with tuberculosis and pneumonia. (Courtesy

Angie Debo: Native Voices

As drought and depression rocked the foundations of the state and nation after 1929, a growing number of people questioned many of the assumptions that had defined the "Oklahoma" experience.

Was the history of Oklahoma a redeeming drama about progress and manifest destiny? Was it a story of courageous pioneers carving a civilization out of the wilderness? Or, as some asked, was the history of the state a reflection of the bad as well as the good, a story that recognized the experiences of the common folk, many of whom had not feasted on the fruits of progress? One writer who gave voice to both perspectives was Angie Debo.

Born in 1890 on a rented farm in Kansas, Debo moved with her family to Oklahoma Territory when she was nine years old. She attended rural schools through the eighth grade and earned her teacher's certificate when she was 16. At the age of 23, after reading every book she could borrow, she graduated from high school and enrolled at the University of Oklahoma.

There, she met Dr. Edward E. Dale, a fellow pioneer who had risen from his rural life on a Greer County ranch to complete the Ph.D. in History from Harvard, where he studied with Dr. Frederick Jackson Turner, champion of the thesis that successive waves of frontier conquest had defined the American experience. With Dale as her mentor, Debo learned the skills of historical research, honed her native writing abilities, and grew to appreciate the rich possibilities of state and regional history.

After graduating in 1918, Debo taught high school in Enid and enrolled at the University of Chicago, where she completed her master's degree in history in 1924. She joined the faculty at West Texas State Teachers' College in Canyon, Texas, but continued her education as a candidate for the Ph.D. in history at the University of Oklahoma. Once again, she came under the influence of E. E. Dale.

Dale, who was actively building what would become known as the Western History

Angie Debo

Collections to support a regional history program, suggested that Debo use a recently acquired collection of records from the Choctaw Nation for her dissertation. Recognizing a growing awareness of and market for the rich fabric of regionalism, she agreed.

The result was *The Rise and Fall of the Choctaw Republic*, published to great acclaim by the University of Oklahoma Press in 1934. For the first time, a historian with the skills for both analytical research and expressive writing approached Indian history not as a secondary by-product of the march of American expansion, but as a primary story told from the perspective of the Indians themselves. As an early version of ethnohistory, the book sold well and won for Debo the John H. Dunning Prize from the American Historical Association, one of the highest honors granted by the academic community.

Despite earning the Ph.D. and the success of her first book, Debo's career in academia was a casualty of bad timing and discrimination against women. In the summer of 1933, her position on the faculty at West Texas State was eliminated after a 25 percent cut in the school's budget. She was offered a job as a part-time curator at the Panhandle Plains Museum, which she took, but she desperately searched for another faculty position. To her everlasting disappointment, the few openings that

survived the impact of the Great Depression were generally filled by men with families.

Debo was not alone among the casualties of the widening financial calamity. By December of 1933, more than a quarter of all Oklahomans were unemployed. In Oklahoma City, one survey noted that 576 families were living in cardboard shacks and hand-dug caves along the banks of the North Canadian River. When the federal government launched a "make work" program called the Works Progress

Administration in May of 1935, more than 93,000 unemployed Oklahomans were soon enrolled and earning enough to at least buy groceries.

Desperate for work and an opportunity to write again, Debo sought help from Grant Foreman, a friend and self-taught historian who was director of the Federal Writers' Project of the Works Progress Administration. In January of 1937 she was hired as an editor for a bold new initiative

(Facing page) Angie Debo's portrait was painted by Charles Banks Wilson when she was 95 years old. It was painted in her home in Marshall, Oklahoma, and is displayed in the State Capitol. (Courtesy Oklahoma Arts Council)

In addition to professional historians such as Angie Debo, interested amateurs and city officials have preserved Oklahoma's history. For example, this Santa Fe Depot, constructed in 1904, serves as a museum for the Historical Society of Pottawatomie County. (Courtesy Jim Argo)

called the Indian-Pioneer Papers, an inspired project that employed writers to interview Oklahomans who had experienced the Trail of Tears, slavery, the Civil War, Indian government, land runs, and the early stages of becoming a state. The result was a 116-volume set of oral histories that gave voice to the people who had made history.

In 1940 Debo became director of the Oklahoma Guide Book project of the WPA. With a twin mission to compile a portrait of the state and encourage cultural tourism, Debo co-edited *Oklahoma: A Guide to the*

Sooner State, which was published by the University of Oklahoma Press in 1941. Again, she had a hand in celebrating the diversity of the Oklahoma experience.

To supplement her work with the WPA, Debo applied for and received grants from the Social Science Research Council to support work on two books. The first resulted in the research, writing, and publication of *And Still the Waters Run,* a monumental work that uncovered and described in detail the graft and corruption that had defrauded so many Indian people of their allotments in Oklahoma. The second book, told from the perspective of the Creeks, was *The Road to Disappearance,* published by the University of Oklahoma Press in 1941.

During and after World War II, the market for regional history changed and Debo changed with it. First came a booster-inspired narrative history of Tulsa, followed quickly by the innovative historical novel *Prairie City,* in which she captured the spirit and texture of the pioneer life she had experienced first hand. In *Oklahoma: Footloose and Fancy Free,* published in 1949, she stepped back from her more scholarly books to produce a lively, interpretive response to the novels *Cimarron* and *The Grapes of Wrath,* both of which Debo considered "rooted in nowhere."

Despite this shift to books targeted

more at the general reading public, Debo continued her interest in Indian affairs. With a national reputation built on the critical success of *And Still the Waters Run,* she joined others in advocating restitution and assistance to native peoples across the country. In 1951, sponsored by the Indian Rights Association, she produced *The Five Civilized Tribes of Oklahoma: Social and Economic Conditions.* She later added her reputation and skills to the Alaska Native Claims Settlement Act and numerous efforts by the American Civil Liberties Union to protect the rights of individuals.

Writing from her home in Marshall, Oklahoma, Debo penned a steady stream of articles, reviews, and books for the rest of her life. In 1970 she wrote *A History of the Indians of the United States,* her most ambitious survey text, and followed that in 1976 with *Geronimo: The Man, His Time, His Place.* By the time of her death in 1988, her body of work included more than 100 articles and book reviews, 3 edited books, 1 co-authored book, and 9 books written on her own.

Late in life, Angie Debo was asked to describe the motivation behind her historical research and writing. "I suppose I have only one," she said. "To discover the truth and publish it." Through a combination of talent, timing, and courage, she did just that, and in the process, gave voice to the people.

Muriel H. Wright began her career as a young historian and protégé of Joseph B. Thoburn at the Oklahoma Historical Society in the 1920s. Wright was proud of her Choctaw heritage, especially her grandfather Allen Wright, who first used the Choctaw word "Oklahoma," meaning "Land of the Red man." She produced a number of significant books on Indian and Oklahoma history and for decades was editor of the *Chronicles of Oklahoma.* Although Wright and Debo had their disagreements and were rivals, both of them played significant roles as historians. (Courtesy Oklahoma Heritage Association)

The ability to enjoy the dramatic view from the top of Mt. Scott of the Wichita Mountains in the Wichita Mountains National Wildlife Refuge was made possible by employees of the Works Progress Administration during the 1930s who constructed the road to the top. Many significant projects were completed in Oklahoma by the WPA, a federal agency created to provide meaningful employment for individuals during the Great Depression. (Courtesy Jim Argo)

Constructed in 1935 by the WPA to provide a summer home for Oklahoma Governor William H. Murray, Tucker Tower is a striking building that looks like a lighthouse on a cliff overlooking Lake Murray. The structure is within the grounds of Lake Murray State Park, Oklahoma's oldest and largest state park. It now houses local artifacts and state naturalists conduct nature programs and activities there. (Courtesy Jim Argo)

The development of the Interstate Highway System begun during the 1950s continued into the following decades. When Interstate Highway 35 was completed through Oklahoma, the efficiency of travel through the state north to south was enhanced significantly. In the Arbuckle Mountain region in southern Oklahoma, the highway construction cut through hillsides exposing interesting geological strata. (Courtesy Jim Argo)

Sports Heroes

During the Great Depression and World War II, sports provided a welcome diversion for Americans. Oklahomans were no exception. With the rapid growth of the radio industry, Oklahomans could easily follow the fortunes of Major League Baseball teams. The state produced numerous baseball stars, of which two of the brightest were Carl Hubbell and Warren Spahn. The late 1940s and the 1950s brought new prosperity to Oklahoma, and while baseball retained its popularity, individuals like Henry P. Iba and Charles B. "Bud" Wilkinson stimulated a growing interest in and support for collegiate athletics.

Hubbell grew up on a farm near Meeker, Oklahoma. After leading Meeker to the Class C high school state championship in 1923, the lanky lefthander played minor league ball for five years, perfecting his trademark pitch, the screwball. In 1928 he began a 16-year Major League career with the New York Giants, becoming the only pitcher in peacetime to win the Most Valuable Player Award twice, in 1933 and 1936. Hubbell won an amazing 34 games in a row in late 1936 and early 1937. His most famous feat came during the 1934 All-Star Game when he struck out five of the game's greatest hitters—Babe Ruth, Lou Gehrig, Jimmie Foxx, Al Simmons, and Joe Cronin—in succession. Hubbell retired in 1943 and was elected to the Baseball Hall of Fame in 1947.

A native of New York, Spahn pitched a few games for the Boston Braves in 1942 before he was drafted and sent to Oklahoma for basic training. There he met his future wife, Lorene; from that time he was an Oklahoman. A combat engineer, he was wounded at Remagen, Germany. His Major League career was delayed by his service until the 1946 season, and from 1949 to 1963 he was a dominant pitcher for the Braves. He holds the record for the most victories by a lefthander at 363,

Charles B. "Bud" Wilkinson was head coach of the Oklahoma Sooners football team from 1947 to 1964. His teams won conference championships his first 13 years as coach. Between 1953 and 1957 his teams won an amazing 47 consecutive games, an NCAA record that still stands. He also won three national championships during his tenure at the University of Oklahoma. (Courtesy Oklahoma Historical Society)

and he had 13 seasons in which he won 20 or more games. He also tossed two no-hit games and hit 35 homeruns, more than any other pitcher in National League history. After his retirement from baseball in 1966, he managed the Tulsa Oilers for four years. He was inducted into the Baseball Hall of Fame in 1973 and died in 2003.

Known to his players as "Mr. Iba," Iba was born in Missouri in 1904. His first head coaching experience came at Classen High School in Oklahoma City from 1927 to 1929. After coaching at a small college in Missouri and at Colorado University, Iba was hired to coach Oklahoma A&M University in 1934. He would coach there until 1970. Iba became one of the most influential coaches in the history of basketball, developing a tenacious style of man-to-man defense and a deliberate offense. His teams won the NCAA Championship in 1945 and 1946, and he retired with 767 collegiate wins.

Iba's effective use of Bob Kurland, one of the first great post players in college basketball, prompted rules against goal tending and "camping in the lane." Iba also was the only coach in history to win two Olympic Gold Medals and was prevented from winning a third by some highly controversial calls by referees. He was a revered figure on the campus of Oklahoma State University until his death in 1993.

A native of Minnesota, Wilkinson arrived at the University of Oklahoma as an assistant football coach in 1946 at age 30. One year later, Coach Jim Tatum departed and the unproven Wilkinson became head coach. Over the next 16 years he elevated the Sooner program to elite status. During those years, his teams had an .826 winning percentage, won 14 league championships, and captured three national championships. During the 1953 season, Bud's teams began a 47-game winning streak that is still unmatched by any other NCAA Division I program.

Highly organized and detail oriented, Wilkinson's team ran the split-T formation to perfection. He also borrowed from Hank Iba in preparing for opponents, carefully replicating in practice what his players would see in games. He was a master strategist and motivator. Following his career at OU, Wilkinson unsuccessfully entered the political arena and coached in the National Football League. He did have a highly successful career as an analyst for college football telecasts for ABC and ESPN. He died in 1994. Eddie Crowder, who played quarterback at OU for Wilkinson and later coached at Colorado University, observed that he had only known one genius—"His name was Bud Wilkinson."

Oklahoma State University head basketball coach and athletic director Henry P. "Hank" Iba as he appeared late in his coaching career. Iba generally is regarded as one of the most influential coaches in the history of college basketball. (Courtesy Oklahoma Heritage Association.)

A busy day in May 1940 in downtown Pawnee. This photo shows only one side of the square that surrounds the county courthouse in the community. Given the number of vehicles on the streets and people on the sidewalks, this photo likely was taken on a Saturday when people from the surrounding countryside came to town to shop, sell eggs or other items, and visit with friends. (Courtesy Oklahoma Publishing Company)

The St. Gregory's Abbey Chapel on the campus of St. Gregory's University in Shawnee was built in 1942 and features beautiful, intricate stained glass windows that are the focus of visiting tour groups. Public tours can be scheduled. (Courtesy State Historic Preservation Office, Oklahoma Historical Society)

Joseph Danne: Man of the Soil

By the late 1930s most farmers and ranchers in Oklahoma were struggling to survive. The first challenge had been the Great Depression with ruinously low prices for their crops and livestock, followed by years of record drought and terrifying dust storms. Some hunkered down and fought back with the help of family, friends, and government assistance. Others simply walked away, joining the army of drifters riding the rails and roaming the highways.

One farmer who fought back in his own unique way was an eccentric, self-taught plant geneticist who spent three decades patiently breeding different strains of wheat in the search for a plant that would increase harvests and improve profit margins. Thanks in large part to his efforts, farmers on the Southern Plains produced record harvests during World War II and had a fighting chance to survive the environmental challenges and volatile markets of the post-war era. That man of the soil was Joseph Danne.

Danne was born in 1887 on a farm in western Nebraska. When he was six, his German-born parents bought a farm four and a half miles northwest of Kingfisher and joined thousands of other pioneers making the rocky transition from self-sufficient, subsistence-style farming to the production of cash crops intended for the marketplace.

Young Danne grew up marching to the beat of his own drum. He was a loner and lifelong bachelor who earned a reputation for thrift and hard work. Even late in life, he rarely used his tractor, preferring to plow behind two mules. He never installed electricity or plumbing

Joseph Danne

in his homes, getting by with well water and outhouses. Despite the limitations of his eighth-grade education, he was a voracious reader with considerable knowledge of ancient history and astronomy. He spoke German, English, and Spanish, invented practical devices such as a scale that could weigh a single grain of wheat, and was known for inflexible honesty. When a neighbor bound his crop of oats and left without being paid, Danne showed up at his house before daylight the next morning with cash in hand.

At the age of 13, armed with a clear disposition for self-discipline and blessed with a boundless sense of curiosity, Danne read a magazine article that changed his life. The article described the work of Luther Burbank, the world famous plant geneticist who had developed new techniques of plant breeding. Using scientific methodology, Burbank surgically cross-bred plants to create new hybrids that shared the best qualities of the parents. In a world where crops had long been improved by simply saving the best seeds of one variety, the possibilities of creating new hybrids through surgical manipulation and selective breeding were revolutionary.

In 1908 Danne conducted his first cross-breeding experiments using cotton. From there, he expanded his efforts to cross-breeding oats, barley, wild flowers,

(Facing page) Joseph Danne, shown here checking the development of some of the plants in his experimental plots, was an eccentric genius who made magnificent contributions to mankind through his creation of wheat varieties that thrived in the environment of the Great Plains. (Courtesy Oklahoma Historical Society)

Joseph Danne's work helped spur increased prosperity among wheat farmers in western Oklahoma and far beyond. Evidence of that prosperity can be seen in the Pioneer Day parade in Guymon in 1950. An estimated crowd of 45,000 lined the streets for 15 blocks. Attendees came from Oklahoma, Kansas, Colorado, New Mexico, and Texas. (Courtesy Oklahoma Publishing Company)

and lilies. He even tried breeding corn with sorghum and corn with Johnson grass. For the barnyard, the budding scientist crossbred hogs and worked on a cross of a White Leghorn chicken with a Barred Rock chicken in an attempt to produce chicks with colorization that did not attract the attention of hawks. His greatest challenges, however, as well as his greatest achievements, came with the cross breeding of wheat.

On the rich soils of the Southern Plains, conditions did not favor cotton, the preferred cash crop of the era, so most farmers turned to wheat. For more than 6,000 years wheat had been known as the "staff of life," the "perfect food" with a unique combination of carbohydrates, fats, proteins, vitamins, and minerals. And it was perfect for the Southern Plains, a natural environment for native grasses and their genetic cousins, the various varieties of wheat.

Wheat had been introduced to Oklahoma by Indian farmers who grew the grain for domestic use. After the land runs, German and Russian farmers brought with them the hard winter wheats that had grown so well on the steppes of Turkey and Russia and later the plains of Kansas and Nebraska. By 1924, through the ancient process of selecting the biggest and strongest heads for seed stock, the most popular varieties for conditions in Oklahoma were Kansas Red and Blackhull.

During the first three decades of his life, Danne witnessed the great wheat bonanza. In 1896, when the price of a bushel of wheat was only 48 cents, territorial farmers planted a mere 250,000 acres of the grain. By 1919, with the price at $2.10 a bushel, farmers planted wheat on 4,178,000 acres. Then came mechanized farm machinery, a decade of increased rainfall, and the spread of the wheat boom to the former grasslands of the Oklahoma Panhandle. Texas County produced more wheat than any other county in the nation in 1921, 1926, 1928, and 1929.

Throughout this "golden age" of wheat production, farmers desperately searched for seeds with five primary qualities. Most of all, they wanted greater yields per acre, followed closely by drought resistance, disease resistance, uniform height, and improved baking quality. In 1924, when Joseph Danne started his quest to find a new wheat that shared these qualities, the challenge must have seemed daunting. One single cross of 2 wheat plants created more than 10 billion genotypes, and of those, more than 2 million genotypes could reproduce again.

He started by crossing the two most popular pure bred lines, Kansas Red and Blackhull. The resulting plants, classified as C1, grew well. Carefully, Danne separated the harvested heads based on perceived qualities, using his own intuition and powers of observation. He then planted each of the

types in 16-foot-long rows and repeated the process each year thereafter. By 1928 he noticed that one type, C1H68B, yielded more than its cousins, so he focused on it and planted bigger plots. Within ten years, the new variety out-yielded Blackhull by six bushels per acre, had a stronger straw, and matured two days earlier. He called it Reliant and released it for sale for the first time in 1939.

Another lineage began in 1925 when Danne crossbred a Burbank Quality spring wheat with one of the first Kansas Red-Blackhull hybrids. Within two years, he noticed among the progeny a small amount of wheat that created only three small heads. Normally, he would have destroyed such underperformers, but he noticed that they had been the first to ripen. He classified the strongest seeds as C7H, planted more rows, and continued watching it develop year after year. By 1931 it was ripening ten days earlier than other varieties and producing an average of 34 bushels per acre. Nine years later, when he put the new hybrid on the market, he called it Triumph.

For the rest of his life, Danne would continue improving and promoting his wheat varieties, always searching for the qualities that would produce more grain and give farmers a better chance at surviving the challenges of fickle weather, volatile prices, and inconsistent federal farm policy. By the

time of his death in 1959, more than 6 million acres in Texas, Oklahoma, and Kansas were planted in Danne wheat. Within another 10 years, the eccentric scientist-farmer's varieties made up 58.8 percent of all wheat grown in Oklahoma.

Danne's legacy survived his death. In his will, he left $250,000 to a foundation for the support of orphans and others in need. To the United States Department of Agriculture and Oklahoma A&M, he left his priceless collection that included 1,624 samples of seed wheat and detailed journals and notes stored in five-gallon lard cans found in his cellar. His research, under the watchful eyes of others, would continue.

For most people, Joseph Danne's legacy can be seen every year in the wheat fields of western and northern Oklahoma. There, like squares on a patchwork quilt, are wheat fields that emerge a deep green in the winter and turn a blaze gold in the spring. There, in the soil of Oklahoma, is the story of one determined farmer who had the curiosity and discipline to undertake the work of a lifetime.

Two boys, Tommy Lamarr and Tommy Spoke, examine a demolished car in the aftermath of the Woodward Tornado of April 9, 1947. No one knew where the car had come from or to whom it belonged. The deadliest tornado in Oklahoma history struck Woodward at 8:42 p.m. The massive F-5 tornado first touched down near Canadian, Texas, and remained on the ground continuously for approximately 100 miles, eventually lifting in Woods County near Alva. At least 69 people were killed in the Texas Panhandle. As the storm moved across Ellis County, Oklahoma, eight people were killed and 42 injured even though no towns were struck. One person was killed at Tangier in Woodward County before the tornado moved in on the county seat. By then, the funnel was 1.8 miles wide. In Woodward, more than 1,000 homes and businesses were destroyed, 107 people died, and nearly 1,000 others were injured. The storm was so deadly because in 1947 advance warning systems for storms were not in place and the community was taken by surprise. (Courtesy Oklahoma Publishing Company)

Dust Bowl: Myth and Reality

John Steinbeck, as a writer, was a master at spinning a story filled with rich characters, vivid settings, and compelling emotions. John Ford, the movie maker, was armed with similar skills at creating images that transcended reality and captured unforgettable scenes of the human experience. Unfortunately, many people have accepted these gifted artists as sources of historical reality.

In *The Grapes of Wrath*, a novel written by Steinbeck and adapted to the big screen by Ford, readers and viewers entered the lives of the Joad family just as their dust-blown farm was being taken from them by drought, tractors, and the evil forces of bankers and corporations. Their only hope was to flee the environmental wasteland and head to

Two women in Alva, Oklahoma, held handkerchiefs over their noses as they attempted to make their way through a "dirty thirties" dust storm. (Courtesy Oklahoma Historical Society)

California, the new land of milk and honey. To the Joads, the American hearth was no longer on the land; it was in the automobile, rootless and rambling.

The reality behind these wonderful works of art is no less dramatic but much more complex. There are two parts to the story. One was the failure of the tenant-farming and sharecropping economy that had offered another chance to so many families from 1898 to 1918. The other was the Dust Bowl, an ecological disaster that shocked the world. Together, side-by-side with the stock market crash and bread lines, these two chapters of the American frontier experience came to symbolize the hard times of the 1930s.

The opening chapter in this human drama began in the old Indian Territory, largely the eastern one-half of the state, where most of the arable land was allotted to individual Indian families at the turn of the century. Under federal law, they could not sell the land, but they could rent it. And there were plenty of desperate families looking for one more chance, especially cotton farmers from the Old South where boll weevils, tired soil, and perpetual indebtedness had driven them from their homes.

At first, the tenants did well. The soil was fresh and fertile, especially in the well-watered river basins, and an expanding web of railroads drove down the cost of transporting crops out and goods in. Most importantly, the price of cotton rose steadily during the first two decades of the new century, peaking at 35 cents a pound in 1919. As farm immigrants swelled the population of the state, the number of congressmen elected from Oklahoma increased from six in 1907 to nine in 1930. That year 62 percent of all farmers in the state were listed as tenants or sharecroppers.

By the mid-1920s, cracks were appearing in the foundation of this farm economy. The dreaded boll weevils attacked crops, followed by plagues of grasshoppers that spread during periodic spells of drought. Machinery, used for both planting and harvesting crops, encouraged the consolidation of acreage that could be handled by fewer workers. In 1929, after the stock market crash, the price of cotton tumbled as low as five cents a pound, less than the cost to pick it. Among the landless tenant farmers accustomed to moving from one farm to the next virtually every year in the endless search for a better piece of land, the first option was to load the family in the old truck and hit the road.

As this mobile mass migration erupted from the hills and valleys of eastern Oklahoma, east Texas, and Arkansas, a different drama was unfolding far to the west on the Great Plains. As with tenant farming, the roots of the problem had been planted decades earlier. In this case, it was the wheat bonanza during and after World War I when the "perfect storm" created a market for grain that lured a small army of farmers onto what one early explorer had called the "Great American Desert."

First, there was free land. As late as 1900, there were more than 7 million acres of land in western Oklahoma still available for homesteading. Similar opportunities abounded in an area that stretched from Shattuck, Oklahoma, on the east to Clayton, New Mexico, on the west, and from Lubbock, Texas, on the south to the Republican River in Nebraska on the north. Then came high prices for wheat, topping two dollars per bushel, and the means to cultivate and harvest hundreds of acres with new tractors and combines available through easy credit. In 1830 it had taken farmers 58 hours to plant and harvest one acre of wheat. In 1930, armed with machinery, it took only three hours to complete the same work.

Then came the rain. In a region that averaged between 15 and 20 inches of rain per year, the 1920s were wet years on the Southern Plains. As many old timers knew, there had been extended droughts before, especially those from 1893 to 1894 and from 1910 to 1912 when as little as seven inches of rain fell in one year, but those had been of short duration. After all, as many people believed, increased rain supposedly followed the plow. With free land and fertile soil, high prices and unseasonable rains, the rush was on. In less than 20 years, with profits mounting for those willing to take a chance, ever optimistic farmers scraped the grass from more than 33 million acres, an area the size of Pennsylvania.

In 1929 the bubble burst. First came a surplus on world markets, followed quickly by dropping prices that slid to 75 cents a bushel in 1929, 40 cents a bushel in 1930, and 24 cents a bushel in 1931. As buying power sank under the weight of the Great Depression, it still cost a farmer 40 cents a bushel to plant and harvest a crop. Compounding this recipe for financial bankruptcy was an end to the wet years. In 1930 rainfall returned to normal levels, followed by a real drought that started in 1932 when the Panhandle of Oklahoma received only 10 inches of rain.

And then came the wind. For thousands of years, the wind had blown on the Southern Plains, but there had always been a layer of grass to protect the fragile soil. On the surface the grass might look dead, but below were roots ready to sprout new growth with sufficient sun and moisture. After 20 years of the wheat bonanza, that protective layer was gone.

It takes a wind of 30 miles an hour to move dirt. At 40 to 50 miles per

hour, wind can create a dust storm. On January 21, 1932, a day when the wind was blowing 60 miles per hour, a dust storm formed west of Amarillo, Texas, and started moving northeast. By the time it hit the Oklahoma Panhandle it was a dark cloud almost two miles tall rolling across the landscape. Those who survived that black blizzard never forgot the experience. That year a total of 14 "dusters" rolled across the region.

The ecological disaster compounded the financial plight of the Great Depression. By 1934, in one six-county area that included the Oklahoma Panhandle, 4,000 of 5,500 farm families received some form of assistance from county, state, and federal programs belatedly launched to deal with the mounting crisis. In one year, the farmers of Cimarron County produced zero bushels of wheat. The so-called "suitcase farmers" left, perhaps a third of the population, but most of the land owners stayed. As usual, it was one more crop, one more season of hope.

The people of the Oklahoma Panhandle, like their cultural kinsmen on the Southern Plains, adapted to the new world. They limped through the Depression with the help of government programs and prospered once again as prices increased with the outbreak of World War II. Even the land changed. Marginal lands were returned to grass. Fields were terraced. Windbreaks were planted. And ponds were built through conservation districts. By the 1950s, a decade that was drier than even the 1930s, the land and its people were better prepared. The worst hard times were over.

(Above) The dust storms of the 1930s were indeed horrific as seen in this photograph of a dense dust cloud enveloping Keyes, Oklahoma, on May 21, 1937. (Courtesy Oklahoma Historical Society)

Roscoe Dunjee: Advocate for Justice

Although the institution of slavery had ended more than 40 years earlier, African Americans faced severe discrimination in the new State of Oklahoma. The chairman of the state's Constitutional Convention, William H. Murray, in his opening speech to the delegates observed that Negroes "as a rule" were fit only to be "porters, bootblacks, and barbers." In its first decade of statehood, Oklahoma enacted a series of Jim Crow laws that institutionalized segregation of blacks in education, public transportation, housing, and public facilities such as restrooms and water fountains. Such laws were constitutional as a result of a ruling by the Supreme Court of the United States in 1896, which held that separate facilities for blacks were legal so long as they were equal to facilities for others.

In practice, such facilities almost never were "equal." Moreover, segregation clearly was intended to indicate that blacks were inferior, second-class citizens. This message also was conveyed through laws and local practices that made it difficult for blacks to vote. In addition to the legal system, violence and intimidation were employed to keep blacks "in their place." The rebirth of the Ku Klux Klan, which dispensed vigilante justice to drunks, gamblers, and abusers of women and children of all races in addition to racial violence, struck fear into the hearts of blacks. It was in this environment that a young, black newspaperman launched a life-long crusade for justice that would have tremendous impact in Oklahoma and throughout the nation. He believed that within the American system of justice and within the American psyche the seeds of social justice eventually would find fertile ground. His name was Roscoe Dunjee.

Dunjee's father, Reverend J. W. Dunjee, was a former slave who had escaped the bonds of slavery during the Civil War, fleeing to Canada via the Underground Railroad. Four years later, he returned to his home state of Virginia and studied to become a Baptist minister. His wife Lydia Ann also was a former slave. Reverend Dunjee had a successful career founding new churches in various states and in 1892 was sent to Oklahoma Territory to establish churches in the Oklahoma City area. He leased and later purchased a small farm near present Nicoma Park northeast of Oklahoma City on which he raised fruits and vegetables to

Roscoe Dunjee

supplement his meager pastoral earnings. After they settled at their new home, the Dunjees had two daughters and a son, Roscoe, whose job was putting meat on the table through hunting and trapping during a severe drought from 1893 to 1898 that restricted the productivity of the farm.

By the time of his death in 1903, Reverend Dunjee had helped to found Langston University and was a beloved minister, but his estate was tiny and the family was left in desperate straits. Roscoe took over the management of the farm and eventually retired the mortgage on the property. His formal education essentially ended with the eighth grade, but his father's

1,500-book library became Roscoe's university. He read voraciously and soon would demonstrate through his writings that indeed he was well educated.

Roscoe moved to Guthrie following statehood in 1907, took a few high school training courses at Langston University, and learned the printing trade. He began writing stories for local newspapers in 1904. By 1913 he was ready to start a printing and newspaper business when he purchased a small printing plant in Oklahoma City. The first edition of his newspaper, *The Black Dispatch*, appeared on November 5, 1914, and Dunjee began his crusade for justice that would last more than four decades. Although

he would remain a bachelor throughout his life, he was "married" to his newspaper and his fight for racial justice.

From 1914 to 1932 Dunjee, through rousing editorials and political activity, fought against all manner of racial injustice. He railed against Jim Crow laws and bravely condemned the Ku Klux Klan. Governor J. B. A. Robertson responded to Dunjee's efforts by establishing a committee to study problems in race relations in the early 1920s and, after the horrific Tulsa Race Riot of 1921, by frequently asking Dunjee's advice on racial problems. Dunjee became recognized as a political force, and on more than one occasion white politicians attempted to purchase control of

(Facing page) Roscoe Dunjee, as depicted in this painting by Simmie Knox, spent much of his life fighting the "bloody fangs of Jim Crow." The painting is displayed in the State Capitol. (Courtesy Oklahoma Arts Council)

Although the Ku Klux Klan in Oklahoma declined in numbers and influence after the 1920s, it still was sufficiently strong in 1937 to demonstrate openly. On an evening early in November 1937, 25 robed members of the "invisible empire" stood on a ridge near the intersection of U. S. Highways 66 and 77, about three miles east of Edmond. They were illuminated by the glow of a burning cross. Other Klansmen in the woods behind the cliff were busy initiating 32 new recruits to the order. In such an environment, individuals such as Dunjee, who spoke out against racial injustice, indeed were brave individuals. (Courtesy Oklahoma Publishing Company)

were not equal. Dunjee, an active national leader in the National Association for the Advancement of Colored People, spearheaded the filing of a series of lawsuits in the 1940s, attempting to expose the corruption in funding schools for blacks. In 1941 the Legislature responded by strengthening the laws segregating schools from the first grade through colleges and universities. In 1945 Dunjee brought the NAACP's chief legal counsel, Thurgood Marshall, to Oklahoma for meetings with black leaders to determine a legal strategy to combat segregation. Marshall then announced that Oklahoma's segregation laws would be challenged in court.

In January of 1946, Dunjee and Dr. W. A. J. Bullock of Chickasha accompanied Ada Lois Sipuel, a well-qualified, young black woman who wished to enroll in the School of Law at the University of Oklahoma, to the office of Dr. George L. Cross, president of the university. Cross was forced by law, which included a personal fine of $500 per day if he allowed Sipuel to enroll, to deny her admission. Cross did not agree with the law and knew that this situation would provide the basis for a law suit to test the constitutionality of the state law. Dunjee led the effort to raise thousands of dollars to finance the legal action. Filed on May 6, 1946, the case eventually made its way to the United States Supreme Court, which ruled in 1948 that the state must offer Sipuel

his editorial policy. But his opinions and his passion for justice were not for sale. In 1932 Dunjee became a Democrat in response to the candidacy of Franklin D. Roosevelt for president of the United States. Roosevelt forged a new political coalition that included blacks as he held out hope for an improved climate for racial justice in America.

While Dunjee worked hard to alleviate the hardships of hate and prejudice that daily affected blacks in virtually every aspect of their lives, his greatest accomplishments came in the area of assuring equal education for all. Dunjee and other black leaders were painfully aware that the poorly funded separate schools established for blacks

Planning strategy for the integration of the University of Oklahoma Law School in 1948 were, left to right, Dr. W. A. J. Bullock of Chickasha, physician and a regional director of the National Association for the Advancement of Colored People; Ada Lois Sipuel, whose intention was to earn a law degree at OU; and Roscoe Dunjee, editor of the *Black Dispatch*, state president and a national director of the NAACP. (Courtesy Oklahoma Publishing Company)

a legal education equal to that received by white students. The Legislature responded by setting up a sham Langston University School of Law with three professors at the state capitol, in which she refused to enroll. The Langston law school was closed, and Fisher was allowed to enroll at OU. She graduated in 1951 and enjoyed a long career as an educator and civil rights activist.

Dunjee was the catalyst for another important legal action regarding the case of George W. McLaurin, who applied for admission to the Graduate College at OU in 1948. A panel of federal judges ruled that McLaurin must be admitted to the university or the institution could not offer the same graduate program to whites. The state's segregation law was not held to be unconstitutional, however. McLaurin was admitted, but he was required to sit in an alcove in the classroom so the white students could not see him. He also was provided with a separate desk and restroom in the library. Marshall appealed the plan to the United States Supreme Court, and in June, 1950, the Court ruled that the plan violated McLaurin's right to an equal education. The walls of segregation in higher education in Oklahoma crumbled, and four years later, in a case brought by Marshall, the separate but equal doctrine was invalidated by the United States Supreme Court. Segregation in public elementary and

high schools nationwide was outlawed.

Dunjee was 70 years old in 1955 and his health was declining. He sold his newspaper that same year. He noted with satisfaction the gains that had been achieved: "When we first started fighting segregation in Oklahoma City, negroes could not live north of Second Street. Today 30,000 black men live unmolested all over the municipality." His efforts had never been calculated to make white men angry. "All we have done is try to make them think." Also in 1955 Thurgood Marshall, who was destined to become the first black justice of the United States Supreme Court, was the featured speaker at a testimonial dinner held in Dunjee's honor. Dunjee spoke briefly and told the appreciative audience, "Negroes can do anything that they want to do, if they have enough patience, courage, and integrity."

Upon Dunjee's death in 1965, civil right's leader Jimmy Stewart observed that "no one during my lifetime caused so much change on issues of human relations as Roscoe Dunjee." During Dunjee's funeral, Marshall remarked that Dunjee had provided the inspiration to "get the job done." And, Marshall revealed, Dunjee had raised all the money or paid legal fees, court costs, and travel expenses out of his pocket for all the landmark civil rights cases that had been originated in Oklahoma. Throughout his life, Dunjee indeed had displayed "patience, courage, and integrity" in his crusade for justice.

The Oklahoma City of the 1930s, despite the Great Depression, was buoyed somewhat by the impact of the Oklahoma City Oil Field. The First National Center, the tall building in the center of the photograph, had been completed in 1931. But for blacks, the city, state, and most of the nation did not hold the same opportunities for them as they did for whites. It was against such discrimination that black leaders such as Roscoe Dunjee fought. (Courtesy Oklahoma Historical Society)

Serving the Nation: Oklahoma's Military Heroes

Members of the 279th Infantry Regiment of the 45th Infantry Division left their bunkers near the front lines in Korea in May 1952 in response to mail call, hoping to get one of those precious letters from home. (Courtesy Oklahoma Publishing Company

Oklahomans are a patriotic people. In times of war, Oklahomans in impressive numbers have served their country, either as citizen soldiers, draftees, or volunteers. Others have made military service their careers. From the Spanish-American War through the conflict in Iraq, Oklahomans have served with distinction. Ironically, the veterans of some wars were treated differently from those who served in others. Veterans of World War II, for example, have been regarded as being part of "The Greatest Generation," while those who served in Vietnam either were ignored or treated shamefully when they returned home. Veterans of the Korean War often were neither vilified nor praised, but simply ignored or forgotten.

When the Korean War erupted, thousands of Oklahomans served in Korea as part of the famed 45th Infantry Division, which had acquitted itself with distinction in World War II. Others served in the regular Army or in other branches of the military. Two Oklahomans received the Congressional Medal of Honor for their heroic service in Korea—First Lieutenant Frederick Funston Henry of Clinton and Sergeant First Class Tony Kenneth Burris of Blanchard.

Henry was one of six brothers who had fought in World War II, during which he received a Bronze Star for Gallantry as a member of the 5th Infantry Division. Four of the Henry boys, including Frederick, also served in Korea. A native of Vian, Frederick moved with his parents, Mr. and Mrs. James P. Henry, to Clinton when he was a small child. After World War II, Henry left the army for several years but rejoined and went to Korea as a First Lieutenant in the 38th Infantry Regiment of the 2nd Infantry Division.

On September 1, 1950, Henry was in command of a platoon holding a strategic ridge near the town of Am-Dong when it was attacked by a superior enemy force augmented by heavy mortar and artillery fire. During the attack Henry left his foxhole to rally his men to hold their positions, and they managed to halt the enemy's assault. Communications had been disrupted, however, and Henry could not determine the status of the line of resistance beyond his immediate area.

Congressional Medal of Honor Recipients from Oklahoma
August 24, 2006

NAME, PLACE OF BIRTH, HOME OF RECORD, OR ENTERED SERVICE, RANK, BRANCH

INDIAN WARS

Amos Chapman, Camp Supply (ES), **Seiling** (HOR), Scout (Civilian)

PHILLIPPINE INSURRECTION

Joseph L. Epps, Indian Territory (POB), **Muskogee** (Buried), Private, U.S. Volunteers

WORLD WAR I

George Price Hays, Okarche (ES), First Lieutenant, U.S. Army
Harold L. Turner, Seminole, (ES), Corporal, U.S. Army
Samuel M. Sampler, Altus (ES), Corporal, U.S.Army

WORLD WAR II

Ernest Childers, Broken Arrow (POB), **Tulsa** (ES), Second Lieutenant, U.S. Army
John R. Crews, Golden (POB), **Bowlegs** (ES), Staff Sargeant, U.S. Army
Ernest Edwin Evans, Pawnee (POB), Commander, U.S. Navy
Donald J. Gott, Arnett (ES), First Lieutenant, U.S.Army
Harold G. Kiner, Aline (POB), **Enid** (ES), Private, U.S. Army
Richard Miles McCool, Tishomingo (POB), Lieutenant, U.S. Navy
Troy A. McGill, Ada (ES), Sergeant, U.S. Army
Jack C. Montgomery, Long (POB), **Sallisaw** (ES), First Lieutenant, U.S. Army
John N. Reese, Jr., Muskogee (POB), **Pryor (ES),** Private First Class, U.S. Army
Ruben Rivers, Tecumseh (POB), **Hotulka** (HOR), Staff Sergeant, U.S. Army
Albert Earnest Schwab, Tulsa (ES), Private First Class, U.S. Marine Corps.
John Lucian Smith, Lexington (POB), Major, U.S. Marine Corps.
Jack L. Treadwell, Snyder (ES), Captain, U.S. Army

KOREAN WAR

Tony K. Burris, Blanchard (POB; ES), Sergeant First Class, U.S. Army
Frederick F. Henry, Vian (POB), **Clinton** (ES), First Lieutenant, U.S. Army

Note: This list includes individuals who either were born in or entered the service from Oklahoma Territory, the Indian Nations, or the State of Oklahoma. Also listed are individuals whose "Home of Record" at the time they were honored was in Oklahoma or in one of the "Twin Territories." Where towns are listed, Place of Birth (POB), Entered Service (ES), or Home of Record (HOR) is indicated. Ranks shown are those held at the time of the actions for which the awards were conferred.

A memorial to Oklahomans who have fought and died for their country is located on the grounds of the Wiley Post Building, formerly the home of the Oklahoma Historical Society. The historic building now is the home of the Oklahoma Supreme Court. In the foreground is one of the statues honoring Oklahoma's fighting men and women, and in the background is the Oklahoma State Capitol. (Courtesy Jim Argo)

Fort Gibson National Cemetery was established in 1868. Among those interred are two Congressional Medal of Honor recipients, First Lieutenant Jack C. Montgomery of Sallisaw and Private First Class John N. Reese, Jr. of Pryor. Both Montgomery and Reese earned their medals in World War II. The beauty and precision of the headstone placements and the sacrifice each headstone represents makes visiting the cemetery a memorable experience. (Courtesy State

Although Henry was severely wounded, he ordered the evacuation of the wounded and had all their weapons and remaining ammunition brought to him. He then established a one-man defensive position and ordered the surviving members of his platoon to withdraw. The enemy attack resumed, and Henry covered the platoon's retreat. When last seen by his men, he was firing his weapons so effectively that he caused an estimated 50 enemy casualties before exhausting his ammunition. His position was overrun and he was killed. Henry had saved his platoon and had sufficiently delayed the enemy advance to allow his comrades time to successfully repulse the enemy.

Burris was one of ten children born to Samuel and Mabel Burris. Burris grew up near Blanchard, and he and his siblings were proud of their Choctaw heritage. Burris graduated from Blanchard High School in 1947, and a few weeks after the invasion of South Korea he volunteered for service in the United States Army. A year later he was on the front lines in Korea as a member of the 38th Infantry Regiment of the 2nd Infantry Division. On October 8, 1951, Burris and his comrades were engaged in a bloody battle for control of Heartbreak Ridge. During the battle, Burris and his men came under intense enemy fire from entrenched enemy forces. Burris alone charged the enemy position and, throwing hand grenades, killed 15 of his adversaries.

The following day, Burris was wounded while leading an assault on another enemy position. He continued to lead the attack, reached the crest of the ridge ahead of the rest of his unit, and received a second wound. He then called for the advancement of a 57mm recoilless rifle team and deliberately exposed himself to enemy fire to reveal their position, allowing the rifle team to destroy the enemy machine gun emplacement. The assault on other enemy positions continued as the twice wounded Burris refused evacuation. He then charged and destroyed another enemy gun emplacement and its six-man crew. He assaulted yet another enemy position and destroyed it with his last grenade just as he was mortally wounded. Inspired by his actions, his men renewed a spirited attack and secured Hill 605, a strategic position in the battle for Heartbreak Ridge.

Thousands of Oklahomans have served their country in combat. Their bravery and sacrifice, regardless of the specific war or action in which their valor was demonstrated, deserves to be viewed with respect and appreciation.

The sheer joy of a combat soldier and wife being reunited after being separated for an extended period was expressed on the faces of Sergeant First Class and Mrs. Billy W. Shough of Elk City in May of 1952. Shough had just returned home from combat in Korea, and his wife and child met him upon his arrival by train at Fort Sill. (Courtesy Oklahoma Publishing Company)

Frederick A. Daugherty: Citizen Soldier

Oklahomans always have served their country in times of war with great distinction. Twenty Oklahomans have received the Congressional Medal of Honor, the nation's highest award in recognition of heroism on the field of battle. Thousands have fought bravely and have given their lives to defend America. Some joined the military as volunteers; others were drafted in time of war; while still others were "citizen soldiers" whose militia or national guard units were federalized and sent into combat. Frederick A. Daugherty of Oklahoma City was one such citizen soldier who gave distinguished service as an officer in two wars and as a state and federal judge.

Born in 1914 in Oklahoma City, Daugherty graduated from Central High School in 1932 and enrolled at Cumberland University at Lebanon, Tennessee, where he studied for two years. Knowing that he wanted to enter the legal profession, he returned to Oklahoma City in 1934 and enrolled in Oklahoma City University to complete his undergraduate education. Daugherty for several years had admired William S. Key, the father of one of his friends at Central High School. Key was a prominent business and civic leader who also was an officer in the 45th Infantry Division. In 1934, inspired by the example of Key and motivated by a desire to serve his country, Daugherty decided to join the National Guard at age 20.

Daugherty was enlisted as a private in Headquarters Company, 1st Battalion, 179th Infantry Regiment, 45th Infantry Division by First Lieutenant Ross H. Routh, who took the young man under his wing. As Daugherty later recalled, Routh gave him and others "strong

Frederick A. Daugherty

support and encouragement, not only for advancement in the military but to become responsible young men in our society."

Intelligent and highly motivated, Daugherty quickly rose to the rank of sergeant but had to transfer to a unit headquartered at Atoka in order to make second lieutenant when there were no officer vacancies in the Oklahoma City Headquarters Unit. He was commissioned a second lieutenant in 1935. In 1936 he enrolled at the University of Oklahoma and in 1937 graduated with his LLB degree. He was admitted to the Oklahoma State Bar that year and entered into the general practice of law, all the while meeting his National Guard service obligations. Daugherty was promoted to first lieutenant in July of 1940, just as it appeared likely that the United States would ultimately be drawn into the war that had begun in Europe the previous year. When the 45th Infantry Division was called into federal service just two months later, Daugherty became a full-time soldier.

The United States declared war on Japan, Germany, and their allies after Japanese forces attacked United States military installations at Pearl Harbor, Hawaii, on December 7, 1941. Daugherty's intelligence, organizational skills, and devotion to duty did not go unnoticed. When Daugherty graduated from the Command and General Staff College, Lieutenant General Walter Krueger, Commander of the Third Army, wanted Daugherty for his staff. Major General William S. Key, now in command of the 45th Infantry Division, told Krueger that Daugherty was "unavailable." Krueger asked Key to reconsider, which he refused to do. The next communication on this issue came as an order from Krueger to Daugherty to report for duty at the headquarters of the Third Army, where he was promoted to the rank of captain. At the outset of the war, the Third Army's role was to train the huge influx of draftees entering the United States Army.

A 60-year-old German immigrant, Krueger had fought in the Spanish American War, had taken part in the Mexican Punitive Expedition, and had seen combat in World War I. He was an expert on military discipline and training, and he expected absolute competence and devotion to duty among his officers. While serving on Krueger's Third Army staff, Daugherty was promoted to major in December of 1942, and when Krueger was promoted to general and given command of the newly activated Sixth Army in January of 1943, Daugherty went with him to Australia as a key staff member. In this position, Daugherty was involved in planning the Sixth Army's major operations for the duration of the war, including the campaigns of Bismarck Archipelago, New Guinea, South Philippines, Luzon, and Leyte. The Sixth Army was slated to provide the ground forces for the initial invasion of Japan, but the Japanese surrender precluded the need for such an assault. Daugherty continued to advance in rank through the course of the war, rising to lieutenant colonel in March of 1944 and colonel in June of 1945.

Following his discharge after the war, Daugherty returned to Oklahoma City, where he resumed his service with the 45th Infantry Division as commander of the 179th Infantry Regiment, the unit in which he once had served as a private. He resumed his legal career in 1946 as a member of the firm of Ames, Ames, and Daugherty, and the following year he married Marjorie E. Green of Oklahoma City. At age 32, Daugherty had a wife and a promising legal career and could have been forgiven if he had determined that he had given sufficient military service to his county and had resigned from the National Guard. Yet his sense of duty caused him to remain in the military.

Daugherty's comfortable civilian life was interrupted in September of 1950 when the 45th Infantry Division was called to active duty to serve in the Korean War. As Commander of the 179th Infantry Regiment, Daugherty accompanied his men to Camp Polk, Louisiana, for training among the "tall pines and wild hogs" that would prepare them to face combat. Among the men in his command was Sergeant First Class

(Facing page) General Fred Daugherty on the ground in Korea. Daugherty's career as a citizen soldier spanned 30 years. (Courtesy 45th Infantry Division Museum)

Dan Blocker, who some years later played the role of Hoss Cartwright on the television show *Bonanza*.

To the men, Daugherty seemed to be everywhere checking on training operations.

Fred Daugherty in 1958 was a state district court judge. He was appointed by President John F. Kennedy to the federal judiciary in 1961. (Courtesy Oklahoma Historical Society)

He did have one mishap, however, when he followed one group after they had completed a practice landing. Daugherty stepped into some quicksand and sank to his chest before sufficient help arrived to pull him out of the morass. Finally, on March 29 Daugherty and his men departed Camp Polk via train for New Orleans, where they boarded the troop ship *Marine Lynx* for the 30-day trip to Japan. There they received additional training before facing their North Korean and Chinese enemies in combat.

A little more than six months was spent training in Japan. On December 5, 1951, the advance party of the 179th entered Korea at Inchon. The remainder of the regiment soon followed. Over the next 18 months, the 179th saw heavy combat action as they fought North Korean and Chinese forces for control of strategic hilltops and outposts. In addition to their human enemies, the Americans battled bitterly cold weather. At places like Pork Chop Hill, Old Baldy, and Outpost Eerie they fought bravely and effectively. When they were pulled into a reserve position in June of 1952, Daugherty returned home. In November he was promoted to brigadier general and assumed the position of second in command of the 45th Infantry Division. He also returned to the practice of law with the firm of Ames, Daugherty, Bynum and Black.

Daugherty's legal career took a different direction in 1955 when he was appointed to a state district court judgeship by Governor Raymond Gary. He served in that capacity until his appointment by President John F. Kennedy as United States district judge for the Western, Eastern, and Northern districts of Oklahoma on October 11, 1961. He served with distinction in this position, taking senior status in 1981 and retiring in 1996 at age 82. His military career did not end when he became a judge, however. Upon the retirement of Major General Hal Muldrow, Daugherty assumed command of the 45th Infantry Division and was promoted to Major General in 1960. He was the only individual to command the 45th who had joined the organization as a private.

Early in 1964, Marjorie, Daugherty's wife of 17 years, died. Later that same year, he retired from the military to focus on his judicial career and a wide range of civic activities, including volunteer service for the American National Red Cross, United Fund of Greater Oklahoma City, Oklahoma County Association for Mental Health, Oklahoma City Council on Alcoholism, and many other organizations. By 1982 he had become the highest ranking Scottish Rite official in Oklahoma. He was supported in all his activities by his second wife, Betsy F. Amis, whom he married on December 15, 1965. Fred Daugherty completed his life of service to his city, state, and nation when he died on April 7, 2006, at age 91.

The home of Herbert Hiram and Jane Champlin in Enid was constructed in 1939 by the Bass Construction Company of Enid, headed by H. B. "Heinie" Bass. Champlin was one of the founders of the Champlin Petroleum Company and together the Champlins were civic and cultural leaders in the community. The Tudor Revival style house and grounds were added to the National Register of Historic Places in 1993. (Courtesy State Historic Preservation Office, Oklahoma Historical Society)

Designed by famed architect Frank Lloyd Wright to serve as the headquarters for the H. C. Price Pipeline Company in Bartlesville, the Price Tower was the only skyscraper that Wright designed during his distinguished career. The building was completed in 1956. It now houses the Price Tower Arts Center and the Inn at Price Tower and is a major tourist attraction for Bartlesville. (Courtesy Jim Argo)

By 1939 The Oklahoma City Oil Field had expanded north from south Oklahoma City to the State Capitol complex on Lincoln Boulevard, north of Northeast 13th Street. (Courtesy Oklahoma Publishing Company)

Although the State Capitol did not have the dome architects originally intended, inside the structure the illusion of a dome was created in glass. (Courtesy Jim Argo)

The Tulsa Fairgrounds Pavilion is an example of Tulsa's numerous art deco buildings. Designed by Leland I. Shumway, the Pavilion features blond-brick construction with terra cotta ornamentation. Built in 1932, the structure has a seating capacity of 10,000. (Courtesy State Historic Preservation Office, Oklahoma Historical Society)

CHAPTER FOUR

"You're Doin' Fine"

Reaching for New Horizons

George Shirk: Art of the Possible

Emerging from World War II, the people of Oklahoma found themselves at a crossroads. The economy, which had attracted national attention during the protracted boom from 1898 to 1929, was adrift as both farmers and oilmen suffered low prices and static production. The population of the state, reflecting the slowing economy, was smaller in 1950 than it had been in 1930. On top of that was a deflated self image, battered and bullied by the fertile imaginations of John Steinbeck and John Ford in the book and movie versions of *The Grapes of Wrath*.

The economic struggle ushered in a crisis of leadership. The titans of the earlier era, attracted by the lure of land runs, statehood, and the oil frontier, had not been replaced in the 1930s and 1940s by a new generation of hungry and ambitious immigrants armed with innovation and youthful energy. With a few notable exceptions, the first generation of native-born leaders was too young to guide the ship of state in the 1930s and was diverted by the national crisis during the war. With peace, however, came what some have called the "Greatest Generation" who believed that anything was possible if people worked together for the common good. One of those young, new leaders was native son George Shirk.

Shirk, born in 1913, was the oldest child of John Shirk, an attorney who had migrated to Oklahoma City in 1903 just as the town was booming and attracting urban pioneers such as Anton Classen, Charles Colcord, and E. K. Gaylord. With access to that generation of leaders and their families, young George formed friendships that would last a lifetime. He attended the University of Oklahoma, earned his law degree, and entered active duty in the Field Artillery in 1940. By 1946, when he was discharged, Shirk was a full colonel on the headquarters staff of Dwight D. Eisenhower.

Out of uniform, Shirk rushed headlong into the social, political, and professional life of Oklahoma City. He joined organizations such as the Men's Dinner Club, which dated to 1908, and the Oklahoma City Bachelors' Club, of more recent vintage. So he could entertain friends and associates, he built a log cabin and homemade swimming pool in a wooded area northeast of town. He ran unsuccessfully for county judge, joined the Young Republicans for Eisenhower Club, and studied the political landscape under mentors such as Federal Judge Edgar Vaught.

George Shirk

Shirk joined his father's law firm and quickly established his own reputation. During the war, an oil company had drilled on the land of a friend but had not paid the anticipated royalties or fees. Shirk took the case all the way to the United States Supreme Court, where he won a million dollar settlement. The fee provided a level of financial security that allowed the budding scholar to indulge himself in his lifelong passions for stamp collecting, local history, and civic affairs.

During the late 1940s Shirk wrote and published a series of articles about the post offices and cancelled covers of Indian Territory, a hobby that dated to his youth. A year later, from his collection of 2,500 envelopes, he loaned 325 pieces for a museum exhibit in Muskogee. It was during this period that he met and befriended Muriel Wright, the heart and soul of the Oklahoma Historical Society who shared his passion for discovering and visiting historic sites. They would become lifetime partners in the adventures of history for the next thirty years.

George invested similar energy in the civic affairs of Oklahoma City. In 1953 he was asked to join the Committee of 100, a well-established group of concerned citizens who advocated changes in the city charter. Working together, they ultimately achieved all of their goals, including equitable

redistricting, a vote for the mayor on all issues, and due process for protecting the city manager from the whims of political warfare. The next year Shirk was asked to join the City Safety Council, a group concerned with better police and fire protection.

In 1955 Shirk joined the Committee of 19, whose task was to search for a solution to the water needs of Oklahoma City. The city was growing, not just in population, but also in size as suburban housing additions spread in all directions. Adding to the pressure was the fact that the drought of the 1950s was worse than the Dust Bowl days of the 1930s. If Oklahoma City was to realize its dreams of becoming an industrial and

(Facing page) George Shirk served the community as an attorney, as mayor of Oklahoma City, as president of the Oklahoma Historical Society, as a civic leader, and as an historian. (Courtesy Oklahoma Heritage Association)

Mayor-elect James Norick joined Mayor Shirk on April 11, 1964, in a "brick breaking." Using gilded chisels, Shirk and Norick were joined by other civic leaders in chipping bricks from one of the buildings that soon would be demolished by the Oklahoma City Urban Renewal Authority to make room for the Mummers Theater. The entire block bordered by Sheridan, California, Hudson, and Walker Streets was cleared for the new theater, now known as Stage Center. (Courtesy Oklahoma Publishing Company)

manufacturing center, a secure source of water had to be found.

The committee members considered three options. Two involved dams on the South Canadian River, but the waters of that prairie stream were saturated with salt and other minerals. The better solution, they reasoned, was to build a lake in the well-watered southeast section of the state and to construct a pipeline to a holding reservoir on the outskirts of the city. The question was how to pay for the project.

With Shirk providing legal counsel, the committee suggested an innovative use of private bonds to build the system, with revenues from water sales dedicated to retiring the debt. When the concept was tested in court, Shirk took up the fight and won. In 1959 work on the Atoka Reservoir began with a $24 million bond issue and was completed in 1964 with the dedication of Lake Stanley Draper. With this one project, Oklahoma City had a secure source of water for the next century.

Water was only one challenge facing urban leaders in Oklahoma during the late 1950s and early 1960s. Even more troubling was declining revenue at a time when most people expected more services from their city governments. At the core of the problem was suburban sprawl, the result of new highways, scattered housing additions, and a migration of retail businesses from the central city to shopping malls in the suburbs. By 1964 the results were virtual bankruptcy, a decaying city center, and a crisis in city services. That same year, George Shirk stepped onto this battlefield as mayor of Oklahoma City.

As mayor, Shirk worked with various coalitions to tackle the challenges. To jumpstart the urban renewal program, which had come to a virtual standstill after a celebrated beginning in 1961, he and a majority of council members adopted the Pei Plan, a comprehensive vision for the redevelopment of the inner city. Within four years the results included the Kerr-McGee Tower, Liberty Tower, and Fidelity Plaza. The urban renewal program soon expanded to include an ambitious Health Sciences Center component.

In 1965 Shirk and his urban allies lobbied the State Legislature for authorization to levy a city sales tax. With passage of the bill, Shirk led the public relations effort to convince voters that a penny sales tax was in their best interests. The authorization passed two to one. He also helped navigate the transition to a new generation of city trusts that had the ability to issue tax-exempt bonds for industrial firms looking to expand or relocate. When he left office, Shirk became the first director of the Oklahoma Industrial Authority, which played a major role in the growth of Ling-Temco-Vaught, Unit Parts, Dayton Tire and Rubber Company, Mercy Hospital, and General Motors.

Shirk used the powers and prestige of the mayor's office to champion his enduring love of history. Since 1958 he had been president of the Oklahoma Historical Society, and in 1959 he had been appointed to the State Civil War Centennial Commission. The latter included the usual celebrations and reenactments that most people expected, but Shirk used the opportunity to invest in the future. By 1965 the commission had acquired for the Oklahoma Historical Society three historic sites critical to the story of the Civil War in the Indian Territory—Honey Springs Battlefield, Fort Washita, and Fort Towson.

As mayor, he energized early efforts to protect historic neighborhoods and buildings. In 1967, when a highway was proposed through the near-north side of the city, he worked with urban leaders to organize Historic Preservation, Inc. (Heritage Hills) and prodded city staff into drafting an ordinance protecting historic neighborhoods. The result was the Historic Preservation Commission with the authority to set zoning standards for the appropriate rehabilitation of homes. His devotion to history contributed to other local achievements such as the survival of the Colcord Building, the conversion of the Overholser Mansion to a museum, the

protection of the Harn Homestead, and the beginning of the Firefighters Museum.

In many ways, the post-war generation performed a balancing act. They were confronted with a stalled economy, a decaying inner city, and a lack of confidence that the future would be better than the past. Out of necessity, they searched for new economic formulas, developed public-private partnerships on a monumental scale, and looked to their history to instill a sense of hope for the future. For George Shirk and his contemporaries, their best tool for leadership was the art of the possible.

Tinker Air Force Base continued to grow as a driving force in the economy of central Oklahoma after World War II. In 1960 approximately 23,000 Oklahomans were employed in the overhaul, maintenance, and supply of aircraft at Tinker. In 1960 the "newest tenants" in the mile-long overhaul and modifications line were these KC-135 aerial tankers of the Strategic Air Command. B-52 Stratofortress Bombers also were being maintained at Tinker at this time. (Courtesy Oklahoma Publishing Company)

Search for the
Middle Ground:
Politics, 1959-1982

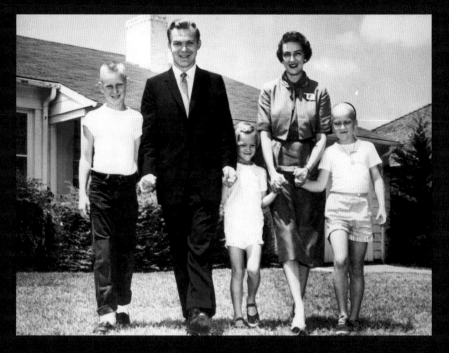

J. Howard Edmondson, elected governor in 1958, ushered in a new era of politics in Oklahoma. He was the first to use television during a campaign. He was a Democrat with his strongest support in urban areas, and he used enforcement of the law to change a law he thought was outdated. Urban voters strongly supported the "Big Red E" campaign of J. Howard Edmondson, and he was elected by the largest majority ever given to a candidate for governor in the state's history to date.

Oklahoma had been a "dry" state since 1907, but so many Oklahomans ignored the law that "moonshiners" and bootleggers prospered. Will Rogers once observed that Oklahomans would vote to retain prohibition so long as they could stagger to the polls. When Edmondson vigorously enforced the state's liquor laws, drying out the state, voters subsequently voted heavily in favor of an amendment to the state constitution repealing prohibition.

Another first in politics was the election of Henry Bellmon as the first Republican governor in Oklahoma history. A former United States Marine

J. Howard Edmondson made a major impact on Oklahoma government. Here he was photographed with his family in front of the family home. From left to right: Jimmy, J. Howard, Patty, Jeanette, and Jeanne. (Courtesy Oklahoma Historical Society)

and a wheat farmer from Billings, Bellmon sparked a Republican Party renaissance in the state that would lead to a competitive, two-party system during the ensuing decades.

The matter of legislative reapportionment was resolved during Bellmon's administration, not by the Legislature but by the federal courts in various legal actions that finally resulted in a United States Supreme Court ruling that provided that both houses of the Legislature must be apportioned strictly by population. The districts were redrawn and a special election was held on September 29, 1964, to select the members of the Thirtieth Legislature. Democrats secured control of both houses by comfortable margins. During Bellmon's term, a state human rights commission was established, as was a bi-partisan highway commission. In addition, the state constitution was amended to allow for governors to be elected to two successive terms. Previous governors were limited to one four-year term and thus were "lame ducks" when they entered office. Upon completing his term, Bellmon was elected to two, six-year terms in the United States Senate.

Bellmon was succeeded as governor by another Republican, Dewey F. Bartlett, an independent oilman from Tulsa. Bartlett had served two terms in the State Senate, and he focused his efforts on promoting economy and efficiency in state government. Early in his term an embarrassing situation in state government was addressed by reforming the process by which state Supreme Court justices are selected. This effort was spurred by revelations that three justices had accepted bribes in exchange for favorable rulings. The new procedures, which were praised nationally, established a selection process based on merit for the Supreme Court and the Court of Criminal Appeals.

Bartlett was the first governor eligible to stand for reelection, but he was defeated by David Hall of Tulsa in the closest gubernatorial election in state history. Hall promoted increased funding for education, prison reform, and road construction. He was followed by David L. Boren of Seminole, whose campaign featured a "broom brigade" to sweep out the "old guard." The son of former United States Congressman Lyle H. Boren, the young governor was a Rhodes Scholar who had served in the State House of Representatives since 1967. Buoyed by a strong state economy, Boren pressed various education programs, including the Oklahoma Summer Arts Institute at Quartz Mountain State Lodge. From 1976 to 1978 Oklahoma ranked first in the nation in percentage of increase in funding for higher education. The executive branch of the

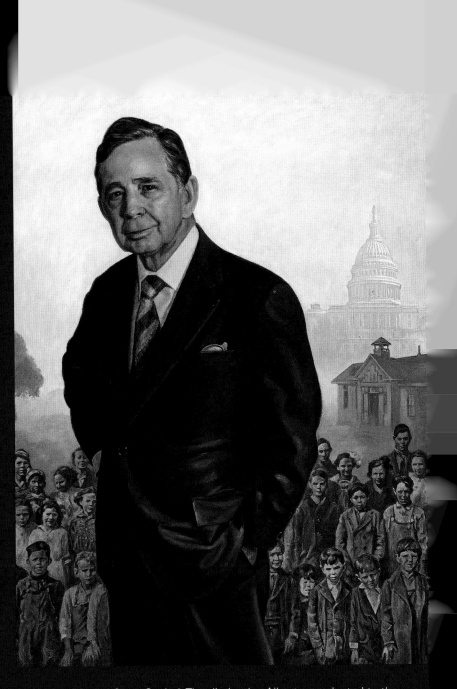

Charles Banks Wilson's portrait of Carl B. Albert, the "Little Giant from Little Dixie," is displayed in the State Capitol. The diminutive Albert was elected to the United States House of Representatives in 1947 and served in that body for 30 consecutive years. From 1971 to 1977 he was Speaker of the House. The son of a coal miner, Albert grew up in Bug Tussel, near McAlester, attending a one-room school, depicted by Wilson in the background of the portrait along with the United States Capitol Building. A champion debater in high school, Albert was a Rhodes Scholar at Oxford University and a veteran of World War II. Following his retirement from Congress, he returned to McAlester where he remained a revered figure until his death in February 2000. (Courtesy Oklahoma Arts Council)

state's government also was streamlined, and the budget balancing amendment was modified to reduce boom and bust financing. Boren won election to the United States Senate and served in that body until becoming president of the University of Oklahoma in 1994.

George P. Nigh, a high school history teacher from McAlester, was elected governor in November, 1978. Nigh's political career began as a member of the House of Representatives in 1952 and had served three terms before being elected lieutenant governor in 1958. He was elected to that office again in 1966, 1970, and 1974. With revenues expanding dramatically because of the oil and gas boom the state was enjoying, Nigh was able to push through 17 different tax cuts and still expand state funding for important programs. He became the first person in state history to be elected to a second term as governor, carrying all 77 counties, another "first" in state history. Times were good, but storm clouds were gathering on the political and economic horizons.

Benjamin Harrison Hill of Tulsa was pastor of the Vernon AME Church. A civil rights leader, journalist, and state legislator, he was elected to the Oklahoma House of Representatives in 1968. This portrait of Hill by Simmie Knox may be viewed in the State Capitol. (Courtesy Oklahoma Arts Council)

President John F. Kennedy, left, traveled to eastern Oklahoma on October 29, 1961, to dedicate U. S. Highway 259. His participation was requested by Oklahoma's senior United States Senator Robert S. Kerr, Sr., right, whose support was vital for Kennedy if he hoped to get his legislative agenda through the Senate. Others participating in the ceremony were Oklahoma Governor J. Howard Edmondson and Oklahoma's junior United States Senator A. S. "Mike" Monroney. An estimated crowd of 25,000 gathered to see and hear Kennedy speak amid the autumn splendor of the Kiamichi Mountains. (Courtesy Oklahoma

Jack Zink: The Will to Win

By the 1950s Tulsa was struggling to retain its crown as the Oil Capital of the World. The city had earned the title during a series of sensational oil discoveries in Oklahoma from 1902 to 1928, but the accumulated impact of the Great Depression, World War II, and declining production had stalled the growth of the oil patch in the state. Coastal cities, with direct access to crude oil shipped from overseas fields in the Middle East and South America, were emerging as the new centers of oil trading and refining.

One Tulsa-born business affected by that transition was the John Zink Company, founded in 1930 to produce burners for the oil industry where the application of heat was needed to break crude oil into its component parts. By 1950, with oil production declining and refinery construction drawn to Texas, Louisiana, and New Jersey, the company had turned to consumer products such as floor furnaces, water coolers, and space fans to survive. John Steele Zink and his 20 employees needed a new direction. They found it with the help of the founder's son, Jack Zink.

John Smith Zink, known all his life as Jack, was born in Tulsa in 1928. His father, a large, powerful man, taught him to work with his hands and to solve technical problems through teamwork and experimentation. His mother, Swannie, was a scholar who taught him the joys of learning and the freedom of living life on his own terms. After years of fun, football, and working in the family-owned foundry and plant, Jack attended Oklahoma A&M where he graduated in 1950 with a degree in mechanical engineering.

Jack joined the John Zink Company as a sales engineer, a position his father hoped would reinvigorate their position in the oil industry outside the state. Throughout much of the decade, Jack was on the road more than 200 days a year, working with industrial clients who needed controlled heat applied to a variety of tasks ranging from refinery crackers to smokeless flares.

Jack Zink

To win that industrial battle, Jack and his team at the company designed and built the first test furnace in the burner industry. It was a ten-feet by fourteen-feet box within a box, surrounded by water to absorb the vast amounts of heat generated in the testing process. There, under carefully controlled conditions, Jack and his team calculated and measured the endless variables of fuel mixture, thermal input sizes, heat transfer demands, heat release and turndown, firing positions, and shape of the flame.

One application of this methodical process was the development of a smokeless flare for a Mobil Oil Company refinery in East St. Louis, Missouri. To eliminate the billowing clouds of black smoke coming from the flare stack, Jack did his measurements, conducted his experiments in the test furnace, and installed a new burner that introduced steam around the perimeter of the stack. As waste gasses were discharged, they would be mixed with steam to raise the heat high enough to burn both the gas and the smoke it created.

With a crowd of Mobil officials watching, Jack pushed the button to ignite the pilot light for the first time, but nothing happened. He pushed it again, but they could neither see nor hear anything. The only option was to climb the 150-foot tower to do a visual inspection. Without harness or safety net, Jack pulled himself up one step at a

time until he got close to the top. Then he discovered what was wrong. The design worked too well for them to see any smoke or even hear the roar of the flame from the ground. It was working perfectly.

With his father taking care of manufac-

turing at home, Jack pursued business around the world. In 1960, to avoid the international trade barriers that protected foreign markets from American competition, he took the John Zink Company international. He established an office

(Facing page) John Smith "Jack" Zink of Tulsa was a popular industrialist, philanthropist, civic leader, and motor sports innovator. (Courtesy Oklahoma Heritage Association)

Jack Zink loved to drive vehicles in grueling, off-road races, which he frequently won. In this photo, all four wheels of Jack's racer were off the ground as he sped along the rugged course. (Courtesy Zink Ranch)

in Mexico to sell burners to Pemex, the national oil company, and followed with subsidiaries and manufacturing plants in London, Paris, Frankfurt, and Rome.

Jack also pioneered burners, incinerators, and oxidizers for pollution control in the 1960s as environmental standards forced companies to do something about the quality of water, air, and soil. By 1972 the John Zink Company was the largest family-owned business west of the Mississippi River with two plants in Tulsa employing 600 people to satisfy the demands for its various applications of burners.

The success of the company was a reflection of the qualities shared by Jack and his father. They were innovators who emphasized teamwork. They were fierce competitors who balanced caution with courage as they moved steadily ahead. And they shared an overdeveloped sense of tenacity. As Jack frequently said, there are five rules for success: "Never, never, never, never, never give up." These same qualities took the Zink team to the highest levels of automobile racing.

Jack could not remember a time when he did not enjoy speed. He had a Harley-Davidson 45-cubic-inch motorcycle in high school, raced the family coupe around a track he laid out behind the plant, and built a home-made midget race car from junk parts by the time he was 19. When his father asked

if he could put a better car on the track if he had some financial backing, he said "yes." In 1947 they purchased a kit and assembled a Kurtis-Kraft midget with a four-cylinder Offenhauser engine. The Zink Racing Team was born.

While the Zink midget cars were winning on the regional circuit from Kansas City to Houston, Jack purchased and drove his first stock car, a '37 Ford sedan, and followed by putting on the track a succession of other stock cars, including a Chevy and an Oldsmobile. By 1952 he was called in one publication, "the best known name in the circuit right now…he likes to win and he gives everything he has." With chief mechanic Dennie Moore and drivers such as Jimmy Reece and Buzz Barton, the Zink Racing Team dominated tracks across the state.

In 1952, ready for the next challenge, Jack purchased and ran a car in the Indianapolis 500. With Oklahoma City native Jimmy Reece in the cockpit, they came in a surprising seventh. Three years later, in yet another car, Bob Swiekert drove the Zink Special to a first place finish. A year later, the Zink entry with Pat Flaherty aboard won for a second consecutive time, a rare feat in a world where machine, driver, team, and luck all played a role in success.

Jack did not stop there. He continued putting cars on the speedway at Indianapolis

until 1967, including the first experimental race car equipped with a turbine engine. In 1962 the car ran several fast laps, good enough to qualify, but not fast enough to win. Jack, never content with just competing, did not run it in the race. Instead, he put his energy into developing one of the first rear-engine, Grand Prix-style cars to run at Indy. In the team's last race at the Speedway, the innovative Zink Special came in fourth.

Jack was not finished with racing, however. In 1967 he purchased the best off-road motorcycle available and competed in the Mexican-1,000, a grueling test of courage and endurance down the Baja peninsula. He followed that by designing and building a two-seat dune buggy that he ultimately drove to first place finishes at the Baja 500, the Parker 500, the Sandmaster, and other races. When his chief mechanic and teammate, Dennie Moore, noticed that all the dents were on the passenger side of the car where he sat, he built a one-seat car for Jack, powered by a juiced-up Porsche engine. Once again, Jack drove the car to numerous victories across the country.

For Jack, his sister Jill, and their father, John, winning in the worlds of business and racing was not enough. They wanted to make a difference in the lives of their neighbors. Through their foundations, they invested in organizations such as the Boy Scouts, the Tulsa Fairgrounds, the Salvation

Army, and the National Conference of Christians and Jews. One of the most visible results of their generosity and leadership was the Tulsa River Parks Project, which contributed to a sense of community with trails, public art, and a low-water dam that created a body of water city officials named Zink Lake.

Late in life, when he was asked to name his most cherished accomplishment, Jack Zink did not suggest the racing victories he had won, the inventions he had pioneered, or the business empire he had expanded. Instead, he said he was most proud of the Zink Ranch, a nature preserve on the outskirts of Tulsa his father had started in 1931 and he had grown to 33,000 acres. To Jack, it was more than land and woods, more than a place for Boy Scouts and outdoor recreation. The Zink Ranch was a place where people could get close to nature, test themselves, and rediscover the joys of being with friends and family. For a man who loved to win, there was no better reward.

Another enduring symbol of petroleum's legacy and cultural richness is the Philbrook Museum of Art, originally made possible by the donation of Villa Philbrook, the elegant house and beautiful grounds of Waite and Genevieve Phillips. The home featured 72 rooms on 23 acres of grounds. A brother of Frank and L. E. Phillips, founders of Phillips Petroleum Company, Waite was a prominent independent oilman known for donating his Philmont Ranch in New Mexico to the Boy Scouts of America. Waite and Genevieve donated their home to the City of Tulsa in 1938, and the museum was opened in 1939. A large, new wing has been added in recent years, and the museum is internationally recognized for its large, diverse collection of fine art. (Courtesy Jim Argo)

Voices of the People: Newspaper Families

On September 25, 1844, Volume 1, Number 1 of the *Cherokee Advocate* was published at Tahlequah, Cherokee Nation. It was the first newspaper published in the region that would become the State of Oklahoma in 1907. Hundreds of other newspapers, large and small, daily and weekly, would follow. As new communities were founded, newspapers were among the first civilizing elements to be established, along with churches and schools. Publishers became the conscience of their communities. Chain ownership of newspapers was introduced to Oklahoma when Eugene C. Pullium purchased seven daily newspapers in western Oklahoma in 1929 and 1930. From that point, independently-owned newspapers in the state began to decline in number, following the national trend.

By the 1970s newspaper chains were scrambling to purchase prosperous, independently-owned newspapers in the state. Often the offers were "too good to pass up." Yet through the decades a number of newspapers in Oklahoma, including its two largest daily newspapers, remained in the hands of several generations of one family.

The Daily Oklahoman was started in 1889 in Oklahoma City by Reverend Sam Small, who quickly ran into financial difficulties. By 1902 the paper was under the control of Roy E. Stafford who joined with E. K. Gaylord in 1903 to form the Oklahoma Publishing Company. By 1918 Gaylord was in control of OPUBCO and remained the publisher of the paper until his death at the age of 101 in 1974. By then, *The Daily Oklahoman* was the state's largest newspaper. Control of OPUBCO passed to Gaylord's son, Edward L. Gaylord, who continued to publish the newspaper and build an extensive business empire. Upon his death in 2003, his daughter Christy Gaylord Everest became publisher. For more than a century, the Gaylord family has played a prominent roles in civic leadership, political debate, and philanthropy in Oklahoma.

Oklahoma's other large daily newspaper, the *Tulsa World*, also remained family-owned as the state approached its centennial year. A Missouri native, Eugene B. Lorton was an experienced newspaper editor when he came to Tulsa in 1911 as editor and part-owner of the paper. He purchased full ownership of the enterprise in 1917. For the next 32 years he enhanced the quality of the paper and the size of its circulation while working constantly for civic improvements for Tulsa. Upon his death in 1949, his wife, Maud, assumed the role of publisher, as their son, Robert Eugene Lorton, had died in 1938 as the result of a swimming accident. Following her death in 1962, the paper was operated by attorney Byron E.

Edward L. Gaylord was publisher of *The Daily Oklahoman* from 1974 until his death in 2003. His father, E. K. Gaylord, was co-founder of the Oklahoma Publishing Company in 1903 and was publisher of the paper from 1918 until his death in 1974. Edward was a talented entrepreneur with extensive business interests in the entertainment industry, hotels, and broadcasting in addition to the newspaper. He also was a generous philanthropist. The newspaper remains in the hands of the Gaylord family with Edward's daughter Christy Everest serving as publisher. (Courtesy Oklahoma Heritage Association)

Boone until a grandson of Lorton's, Robert E. Lorton, Jr., assumed control of the paper in 1968. He and his wife, Roxana Lorton, continued the family tradition of community involvement and philanthropy. In 2006, the *Tulsa World's* centennial year, Lorton turned over the daily management of the paper to his son, Robert E. Lorton, III.

Oklahoma has benefited from the contributions of newspaper families who operated newspapers in communities throughout Oklahoma. Among them were the Muchmore family in Ponca City, the Bentley family in Lawton, the Bellatti family in Stillwater, the Phillips family in Seminole, the Lockey family in Tishomingo, and the Riesen family in Ardmore. These families, and many others, contributed more than delivering world, national, state, and local news to their customers' doorsteps; they also worked hard to help build better communities for their families and their fellow citizens.

H. Milt Phillips returned to Oklahoma after serving in the United States Navy during World War II and purchased the *Seminole Producer* in 1946. In the 1950s, Phillips and his son Ted consolidated their paper with another in Seminole to form the *Seminole Daily Producer*. Phillip's stature in the journalism community in Oklahoma was recognized in 1978 by the Oklahoma Press Association when it created the Milt Phillips Award to be given on an annual basis to an individual based on "publishing a high-quality newspaper; contribution to the profession and the newspaper industry; years of service to the community, state and nation in a variety of volunteer activities and strong love and dedication to the family." (Courtesy Oklahoma Heritage Association)

Eugene B. Lorton came to Tulsa in 1911 as editor and part owner of the *Tulsa World*. He obtained full ownership of the paper in 1917, and it has remained in the Lorton family to the present. (Courtesy Oklahoma Historical Society)

155

Mary Coletta: Sister of Mercy

By the 1960s many of the economic, social, and political forces affecting life in Oklahoma were changing at an unprecedented pace. From industrialization and decline of inner cities to racial integration and a growing role for government in the daily lives of people, these changes were putting pressure on older institutions and fueling a revolution in the life of the community.

Health care, one of the most important qualities of life, was not spared from this revolution. Aging buildings, shifting demographics, costly technologies, and national health care programs increasingly tested the old business plans that had fostered the growth of hospitals run by charities and not-for-profit organizations. By the 1960s more than ever before, health care needed a new direction and new leadership. One of those new leaders was a petite woman of faith—Florence Johanna Massoth, known for most of her life as Sister Mary Coletta.

Florence was born on a western Kansas farm in 1919. She attended a church school in her predominantly Catholic community, but moved to Oklahoma City in 1935 to attend St. Joseph's High School, where she graduated in 1937. Two years later, following the path of life chosen by several aunts, uncles, and cousins, she dedicated her life to service in the church. After completing six months as a postulant, she took a new name, Mary Coletta, and began a new life as a Sister of Mercy.

The Sisters of Mercy, founded in 1831 in Ireland, lived by the motto, "service to the poor, the sick, and the ignorant." The order first came to the Indian Territory as educators in 1884 to operate St. Mary's Academy for Indian Girls in the Choctaw Nation. Seven years later they came to Oklahoma City to run the school associated with St. Joseph's Church. Reflecting a greater commitment to health care, the order opened a Mercy Hospital in McAlester in 1902.

Sister Mary Coletta

Health care in Oklahoma during the first half of the twentieth century was a mixture of small municipal hospitals, doctor-owned hospitals, and institutions affiliated with churches. There were 85 hospitals in the state by 1943, including St. John's and St. Francis in Tulsa and St. Anthony, Deaconess, and Baptist hospitals in Oklahoma City. The state, through the University of Oklahoma School of Medicine, operated University Hospital near the State Capitol on N.E. 13th Street.

In 1946, looking for new opportunities to serve the community, the Sisters of Mercy purchased the old Baptist Hospital in Oklahoma City, which had been renamed General Hospital. Built in 1917 at 12th Street and Harvey Avenue, the privately-owned hospital had been expanded to 145 beds and 25 bassinets. Sister Mary Coletta, just finishing a four-year assignment as a teacher at St. Josephs, was named director of the School of Nursing.

In her new position, Sister Coletta oversaw a staff of three and served as instructor, recruiter, social director, disciplinarian, counselor, and administrator. Her superiors in the order noticed her potential for leadership and sent her to Catholic University in Washington, D.C., where she completed her master's degree in nursing with a major in administration. In 1956, despite her youth, she was named

administrator of Mercy Hospital.

For the next six years, Sister Coletta lived up to the bold and independent reputation earned while teaching at St. Joseph's. She approached Stanley Draper, Sr., long-time director of the Oklahoma City Chamber of Commerce, about organizing a lay advisory committee to help raise money to expand and improve the hospital. Soon, she was surrounded by admiring civic leaders such as William T. Payne, chairman of Big Chief Drilling Company, Sylvan Goldman, a wealthy grocer and real estate developer, and John Kirkpatrick, a noted philanthropist who was in the process of creating the Oklahoma City Community Foundation.

Although none of the three men were

(Facing page) Sister Mary Coletta was a talented hospital administrator and visionary in the health care industry. (Courtesy Mercy Hospital)

Sister Mary Coletta was adept at public relations and had the ability to inspire civic leaders and philanthropists of varied religious faiths to support Mercy Hospital. Here she is accepting an award for lighting design at the hospital from Richard Lipe, left, and Glen Reagan, ca. 1976. (Courtesy Mercy Hospital)

Catholics, they helped Sister Coletta raise enough money to open a Heart and Research Center, build a new wing with 57 beds, and create a Cardiovascular Diagnostic Center. Other notable advances achieved under the rapidly developing leadership of Sister Coletta included the first open heart surgery in a privately-owned hospital in Oklahoma, the first hospital to install a data processing unit from IBM, and the first hospital in Oklahoma to operate its own blood bank.

Typical of Sister Coletta's fearless devotion to service, she created an alcoholic treatment program at a time when few hospitals accepted alcoholics. To her, alcoholism was a disease, not a moral weakness, so she found two physicians to direct the program and told her nurses to treat the suffering patients "like human beings with dignity." In recognition, she received the 1962 service award from the Oklahoma Alcoholism Council.

From 1962 to 1966, while Sister Coletta was on assignment to build a new nursing school in Fort Smith, Arkansas, the health care industry throughout the country was being challenged as never before. Older hospitals such as Mercy were saddled with aging buildings that had been designed for shared rooms and simple technologies. As patients demanded semi-private and private rooms and as new diagnostic and treatment technologies grew more complex, the ability to expand and adapt grew increasingly difficult and expensive.

Then there was the issue of location. Many of the older hospitals, including Mercy, were located in the heart of the inner city, usually with no room for expansion or parking. Compounding the problem was suburban flight, which had lured away from the inner city potential patients as well as the physicians who served them. Fewer patients, fewer doctors, and a drain on cash just to keep aging roofs and environmental systems repaired was a recipe for bankruptcy.

In 1965 two events occurred which convinced the leadership at Mercy Hospital that they had to change directions immediately. One was the passage of legislation authorizing Medicare and Medicaid, which increased the role of the federal and state governments in health care. Along with new laws providing a steady stream of funding for patient care and expansion came new standards that were difficult to meet in the old buildings.

The second turning point was the launching of the Health Sciences Center as an integral part of urban renewal in Oklahoma City. According to the plan, public and private health care facilities would be concentrated in a 200-acre district surrounding the old University Hospital and the University of Oklahoma School of Medicine south of the State Capitol. With private, state, and federal funds available, civic leaders such as Dean McGee, Stanley Draper, and Stanton Young strongly encouraged health care managers throughout the city to move their institutions to the district.

Sister Mary Coletta returned for a second tenure as director of Mercy Hospital just as these forces were converging in 1966. She agreed that something had to be done, and she understood that remaining in the old location was not an option. As a bold and independent person, however, she also determined that moving to the Health Sciences Center was not the only solution.

As she had done in 1956, Sister Coletta organized a lay board of advisors to offer advice and financial support. Then she hired one of the nation's most respected consulting firms to help develop a long range plan. As she had anticipated, they saw the future of Mercy Hospital in an area that had potential population growth, on at least 40 acres for expansion, with good transportation connections, and on a campus that was attractive to physicians. They estimated the cost would be at least $25 million.

With the help of her loyal band of civic leaders, Sister Coletta raised $2 million to start the planning process and the search for land. One bid, submitted by developers who were building The Greens housing addition on the far northwest side of town, offered 40 acres at their original acquisition price. Although 14 miles north and 4 miles west of the central business district, the site was located on the planned belt highway that would someday encircle the city. And according to Sylvan Goldman, one of Sister Coletta's lay advisors, it was in the path of likely suburban growth.

Despite opposition from powerful community leaders, Sister Coletta forged ahead. She purchased the land, convinced city, county, and state leaders to build intermediate roads to the site, and secured federal grants for construction. In 1970 ground was broken for a hospital that featured all-private rooms, the newest innovations in health care, and amenities that would better serve patients, their families, and the health providers who worked there every day. The hospital opened to great fanfare in 1974.

Sister Mary Coletta did not stop there. For several more years, relying on a winning combination of hard work, perseverance, and teamwork, she continued developing the site with a doctors' tower, additional services, and a convent for the Sisters of Mercy. By the time of her death, Mercy Hospital was flourishing as never before, a symbol of service above self, a tribute to the power of dreaming big dreams.

Just as the healthcare in Oklahoma was becoming more available and technologically sophisticated, the state's highway system continued to improve. In 1964 a major project was building Interstate Highway 40 through downtown Oklahoma City. This stretch of the freeway was elevated, an approach which would allow existing north-south roads not to be disturbed and reduced acquisition of right-of-way costs. (Courtesy Oklahoma Publishing Company)

In addition to agriculture, energy, manufacturing, and services, tourism became increasingly important to Oklahoma's economy with the development of better highways and automobiles in the 1950s. All areas of the state boast significant scenic, cultural, and historic attractions. Among them are Autograph Rock in the Panhandle. Located on the Santa Fe Trail in Cimarron County on privately-owned land, permission to visit the site must be obtained from the land owners through the Cimarron Heritage Center at Boise City. A nearby spring lured thousands to the site over the centuries, including traders traveling the trail from Saint Louis to Santa Fe. More than 800 of them carved their names into the soft sandstone rock. (Courtesy Jim Argo)

Significant dinosaur fossils have been found in the Black Mesa region in Cimarron County. Among the dinosaurs that lived in the area during the Jurassic and Triassic Periods were the Apatosaurus, Stegosaurus, Omithopoda, and Allosaurus. As shown here, dinosaur tracks also may be seen in the bed of a creek near Black Mesa. The tracks are believed to be those of an Iguanodon or Camptosaurus. (Courtesy Jim Argo)

At 4, 973 feet above sea level, Black Mesa in Cimarron County, is the highest point in Oklahoma and is a place of scenic beauty. (Courtesy Jim Argo)

The Best: Oklahoma Sports Heroes

As Oklahoma celebrated its first 50 years of statehood in 1957, many of her citizens also celebrated the successes of Sooner State sports heroes. Over the next 25-year period, Oklahoma would produce outstanding athletes who dominated their sport or were the best to play a particular position. Among them were rodeo star Jim Shoulders, basketball legend Marques Haynes, baseball's amazing Johnny Bench, and Heisman Trophy winner Steve Owens.

Born in Tulsa in 1928, Shoulders became a legendary figure in the sport which reflects Oklahoma's cowboy heritage. He participated in his first rodeo at age 14 at Oilton, Oklahoma. One year after he graduated from high school, he had married Sharon Heindselman and was a professional rodeo cowboy. His career spanned 25 years from 1945 to 1970, during which he won 16 world championships, including five all-around cowboy titles, seven bull riding championships, and four bareback bronc riding titles, a feat unequalled as of 2006. He retired from rodeo to his ranch near Henryetta, Oklahoma, but remained active in the sport through personal endorsement contracts and several businesses. He was in the inaugural class of the Professional Rodeo Hall of Fame in 1979 and received the prestigious Ben Johnson Award from the Rodeo Historical Association in 2004. Shoulders dominated his sport and played a major role in its dramatic growth in popularity.

Sand Springs, Oklahoma, native Marques Haynes was recognized as the world's greatest ball handler during his amazing 45-year professional basketball career. Born in 1926, Haynes was an outstanding player at Booker T. Washington High School at Sand Springs, Oklahoma, and at Langston University, where he led the basketball team to 112 wins and only three losses from 1942 to 1946. One of those victories was a 74 to 70 win over the Harlem Globetrotters. As a professional, he played for four professional teams, including two extended stints with the Globetrotters. Counting his college experience, he played in more than 12,000 games,

University of Oklahoma running back Steve Owens of Miami, Oklahoma, set a number of school records and won the Heisman Trophy in 1969. (Courtesy Oklahoma Historical Society)

played before a world record crowd of 75,000 in Berlin, Germany, in 1950, and entertained fans in 97 countries. A "magician" with the basketball, he became the first Harlem Globetrotter to be enshrined in the Naismith Memorial Basketball Hall of Fame in 1998.

Loren E. "Steve" Owens was born in 1947 at Gore, Oklahoma, and was raised at Miami, Oklahoma. Although he was an outstanding athlete in high school, no one could have predicted that he would be voted the nation's best college football player for 1969. A 6-foot-2-inch, 215 pound running back, Owens had an outstanding career at the University of Oklahoma. In 1969, his Heisman Trophy year, he carried the ball 358 times for 1,523 yards and scored 23 touchdowns, all Sooner records. He also carried the ball an astounding 55 times in one game, yet another school record. His career touchdown total of 56 and his 905 career carries also set school records. His professional career with the Detroit Lions was cut short by a series of injuries, although he did become the first 1,000-yard rusher in Lions franchise history. After retirement from the National Football League, he became a successful businessman and civic leader in Oklahoma and served a stint as athletic director for his alma mater.

Born in Oklahoma City in 1947 and raised in Binger, Oklahoma, Johnny Bench became widely recognized as the greatest catcher in baseball history. Following his graduation from high school, he played two years of minor league ball before joining the Cincinnati Reds for a remarkable 17-year career. During that time, he established himself as the best offensive catcher ever, hitting 389 home runs, batting in 1,376 runs, and garnering 794 extra-base hits. In 14 all-star games, he hit three home runs and his batting average was .409. His impact as a defensive player, however, may have been even more dramatic. Beginning with his rookie season, he won 10 consecutive Gold Glove Awards as the best defensive player at his position. He also played in four World Series and earned the Most Valuable Player Award in 1970 and 1972. Elected to the National Baseball Hall of Fame in 1989, Bench enjoyed a successful career in business and as a baseball announcer following his retirement as a player.

Shoulders, Haynes, Owens, and Bench, as well as others such as amateur golfing great Charles Coe and "the Commerce Comet," Mickey Mantle, enhanced Oklahoma's reputation in sports during the period from 1957 to 1982. Their exploits and those of numerous other athletes inspired and entertained millions and set high standards for the Oklahoma athletes who would follow in their footsteps.

Rodeo is a sport that reflects Oklahoma's ranching and cowboy heritage. Henryetta's Jim Shoulders has won more rodeo world championships, 16, than any other individual. (Courtesy Oklahoma Heritage Association)

J. J. "Jake" Simmons, Jr.:
Black Gold–Black Dignity

As age stilled the efforts of Roscoe Dunjee and others of his generation in the struggle for civil rights in Oklahoma, other leaders rose to take their place. Clara Luper, a high school teacher in Oklahoma City, organized young people to stage sit-ins to integrate lunch counters and earned national respect for her efforts. Jimmy Stewart, an executive with Oklahoma Natural Gas Company in Oklahoma City, served on the national executive committee of the National Association for the Advancement of Colored People and worked tirelessly to advance the cause in Oklahoma. Many other leaders emerged, some of whom held political office while others were educators or professionals. One of the most unique of these individuals was J. J. "Jake" Simmons, Jr., of Muskogee, who served as president of the NAACP's Oklahoma Chapter and who, at the time of his death in 1981, was the nation's most prominent African-American oilman. He was a capitalist who was determined to make the system work for and be accessible to black Americans.

Simmons was born in 1901 as the 9th of 10 children born to J. J. Simmons, Sr., of Creek Indian and African-American ancestry and Rose Jefferson, the granddaughter of Cow Tom, a former slave who rose to prominence as a chief in the Creek Nation. Young Jake and his siblings worked hard on their 500-acre ranch, spending much of their time in the saddle, repairing fences, and working cattle. At a young age Jake developed a dislike for such work, although he enjoyed riding horses and by age nine was a jockey, regularly winning prizes in horse races at the Muskogee fairgrounds. But Jake was intelligent, did well in school, and knew he wanted to make his living with his mind.

Jake spent two years at the Tullahassee Mission School, living in a dormitory, but his life changed when Booker T. Washington visited Muskogee in 1914. Easily the best-known black American of his era, Washington operated Tuskegee Institute in Alabama and encouraged blacks to acquire skills that would be valued by society regardless of the race of

J. J. "Jake" Simmons, Jr.

the individual who possessed them. Rather than worrying about social status or racial injustice or integration, Washington urged blacks to work hard and to be valuable citizens. Progress in other matters would come in due course. While in Muskogee, Washington spent time at the Simmons home, and he sold the elder Simmons on Tuskegee Institute. Two weeks later, Jake and two of his older brothers departed for Tuskegee.

Simmons spent five years at Tuskegee Institute, taking the most advanced academic program available. He also trained as a machinist and developed his oratorical skills. Upon graduation, he married a fellow student from Chicago and moved to Detroit where he worked for Packard Motor Car Company. When he created a new style defroster, his employers were not interested because they did not believe a black could invent anything truly useful. Determined that he would never acquiesce to being treated as an inferior person, he quit in disgust and decided he could work only for himself. He returned to Oklahoma at his father's urging, divorced his first wife, and married local girl Eva Flowers, who he had courted when home from Tuskegee in the summers. They established their residence in Muskogee in 1920. When oil was found on Jake's 160-acre allotment that he had received for being a citizen of the Creek Nation, he was ready to enter the oil business.

Jake became a "lease hound," buying and selling drilling leases. He was especially effective in dealing with Creek and black farmers who found it easier to trust him than some white men, many of whom were bigoted toward blacks and Indians. He also established a real estate business in Muskogee. His prosperous business was hit hard by the onset of the Great Depression in 1929, but he rebounded by expanding his lease trading efforts into the East Texas oil fields. By the end of the decade, he was operating in Oklahoma, Texas, Louisiana, Arkansas, and Kansas, and he was dealing with leading oilmen such as Henry Sinclair, William G. Skelly, and Frank Phillips. He continued to build his business, Simmons Royalty Company, with the help of his sons Donald and J. J., III. He also expanded into Hereford cattle and insurance. In the 1960s Jake became an internationally-known oil industry figure by working as an intermediary between major oil companies in the United States and the governments of emerging nations in Africa, helping those countries arrange equitable development deals with the oil companies. All of this was accomplished during an era in which blacks in the oil industry seldom were allowed to rise beyond unskilled labor positions. His prominence was recognized nationally when he became the first black to be appointed to the National Petroleum Council in 1969.

Simmons' remarkable success in the oil business afforded him economic independence. This fortunate situation shielded him from economic pressure that might otherwise have been applied in an attempt to dissuade him from his lifelong fight against racial discrimination. Shortly after returning to Oklahoma in 1919, he joined the NAACP and remained active in that organization throughout his life. He had pride in his African-American and Creek Indian heritage, and he had a "hair-trigger" temper when he or any members of his family were treated poorly because of their color. At 5 feet, 11 inches and 190 pounds, Simmons would back down from no one, once beating up a white milkman who refused to address Eva as Mrs. Simmons.

In 1937 the city leaders of Muskogee proposed, and the voters approved, a $500,000 bond issue to benefit the public schools, but not one penny of this money was to be spent on facilities to benefit black students. Jake and Eva initiated a lawsuit seeking to bar the sale of the bonds as unconstitutional based on the blatant discriminatory nature of the way the money was to be spent. He responded to death threats by training every member of his family to be proficient with firearms. The pioneering anti-segregation case of *Simmons v. Muskogee Board of Education* made its way to the United States Supreme

(Facing page) Members of the Boley Town Council, ca. 1915. Boley was one of more than fifty "all-black" communities founded in the Twin Territories and the State of Oklahoma between 1865 and 1920. Boley was the largest of these communities. Founded in 1903 in the Creek Nation, Boley in a few years had an estimated population of 4,000. The Okfuskee County community in 2006 was home to approximately 300 individuals. (Courtesy Oklahoma Historical Society)

Court in 1939. When the justices ruled against Simmons, he was disappointed but determined to keep up the fight for justice. He became close friends with publisher Roscoe Dunjee of Oklahoma City, and together they battled for civil rights until Dunjee was incapacitated in the late 1950s.

Simmons became an increasingly important political force. By the 1950s black voters, especially in eastern Oklahoma, listened carefully to his opinions on candidates and issues. He was said to be able to deliver 10,000 votes in elections, and he used his influence to support those candidates who seemed more inclined to treat blacks fairly and to oppose vigorously those whom he believed to be bigoted toward blacks. As the civil rights movement gained momentum in the 1950s, he strongly supported taking direct action to force integration. He especially appreciated the efforts of Clara Luper, a school teacher, who headed the Youth Council of the Oklahoma City chapter of the NAACP. Luper and her student activists staged sit-ins over a six-year period beginning in 1958 to desegregate a wide range of business establishments and public facilities. Luper espoused the doctrine of non-violence advocated by Dr. Martin Luther King. She explained to Simmons that he would have to restrain his temper and smile regardless of being spit upon, cursed, or subjected to some other indignity when

he joined her for a protest at the Skirvin Hotel in downtown Oklahoma City. There he was pushed by a burly white man. Livid, Simmons was pulled aside by Luper who realized that he was ready to explode. Simmons told Luper, "I'll kill that man. I have to leave."

Simmons never participated in another sit-in but continued to support Luper's activities. He used the threat of her coming to Muskogee to end segregation of many establishments in that community without one sit-in being staged. Simmons also used his influence to open jobs to blacks at every opportunity. He used his business as a training ground for blacks to gain skills and then helped them find jobs in other businesses. He contributed generously to his church and to organizations to help blacks and others he felt were being treated unfairly. He also worked directly with individuals in need. Until his death in 1981, Simmons often spent half of his day in his Muskogee office listening to people describe their problems. In addition to lecturing them on what they needed to do for themselves, he would either help them find a job, give them some money, or both.

Simmons became president of the state NAACP organization in 1962 and served until 1968. During his tenure he continued to press for immediate action to end discrimination, including the use of sit-ins

and other non-violent actions. "Negroes must press now for their rights by all legal means and by peaceful demonstrations," he argued. He also observed that it was time to "get rid" of politicians who "have played on prejudice, have played Negro against white." The theme of the first statewide conference he headed was, "Full Citizenship Rights NOW. Moderation LATER." He continued to push for equal opportunity for blacks until he died from heart failure at age 80 in 1981.

Jake Simmons, Jr., was proud of his heritage, his accomplishments, and his family. One son, J. J., III, became prominent in the federal government, while Donald followed his father's footsteps into the international oil business. Yet another son, Kenneth, became a Harvard-educated scholar. His daughter, Blanche, did not graduate from college until she was well past 50, but Simmons continued to cajole her until she too became a college graduate. The children's reverence for their father was noticed by others, including Tulsa oilman Henry Zarrow, who observed, "I never saw any children love their parents like those boys did." Simmons set high standards for his family, and he lived up to those same standards in every aspect of his life.

J. J. Simmons appreciated the work of civil rights activist Clara Luper of Oklahoma City. Luper, shown here leading a civil rights gathering at the State Capitol, was an early leader in the sit-in movement in which blacks, often students, occupied lunch counters and other racially-segregated establishments. Luper stressed that sit-in participants demonstrate self-control, responding to verbal and even physical abuse in a non-violent manner. The hot-tempered Simmons simply could not accept insults or physical confrontations without responding in kind. (Courtesy Oklahoma Publishing Company)

On the Air: Early Television in Oklahoma

Popular Oklahoma City television personality Ida Blackburn with the legendary John Wayne in 1962. The *Ida B. Show* was a popular fixture on KOCO-TV in Oklahoma City from the late 1950s to 1975. (Courtesy Oklahoma Historical Society)

On June 6, 1949, a revolutionary new form of communication burst into the lives of Oklahomans. It was television.

Mass communication was nothing new. Newspapers had been published in the Indian Territory as early as the 1840s, followed by motion pictures at the turn of the century and radio in 1921. But television, with its mix of live action and local personalities, was more accessible to a greater audience that ranged from the smallest children to senior citizens.

The first broadcast was made on June 6, 1949, by WKY-TV in Oklahoma City. It was soon followed by KOTV in Tulsa, which went on the air in October of 1949. Other stations followed in quick succession, including KSWO-TV in Lawton (1950), the state educational channel KETA (1953), KWTV in Oklahoma City (1953), KVOO in Tulsa (1954), and KGEO in Enid (1954), which later was renamed KOCO-TV and moved to Oklahoma City in 1956. By 1960, depending on the height of one's antenna, television was streaming into every community of the state.

Typically, early television was a rich mixture of programming from local and national sources. The three networks, NBC, CBS, and ABC, soon dominated the evening hours with wildly popular shows such as *I Love Lucy* and national stars such as Milton Berle. But the unique side of early television was the local programming, which filled the morning and afternoon hours.

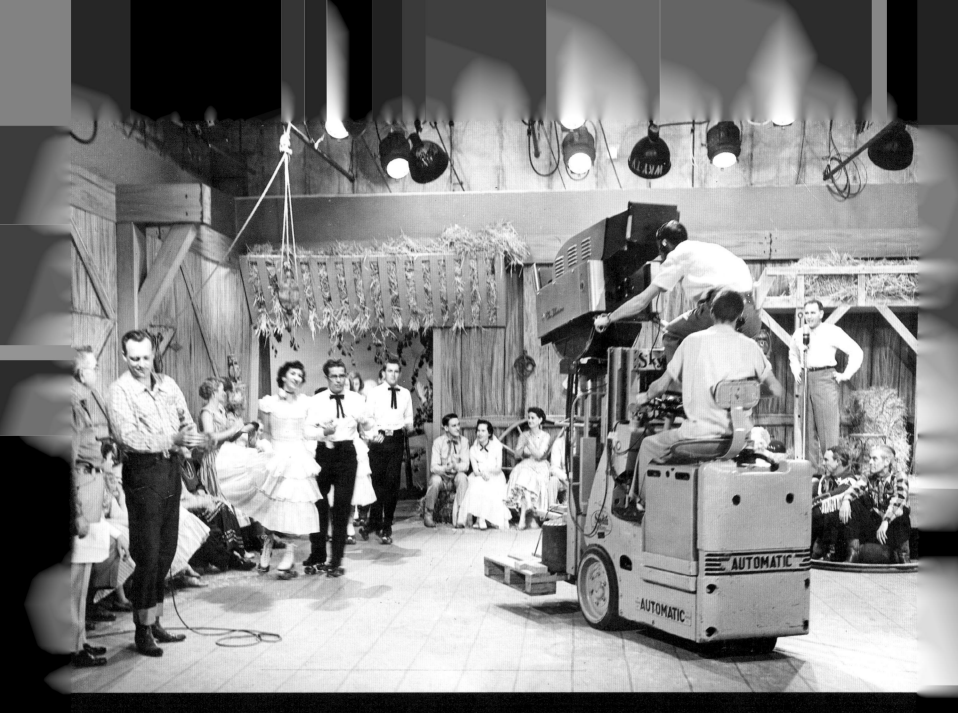

Television station WKY, now KFOR, in Oklahoma City, was owned by Edward King Gaylord, who was known for pioneering in television technology. He placed the first order for a color television camera and finally agreed to let the National Broadcasting Company obtain it. WKY received the second one. Another first for WKY was this telecast of the *National Square Dance Festival* in April 1954, the first NBC-TV colorcast originated by a non-network owned station. (Courtesy Oklahoma

For adults, the noon and evening newscasts became supplements to local newspapers. In Oklahoma City, anchors such as Ernie Shultz and Frank Doyle delivered the news of the day with serious directness, cutting to film clips shot on scene while they provided the voice-over narration. In Tulsa, one of the earliest newscasters people learned to trust was Bob Hower. He started each show with his familiar sign-on of "Good evening all, let's look at the news."

With the baby boomer generation creating a vast market of purchasing power in the 1950s, television filled the demand for advertising with "kiddie" shows. One of the most successful was *The Adventures of 3D Danny*, hosted by the irrepressible Danny Williams and his sidekick, Bazark the Robot. As the master of futuristic machines, such as the physic-tempometer, the synchro-retroverter, and the physco-peerscope, Dan D Dynamo recruited Unicorpsmen for his Universe Science Corps and mailed each member a thunder bolt shoulder patch and interplanetary money, each bill redeemable in star dust.

In Tulsa, at about the same time, a young man named Steve Powell created the character Foreman Scotty. In 1955 he moved his show to WKY-TV in Oklahoma City. Each day, live from the Circle 4 Ranch, Foreman Scotty provided a mixture of cartoons, live adventure dramas, and interaction with children on the stage. The lucky birthday boys and girls got to sit on "Woody the Birthday Horse." The Tulsa market for children's shows was soon filled by *Big Bill and Oom-A-Gog*, *Captain Alan*, and *Uncle Zeb's Cartoon Camp*.

Another market targeted by early television stations in Oklahoma was the homemaker. Talk shows took various formats, such as Tom Paxton's noontime knock-off of the *Tonight Show* on WKY-TV and Betty Boyd's string of shows in Tulsa known as *Woman's Page*, *Hi Neighbor*, and *Boyd's Eye View*. In Oklahoma City, the leading female host was Ida Blackburn, better known as Ida B, who started her career as host of "Romper Room" and went on to create *At Home with Ida B*, *Dateline Hollywood*, and *The Ida B Show*, all on KOCO.

Today, television remains a part of life in Oklahoma, with hundreds of channels available 24 hours a day providing a diversity of programming unimagined in the 1950s. And while local programming is still with us, it is largely confined to early morning talk shows and news, weather, and sports broadcasts. Gone are the days when local men and women came into the home live and up close, like a neighbor joining the family for the next half hour.

Another pioneering television program for children in the 1950s was WKY's *Foreman Scotty Show*. The title character was played by Steve Powell, center, and his companions were "Xavier T. Willard," (Danny Williams), left, and "Cannonball" (Wilson Hurst). (Courtesy Oklahoma Historical Society)

E. T. Dunlap: The Power of Education

The economic and social history of Oklahoma is like a book separated into two volumes. In volume one, before World War II, the dominant stories are farming, oil booms, railroads, and common education. In volume two, after the war, are industry, natural gas, highways, and higher education.

The impact of colleges and universities since the war is the story of intellectual energy, research, and hope for the future. And of all the men and women who have contributed to Oklahoma's system of colleges and universities, there is one whose influence can be seen in all directions at all levels. That man, who fully understood the power of education, was E.T. Dunlap.

Dunlap, the 10th of 13 children, was born in 1914 in rural Latimer County near the town of Cravens. After completing the eighth grade, he rode his horse to high school in Wilburton, the county seat seven miles away, and earned his teacher's certificate. His first job in education was teaching at his old school in Cravens.

From 1936 to 1938 Dunlap served as principal and teacher at Norris, a two-room school that went to the eighth grade. His wife, Opal, was the only other teacher in the school. At the age of 23 the ambitious young educator ran for and was elected Latimer County Superintendent. Two years later, in 1940, he was reelected to another term without opposition.

While earning the meager salary of a teacher and administrator during the Great Depression, Dunlap built bridges to his future. He attended summer sessions at Southeastern State College in Durant, where he earned a bachelor's of science degree in 1940. He joined the Masonic Lodge in McAlester, where he forged bonds with civic, business, and political leaders. He became active in politics, ultimately rising to become county chairman for Democratic candidates such as Carl Albert and Robert S. Kerr. In 1942, with his sights set on running for State Superintendent, he took a job as inspector of high schools with the State Department of Education.

Declared ineligible for military service due to an enlarged heart, Dunlap split the war years between his state job and pursuit of his master's and doctoral degrees in education from Oklahoma A&M in Stillwater. There, he grew close to his advisor and future mentor,

E. T. Dunlap

Henry Bennett, president of the college since 1928 and one of the most powerful forces in Oklahoma politics.

In 1946, while serving as superintendent of the Red Oak School District in Latimer County, Dunlap was elected to a seat in the State House of Representatives. For the next five years, he participated in debates over issues such as desegregation of higher education, the reorganization and centralization of the highway department, and the authorization of the Turner Turnpike. Working his way up to chairman of the Common Education Committee, he pushed through the Legislature a bill starting the painful but necessary process of school consolidation.

This short legislative career strengthened Dunlap's connections with and understanding of the political process long dominated by men from eastern Oklahoma. A few of his contemporaries from Little Dixie included Carl Albert, elected to Congress in 1946; Gene Stipe, elected to the Oklahoma Legislature in 1948; Robert S. Kerr, elected to the United States Senate in 1948; Raymond Gary, elected president pro tempore of the Oklahoma Senate in 1950; and Johnston Murray, elected governor in 1950. In the latter year, a newly-elected member of the Legislature from McAlester joined Dunlap and Stipe for the weekly drive to the State Capitol. That young man was George Nigh.

(Previous page) E. T. Dunlap was one of the most influential figures in the history of higher education in Oklahoma. (Courtesy Oklahoma Higher Education Heritage Society)

In 1951 Dunlap resigned from the Legislature to become president of Eastern Oklahoma A&M College in Wilburton, located about 40 miles east of McAlester. At the time, state supported higher education in Oklahoma consisted of the regional teachers' colleges, the University of Oklahoma in Norman, and the Oklahoma A&M system, which included the main campus in Stillwater as well as the colleges at Langston, Goodwell, Lawton, Miami, Tishomingo, and Wilburton.

In terms of political influence, the A&M system was the proverbial 800-pound gorilla armed with county extension agents in every county. Former Representative Dunlap, with Henry Bennett as his mentor, quickly learned how to recognize and use the levers of power in state government. Five years later, adding another weapon to his arsenal, Dunlap completed his doctoral dissertation, "The History of Legal Controls of Public Higher Education in Oklahoma."

As Dunlap was learning the ways of higher education administration, the system itself was changing and evolving. In 1941 voters had adopted an amendment to the State Constitution establishing the Oklahoma State Regents for Higher Education. This board, with members appointed to nine-year terms, was an attempt to shield colleges from the direct political influence of the Legislature and

governor. Thereafter, appropriations went to the State Regents, who in turn allocated funding, authorized programs, and set standards for all institutions.

The first administrator for the regents was Mell Nash, a political pragmatist who decided to exert the power of the new board slowly but steadily. Throughout his tenure, Nash let others come to him to solve problems and facilitate progress, which incrementally grew the influence of the regents within the political structure of the state. In 1961, when Nash retired, the regents wanted a professional educator who could take their system to the next level, a leader who understood higher education, and a deal maker who had the support network to work effectively with the State Legislature and the governor. That person was E. T. Dunlap.

When he became the second chancellor of the Oklahoma State Regents for Higher Education, Dunlap knew that the old system and the old ways would no longer satisfy the demands on higher education. Anticipating the baby boom generation, he initiated a study to prepare for the impact. He also recognized that federal funding for education was about to explode. Prompted by the Soviet Union's successful launch of *Sputnik*, Congress was eagerly pumping funds into state educational systems in an attempt to promote research in science and technology. Other steady streams of federal money available for educational institutions included urban renewal programs, health and welfare grants, and direct aid to students in the form of loans and G.I. Bill benefits.

Dunlap used these federal funds and the baby boomers' growing demand for access to college to leverage increased support for higher education. When community leaders in Tulsa, Midwest City, and Capitol Hill wanted two-year colleges, they worked with Dunlap and his staff to pass sales tax increases to match federal and state funds. When municipal college administrators in Altus, El Reno, Poteau, Seminole, and Sayre wanted to expand, they worked with Dunlap and his staff to set standards, secure state support, and tap the flow of federal funds.

When University of Oklahoma officials and Oklahoma City civic leaders wanted to expand the medical school and build affiliated institutions of higher education, they approached Dunlap to guide them through the political terrain to secure land, accreditation, and funding. In 1968, when the public approved a bond issue for the Health Sciences Center near the State Capitol, the Legislature allocated $60 million to the State Regents and told Dunlap to spend it wisely. He did, matching every dollar, sometimes two-to-one, from federal and local governments.

As the Health Sciences Center developed, the traditional rivalry between Oklahoma City and Tulsa helped Dunlap generate support for additional units of higher education in Tulsa. The results included a rapidly expanding Tulsa Community College with numerous branches, the Oklahoma College of Osteopathic Medicine and Surgery affiliated with Oklahoma State University, and a Tulsa branch of the University of Oklahoma Medical School. Out of this burst of expansion also came the College of Optometry on the campus of Northeastern Oklahoma State University.

For Dunlap and the State Regents, however, expansion was not enough. They wanted a true system with long range plans, institutional balance, and consistent standards. When a regional university demanded a Ph.D. program, Dunlap resisted and won, even when confronted by a determined governor. He helped organize the State Guaranteed Loan and Tuition Aid Grant Programs, pushed for a statewide "talk back tv" educational network, and led the effort for a Unitized Data System that tracked enrollment, classrooms, laboratories, professors, budgets, and grants.

In 1981, when E. T. Dunlap retired as chancellor of the State Regents, enrollment in Oklahoma institutions of higher education exceeded 160,000, compared to 44,590 twenty years earlier. The budget, which was only $27 million in 1961, was $325 million

when he retired. Yet the greatest measure of his service to the state went beyond the numbers, beyond the institutions. His legacy was greater access to higher education for all who wanted to improve their lives. Thanks in large part to the man who understood the power of education, they got that chance.

For E. T. Dunlap, increasing access to higher education in Oklahoma was a primary goal. (Courtesy Oklahoma Higher Education Heritage Society)

Unique Contributions: Creative Oklahomans

Oklahomans in many different fields of artistic endeavor made unique contributions to American culture from the late 1950s to the early 1980s. Among them were Willard Stone, Louis Ballard, Roger Miller, J. J. Cale, and Leon Russell.

Stone was born at Oktaha, Oklahoma, in 1916. His father died when Willard was an infant, and his mother worked as a sharecropper to support her family. At age 13 an exploding dynamite cap severely damaged his right hand and ended his dreams of being a painter. He eventually learned that he could handle sculpting tools and attended Bacone Indian College, where he was taught and inspired by Acee Blue Eagle and Woody Crumbo. During the 1940s he worked for Thomas Gilcrease for three years. By then he had become a remarkable wood sculptor, whose hands could "transform a block of wood into rhythm and movement and poetry." His work also reflected Native American sensibilities, spirituality, and symbolism. It was not until 1961, however, that he could afford to work fulltime as an artist, which he did until his death in 1985. Much of his work was done in his studio near Locust Grove, Oklahoma, and is found in private collections and museums throughout the United States and Canada.

Louis Ballard was born near Quapaw, Oklahoma, in 1931. Educated at the University of Oklahoma and at the University of Tulsa, Ballard became a critically-acclaimed classical composer, educator, and author. Among his most widely played works are "Scenes From Indian Life," "Incident at Wounded Knee," "Portrait of Will Rogers," and "The Four Moons," a tribute to Oklahoma's famed Indian ballerinas. His music has been premiered in famous concert halls such as Carnegie Hall, Lincoln Center, Kennedy Center for the Performing Arts, and many others. His guidebook with two CDs called *Native American Indian Songs* has been deemed "an American classic." He received a Lifetime Musical Achievement Award from the First Americans in the Arts in 1999 and was inducted into the Oklahoma Music Hall of Fame in 2004.

Another unique songwriter and performer emerged during this period from far Western Oklahoma. Roger Miller was born in Fort Worth, Texas,

Cherokee wood sculptor Willard Stone of Locust Grove was a nationally renowned artist. At age 13 his right hand was severely damaged by an exploding dynamite cap. The budding painter thought his artistic possibilities were ended, but he later discovered he could handle wood carving tools. He spent his adult life transforming blocks of wood into artistic treasures. (Courtesy Oklahoma Heritage Association)

The Union Indian Agency building at Muskogee was constructed in 1875 by the Bureau of Indian Affairs. The building subsequently was used as an orphanage, as a school for Creek freedmen, and after World War I as "The Chateau," where area residents could dance and listen to live bands. The building fell into disrepair after World War II. It was preserved through the efforts of the Da-Co-Tah Club, a group of local women of Indian descent, and the building opened as the home of the Five Civilized Tribes Museum in 1966. The museum holds and exhibits an extensive collection of art and artifacts reflecting the history and culture of the Cherokee, Chickasaw, Choctaw, Creek, and Seminole nations. (Courtesy State Historic Preservation Office, Oklahoma Historical Society)

The Norman home of University of Oklahoma artist and professor Oscar B. Jacobson today is the Jacobson House Native American Art Center. Jacobson, with the help of Susie Peters, "discovered" a group of Kiowa Indian artists, admired their work, and helped expose it to a wider audience during the 1920s. The "Kiowa Five" became international celebrities recognized as fine artists. This helped pave the way for acceptance of Native American art in general among art critics, collectors, and museums. (Courtesy State Historic Preservation Office, Oklahoma Historical Society)

n 1936 but moved to Erick, Oklahoma, a year later to live with one of
his uncles when his father died. "Dirt poor" and desperate to become a
singer-songwriter, he stole a guitar at age 17, turned himself in the next
day, and was allowed to serve in Korea instead of going to jail. He rose
above this difficult beginning on sheer talent and hard work, eventually
winning 11 Grammy Awards for his hit songs. Some of them were novelty
tunes, such as *Dang Me* and *You Can't Roller Skate in a Buffalo Herd*,
while others were sincere ballads such as his signature song *King of the
Road*. He also wrote the musical score for the Broadway musical *Big
River*, earning a Tony Award for that effort. He died of lung cancer in 1992
and was voted into the Country Music Hall of Fame in 1995.

While Ballard and Miller were evolving their distinctive musical styles,
another group of musicians were developing what became known as
"The Tulsa Sound." A mix of rock and roll, rockabilly, and blues music of
the 1950s and 1960s, the genre included a number of musicians, the best
known of which were Leon Russell and J. J. Cale.

Russell was born in Lawton in 1942 but moved with his family to Tulsa,
where he attended Will Rogers High School. He began studying classical
music at age three and learned to play a wide range of instruments. He
started playing professionally at age 14, and his solo career ultimately
spanned rock, blues, gospel, and bluegrass. He started Shelter Records
and had a home in Tulsa during the 1960s and 1970s as well as a
recording studio in the community. Between 1968 and 2002, he recorded
35 albums, the most popular of which was 1972's *Carny*. He also worked
as a session musician and producer, working with many of the legendary
performers in rock.

Another musician associated with "The Tulsa Sound" was J. J. Cale.
Born in Oklahoma City in 1938 and raised in Tulsa, he was an outstanding
guitarist and songwriter. Cale recorded a number of critically acclaimed
albums but did not relish stardom and was somewhat reclusive. His
"loping sense of rhythm and shuffling boogie" style of playing greatly
influenced guitar icons Eric Clapton and Mark Knopfler. Clapton's
recordings of Cale's *After Midnight* and *Cocaine* were huge hits. Years
later, when asked what other musician he would most like to be, Clapton
answered, "Cale," calling him "one of the masters of the last three
decades of music." Cale lived briefly in Nashville and in Los Angeles but
has spent most of his life in Tulsa. In the 1970s and 1980s he became a
cult favorite. He reflected on his Tulsa roots when he recorded the album
To Tulsa and Back in 2004.

Apache artist Allan Houser grew up on a farm near Apache, Oklahoma. His father, Sam Haozous, had been captured with Geronimo and was a prisoner of war
until 1914. Freed at last, Sam decided to remain in Oklahoma instead of returning to New Mexico. Allan, the first Apache child born in freedom, was destined to
become an internationally recognized sculptor. Here he poses with Mildred Cleghorn, chair of the Fort Sill Apache Tribe, at the dedication of Houser's monumental
sculpture, *As Long as the Waters Flow*, on June 4, 1989. Houser was honored by President George H. W. Bush as the first American Indian to receive the National

Thomas P. Stafford: Expanding Horizons

Mary Ellen Patton bumped and bounced her way to Oklahoma in a wagon when she moved from Kansas to Weatherford in 1901. Less than seven decades later her son, Thomas Patten Stafford, would travel into space on top of a rocket. The contrast of those experiences, shared by two generations of one family, is symbolic of the dramatic changes experienced in Oklahoma during the first century of statehood. Although separated by a technological revolution, both shared the spirit of pioneers.

Thomas P. Stafford was born in 1930 and grew up during the years of the Dust Bowl and World War II. He knew from the time he was a small boy that he wanted to fly. Almost every day, as he watched the sky above Weatherford to catch sight of a DC-3 airliner passing overhead, he dreamed of flying one of those magnificent machines. He also was an excellent student and a high school football star.

When Tom graduated in 1948, the slender, six-foot-tall youngster was accepted into the United States Naval Academy. One of his exploits his senior year involved joining a group of friends who managed to burn a large "N" in the turf of the football stadium at the University of Maryland the night before their televised game with the Naval Academy. Fortunately for Stafford, the perpetrators of the deed were never apprehended.

Although the Air Force had been established as a separate branch of the military in 1947, the Air Force Academy had not yet been founded. Tom wanted to fly, and by his junior year at the Naval Academy he hoped to transfer into the Air Force after graduation. He chose the Air Force over Naval Aviation because the Air Force flew the fastest jet fighter at that time, the swept-wing F-86E Sabre Jet. Only about 25 percent of Naval Academy graduates in 1952 were allowed to join the Air Force, but through the luck of the draw, Stafford entered the Air Force as a second lieutenant, ready to face Soviet pilots in mortal combat if necessary. His temperament and intelligence, combined with his flying skills, caused him to be included in September of 1962 in the second group of astronauts selected by the National Aeronautics and Space Administration. America was in competition with the Soviet Union to be the first to land on the moon, and Stafford was destined to play a major role in that Cold War victory.

Thomas P. Stafford

Astronauts already had shown that humans could function in space for short durations in one-person capsules. Stafford began training for the next phase in NASA's program, Project Gemini, which featured a larger space craft that would accommodate two astronauts and remain in space for up to two weeks. Stafford's first adventure into space was as pilot of the Gemini VI mission, commanded by Wally Schirra. This flight was particularly significant because Stafford was to attempt the first rendezvous in space. Plans called for the *Gemini VI* to dock with an Agena rocket booster, but that rocket failed to reach orbit. Consequently, It was determined that *Gemini VI*, the launch of which had been delayed until after the launch of *Gemini VII*, would rendezvous with the *Gemini VII* craft. A successful rendezvous was executed on December 15 as *Gemini VI* closed within a foot of *Gemini VII*. In celebration of the Christmas season and their successful rendezvous, Stafford and Schirra played "Jingle Bells" using makeshift jingle bells and a miniature harmonica.

Stafford's next flight came sooner than expected as the scheduled crew for *Gemini IX* was killed in an airplane crash. On June 3, 1966, *Gemini IX* was launched with Stafford as commander and Eugene A. Cernan as pilot. A series of different types of rendezvous were completed successfully and

the *Gemini* capsule splashed down within one mile of the recovery ship, the closest that had been achieved to date. Following this mission, Stafford was promoted from major to lieutenant colonel.

Next came Project Apollo, the series of flights that would result in the United States putting the first man on the moon. From August 1966 to October 1968, Stafford headed mission planning analysis and software

development for the astronaut group working on Project Apollo. The country boy from Weatherford was the lead member of this group that helped to determine the sequence of missions that ultimately would result in the first lunar landing.

The crew of *Apollo I* was killed when fire flashed through their command module during a pre-flight test. While Stafford and his colleagues knew they were doing

(Facing page) Thomas P. Stafford, left, took a break with Apollo X crewmates, Eugene Cernan, center, and John W. Young during training for their flight. (Courtesy Oklahoma Historical Society)

General Thomas P. Stafford, center, enjoyed a celebration at the Oklahoma Historical Society honoring the 30-year anniversary of his flight to the moon. Visiting with Stafford were Bob L. Blackburn, Director of the Society, and an unidentified guest. OHS staff member Bill Moore is in the background to Stafford's left. (Courtesy Oklahoma Historical Society)

dangerous work, this tragedy brought that danger home in a stunning manner. Stafford and his colleagues wanted the causes of the fire to be found and corrected and the missions undertaken as soon as possible. He believed that the benefits of the space program far outweighed its inherent risks.

Stafford finally got his chance to go back into space as mission commander for *Apollo X*. His crew consisted of John W. Young as command module pilot and Eugene Cernan as lunar module pilot. Using a fully-configured lunar landing module for the first time, Stafford and Cernan descended to 8.4 nautical miles above the lunar surface before rendezvousing with the command module for the return trip to earth. During their descent into the Earth's atmosphere, Stafford and his crew reached a speed of 24,791 miles per hour, a record for the fastest any human had ever traveled. The mission was a success and paved the way for the crew of *Apollo XI* to land on the moon.

Stafford filled major administrative roles at NASA beginning the month after his flight to the moon when he was named head of the astronaut group and was responsible for naming the crews for the remaining Apollo missions and for the upcoming Skylab missions. Two years later he became deputy director of Flight Crew Operations. Stafford was not destined to "ride a desk" for the remainder of his NASA career. He

was selected to command the American crew in the first joint space operation with cosmonauts of the Soviet Union. The Cold War between the United States and the Soviet Union was beginning to thaw, and the Apollo-Soyuz Test Project mission, which took place from July 15 to July 24, 1975, resulted in the joining of the two capsules in space. Stafford and his colleagues had learned to speak Russian while the Russians had learned to speak English. The successful mission contributed to improving relations between the two nations and led to cooperation on future ventures, such as the international space station.

In November 1975 Stafford returned to the Air Force, was promoted to the rank of major general, and assumed command of the Air Force Flight Test Center. He was advanced to the rank of lieutenant general in May 1978 when he became deputy chief of staff, Research, Development and Acquisition for the Air Force. In this position, he was involved in the initiation and development of the F-117A Stealth Fighter. In 1979 he wrote the initial desired specifications for the B-2 Bomber. He retired from the Air Force in November of 1979. By this time, he had received numerous honors, including induction into the Oklahoma Hall of Fame.

Since 1980, Stafford has been active in a variety of successful businesses and headed

major consulting teams for both the first Bush and the Clinton administrations. He received perhaps his highest honor in 1993 when he became only the eighth American to receive the Congressional Space Medal of Honor. Throughout his long, spectacular career, he never forgot his Oklahoma roots, returning frequently to the state and his hometown. When asked to donate some mementos for display at the Weatherford airport, which had been named in his honor, Stafford eventually helped establish an outstanding museum dealing with the history of aviation and space flight. He also helped the Oklahoma Historical Society to obtain the *Gemini VI* module, which Stafford had flown in space, for display at the Oklahoma History Center in Oklahoma City.

Stafford continued to live his life to the fullest in the new century. In 2004 at age 74 Stafford and his second wife, Linda, both had grown children by previous marriages. Yet, Stafford wanted a son to carry on his name and he realized how much he had enjoyed being a father. The couple called on cosmonaut Alexei Leonov, Stafford's close friend from the Apollo-Soyuz mission, for assistance. Leonov helped the Staffords find and adopt two Russian boys, ages nine and 11. Tom Stafford had "flunked retirement" for the third time, but "just because you are retiring," he observed, "doesn't mean you don't have anything left to give."

Exploring a New Frontier: Oklahomans in Space

Just as Oklahomans have been innovators in the energy, aviation, radio, and television industries, citizens of the Sooner State have played important roles in the exploration of space. The "Space Age" began in 1957 when the Soviet Union successfully sent *Sputnik* into Earth orbit. Energized by this threat, the United States government established the National Aeronautics and Space Administration a year later. Oklahoma's powerful senior United States Senator, Robert S. Kerr, Sr., was a strong advocate of space exploration. By 1961 Kerr was known as "the uncrowned king of the Senate" and had become chairman of the Senate's Committee on Aeronautical and Spaces Sciences. In that capacity, he helped procure significant funding for NASA. When the agency needed a new administrator in 1961, Kerr played a prominent role in the selection of Oklahoma City's James E. Webb for that post.

A native of North Carolina and trained in law, Webb had served as director of the Bureau of the Budget and as under secretary of state before accepting a position as assistant to the president of Kerr-McGee Oil Corporation, which Senator Kerr had co-founded in 1953. Serving NASA from February 1961 to October 1968, Webb was a highly effective administrator. He established a balanced program of human space flight and science, with the express goal of benefiting mankind, not just winning a race to the moon. After his retirement from NASA he resumed his service as a director of Kerr-McGee. His dramatic impact on the space program was recognized by many awards through the years but none were more meaningful than NASA's recent decision to name the successor to the Hubbell Space Telescope the James Webb Space Telescope.

Oklahoma has produced a number of astronauts who recognized the dangers inherent in space flight in its developmental stage and chose

Gordon Cooper of Shawnee was a colonel in the United States Air Force with More than 7,000 hours of flying experience when he was selected to be one of Project Mercury astronauts in April 1959. In 1963 he piloted the *Faith 7* spacecraft on a 22-orbit mission, which was the final flight in the Mercury series. He then served as the command pilot of the 8-day, 120-orbit Gemini V mission in 1965, thus becoming the first American to complete a second orbital flight. He later served as backup command pilot for Gemini XII and as backup commander for Apollo X. He retired from NASA and the Air Force in 1970 to enter private business.

to accept the risk. A native of Shawnee and graduate of Shawnee High School, L. Gordon Cooper was a United States Air Force test pilot prior to being selected as one of seven Project Mercury astronauts in 1959 by NASA . His first space flight came in 1963 as pilot of the Faith 7 mission, the last of the one-man orbital flights of the Project Mercury program. The Gemini Project, featuring a larger capsule and a two-man crew, followed with Cooper as commander of Gemini Flight GT-5 in 1965.

A native of Okemah, William Pogue earned undergraduate degrees from Oklahoma Baptist University and Oklahoma State University, as well as a master's degree in mathematics from OSU in 1960. He was a test pilot for the Air Force before being selected for astronaut training in 1966. Pogue served in the support crews for four Apollo missions, including missions VII, XI, XIII, and XIV. The Apollo flights involved three-man crews and eventually resulted in the first lunar landing during the Apollo XI mission. During Apollo XIII, an explosion caused the crew to have to use the Lunar Module as a "life boat" in space, and as an assignment capcom, Pogue was one of the primary individuals communicating with the astronauts during the crises. Pogue flew in space as the pilot of the Skylab 4 mission, the third and final manned visit to the Skylab orbital workshop, from November 16, 1973, to February 8, 1974. This was the longest manned space flight to that time.

Interestingly, the Lunar Module Pilot for the Apollo XIII mission had strong Oklahoma ties. A native of Mississippi, Fred Haise, Jr., earned his bachelor's degree in Aeronautical Engineering from the University of Oklahoma in 1959. From March 1957 to September 1959, he served as a pilot with the 185th Fighter Interceptor Squadron of the Oklahoma Air National Guard.

Yet another test pilot from Oklahoma, Stuart Roosa, was born in Colorado but grew up in Claremore, where he attended grade school and graduated from high school. His higher education was received at Oklahoma State University, the University of Arizona, and Colorado University. Roosa joined the astronaut corps in 1966 and was the command module pilot for the Apollo 14 mission, during which he spent 33 hours in solo orbit around the moon conducting scientific experiments while his colleagues Alan B. Shepherd, Jr., and Edgar D. Mitchell explored the lunar surface.

Owen K. Garriott of Enid was one of six scientist-astronauts selected by NASA in 1965. A graduate of Enid High School and the University of Oklahoma, he received his Ph. D. degree in electrical engineering from

Aviatrix Geraldyn M. "Jerrie" Cobb of Ponca City was the first woman selected to be an astronaut trainee in 1960. She passed all the physical requirements and NASA's rugged training program only to have the agency decide in 1963 that they would not use women as astronauts at that time. Nonetheless, she paved the way for women who in later years were allowed to be astronauts. Cobb set a number of aviation records as a pilot and pursued a remarkable career flying humanitarian aid missions to people in the rain forests of six South American nations. (Courtesy Oklahoma Heritage Association)

Stanford University in 1960. A qualified pilot of jet aircraft and a noted scientist, he flew two missions in space, the first being Skylab 3 Mission in 1973, which set a record for duration to that date—60 days. Garriott's second mission came as part of the crew of the shuttle Columbia, Mission STS-9 in 1983. More than 70 experiments were conducted in the *Spacelab*, mounted in *Columbia's* cargo bay. Garriott also operated mankind's first amateur radio station from space, W5LFL.

Prior to 1978, women were not accepted by NASA to be astronauts. Oklahoma aviatrix Jerrie Cobb had passed all the tests for Project Mercury astronauts and wanted to fly in space, but the agency was not ready to take that step. Frustrated by the experience, Cobb nevertheless helped pave the way for the first six women who were accepted, one of whom was Oklahoman Shannon Lucid of Bethany. A graduate of Bethany High School, Lucid was educated through the Ph. D. degree in biochemistry at the University of Oklahoma. From 1985 to 1996 she flew five missions in space and logged 223 days in space. Her 1996 mission involved an extended stay on the Russian space station *Mir*. As of 2006 she held the international record for the most flight hours in orbit by any non-Russian and the record for hours in orbit by any woman.

Astronaut Neil W. Woodward III, a commander in the United States Navy, was born in Chicago, Illinois, but moved with his family to Oklahoma where he graduated from Putman City High School in Oklahoma City in 1980. After a distinguished career in naval aviation he was selected for astronaut training in 1998 and as of 2006 was serving as deputy director for Constellation Systems in the Exploration Systems Mission Directorate while waiting for his opportunity to fly in space.

A member of the Chickasaw Nation, John B. Herrington was born in 1958 at Wetumka. As a naval aviator, he reached the rank of commander and as of 2006 had logged more than 3,800 flight hours in more than 30 different types of aircraft. He was selected for astronaut training in 1996 and became the first Native American to fly in space in 2002 as a member of the crew of the shuttle *Endeavor*. The mission involved visiting the International Space Station to deliver new crew members and supplies and to install and activate the P1 Truss as part of the ongoing operation to build the space station. While docked with the space station, Herrington performed three space walks totaling 19 hours and 55 minutes.

Upon retiring from NASA and the United States Navy, Herrington moved to Oklahoma City where he is employed as a pilot for Rocketplane Limited, a venture that in 2006 was modifying a jet airplane

to fly into space and return, landing conventionally. The plane was projected to use a 20,000-foot-long runway at the former Air Force base at Burns Flat in western Oklahoma.

In addition to the astronauts, numerous Oklahomans have played significant roles in the space effort, including many highly trained scientists and other technicians who have worked for NASA. Moreover, North American Aviation, with a facility located at Tulsa, was NASA's prime contractor for the Apollo spacecraft. Parts of the Apollo service module were constructed at the Tulsa facility, as were major structural elements of the second stage of the Saturn rockets that were used to propel the Apollo spacecraft and crews into space. All Oklahomans who have in some way served to advance the exploration of space also have helped make possible the rapid progress of technology that the space program has stimulated. Dramatic advances in medical technology, in home appliances and electronics, in aviation safety, and in numerous other technologies were stimulated by the space program, an effort in which Oklahomans likely will continue to pioneer.

James Webb of Oklahoma City served as the administrator of NASA from February 1961 to October of 1968. His contribution to the space effort and the advancement of scientific knowledge was such that the next generation telescope that will replace the Hubble Space Telescope will be named after him. (Courtesy Oklahoma Heritage Association)

In the late 1970s and early 1980s Oklahoma experienced yet another oil and gas boom. Through legislation and Federal Energy Regulatory Commission rulings, the federal government sought to decontrol natural gas prices to stimulate production. As an intermediate step, the price of natural gas found below 15,000 feet was decontrolled in 1978, leading to a dramatic expansion in the price of "deep gas" and a major drilling boom in the Deep Anadarko Basin in western Oklahoma. Elk City became a boom town as the price of gas from deep wells rose as high as $10 per thousand cubic feet of gas. Wells reached depths in excess of 25,000 feet and were incredibly expensive to drill. While drilling the wells appeared to be profitable ventures, the boom came to an end in large part because the supply of gas increased dramatically, outstripping demand. (Courtesy Oklahoma Publishing Company, Oklahoma Historical Society)

The oil boom was on shaky ground when Penn Square Bank of Oklahoma City, an aggressive lender for drilling operations, was declared insolvent. Here investors were lined up at the entrance to the bank hoping to withdraw the funds they had on deposit. With the Federal Deposit Insurance Corporation in charge of collecting money owed to the bank, some oil and gas operators, unable to meet their loan obligations, went bankrupt. The state's economy spiraled downward, taking more than a decade to recover. (Courtesy Oklahoma Publishing Company)

The most severe tornado to strike Oklahoma since the Woodward tornado of 1947 caused extensive damage in central Oklahoma on May 3, 1999, a day during which supercell thunderstorms produced more than 70 tornadoes in north Texas, Oklahoma, and southern Kansas. This tornado was moving through the countryside in Grady County between Amber and Newcastle. It eventually would pass through the Oklahoma City metropolitan area. Among the communities most severely damaged were Bridgeport, Moore, and south Oklahoma City. All together, 40 Oklahomans were killed by tornadoes that day and approximately 675 were injured. The early warning system in the state, including extensive tracking of the storms by television weathermen, undoubtedly prevented the death toll from being much higher. (Courtesy Oklahoma Publishing Company)

The reflecting pool at the Oklahoma City National Memorial, located on the site of the Alfred P. Murrah Federal Building. (Courtesy Jim Argo)

CHAPTER FIVE

Everything's Going Our Way

The Oklahoma Standard

Kent and Helen Ruth: Window on the Past

Oklahomans collectively and individually have faced many challenges, ranging from droughts, depressions, diseases, and disasters, both natural and man made. Oklahomans typically have faced such difficulties with determination, have conquered adversity, or at least have learned how to function effectively in the face of it. Kent Ruth of Geary was a primary example of just such an Oklahoman. Severely crippled by polio as an infant, Ruth, with the help of his sister Helen, nevertheless pursued a career as a travel writer and historian that merited his induction into the Oklahoma Hall of Fame in 1976 and the Oklahoma Historians Hall of Fame in 1998.

Ruth's father, Oscar, was an Illinois native who fought in the Spanish-American War in 1898. Following his service in that conflict, buddy Henry Ringelman was traveling to his home in western Oklahoma and invited Oscar to "go along and see the county." Oscar took Henry up on the offer and eventually met his sister Abigail. They fell in love, were married by a Mennonite minister on January 24, 1901, and moved into a house Oscar had built at 619 North Broadway in Geary. Oscar and Abbie quickly became well known in the community in which they were destined to live the remainder of their lives. They had three children who survived to adulthood—Nelson, Helen, and Kent—all of whom were raised in the Mennonite faith. A fourth child, Helen's twin sister, died in infancy.

Kent and Helen Ruth

Born on Christmas day in 1916, Kent was the youngest of the three children. The next to him in age was his sister Helen, who was 10 years older. The family was stunned when Kent was diagnosed with polio at seven months. A disease that had plagued mankind since ancient times, polio is a viral illness that reached epidemic status in the United States in the first half of the twentieth century until Dr. Jonas Salk's polio vaccine became widely available in 1955. By 1979 the disease had been eradicated in the United States. In 1916, and for the next 40 years, polio was a widely feared menace, especially the version of the disease referred to as paralytic polio, which represented an estimated 2 percent or less of all cases. Baby Kent was in that unfortunate minority and was severely crippled by the disease.

As the Ruth family was to discover, Kent's twisted and paralyzed body did not diminish his will to live as full and productive life as possible. Kent was intelligent and determined to get his education. Kent often rode in a wagon to school while his cousin Otto Krehbiel pulled. Other children in the neighborhood sometimes pushed the wagon while Kent steered. Kent's classmates included him in their games on the playground as scorekeeper. Helen eventually went to college at Bethel Mennonite College at Halstead, Kansas, earned her teaching

certificate and ultimately a master's degree. She returned to Geary, lived in the family house, and taught school in Geary until her retirement. A revered teacher, she earned recognition as Oklahoma History Teacher of the Year. Kent, determined to become a writer, earned bachelor's and master's degrees in English and German at the University of Oklahoma, where, as a senior, he sold his first story for $5.00 to *Wild West Weekly*, a popular pulp magazine which Kent observed "couldn't get any 'pulpier'."

After completing his education, Kent returned to the family home in Geary, worked for the Chamber of Commerce, and continued writing for magazines and newspapers. His physical disability caused him to wear braces on his legs, and as time went by, his disability continued to grow in severity. In 1950 at age 34 he was hired by *The Daily Oklahoman* to write a weekly column on travel. This was timely for Americans who were starting to enjoy an unparalleled era of prosperity. Highways, automobiles, and tires were improving, and people began to realize that they could afford to take extended vacations. Ruth later observed that previously "folks just went to see Grandma."

Every summer for almost 50 years, Helen and Kent hit the road twice a year on extended trips, usually in the American West, to find places, people, and historical sites for Kent to write about.

(Facing page) Oklahoma historian and travel writer Kent Ruth was inducted into the Oklahoma Hall of Fame in 1976. (Courtesy Oklahoma Heritage Association)

Kent Ruth and his sister Helen were lifelong residents and beloved citizens of Geary, Oklahoma. Both loved history and travel. Together they made an effective team. (Courtesy Jim Argo)

Often accompanied by their friend Betty Armstrong, Helen was the "pilot" while Kent served as "navigator." They complimented each other well, Kent observed, because Helen enjoyed driving but "had no sense of direction." Kent quickly learned never to say "east or west, but left or right." As a travel writer, Kent understood that to really know a state or region one had to "get off the main road" and "talk to the natives who know and love the area from first-hand experience."

As Kent's travel writing matured, he increasingly added more regional, state, and local history to his stories. He became knowledgeable about the history and geography of the West and became an authority on Oklahoma. In 1956 he published *How to Enjoy Your Western Vacation* with the University of Oklahoma Press. The next year his classic *Oklahoma: A Guide to the Sooner State* was published by the same publisher. Nine more books followed with OU Press, Nebraska University Press, Colorado University Press, and Alfred Knopf, Inc., among others. Among the best known of these books were *Touring the Old West*, published in 1963, and *Oklahoma Travel Handbook*, which appeared in 1977. He also continued writing articles, many of which were published in *Oklahoma Today* magazine.

In 1969 Ruth was hired by the Oklahoma Historical Society to prepare nominations of historic structures and sites for the National Register of Historic Places. Writing the nominations required significant research, and over a period of years, Ruth produced almost 500 completed forms. This further stimulated his interest in and knowledge of Oklahoma's history and led to additional writing opportunities, including a regular column "Window on the Past" for *The Daily Oklahoman* and a book by the same title for the Oklahoma Historical Society.

As Kent grew older, he had to wear a brace on his upper body, and it became increasingly uncomfortable for him to travel. Although it took time and effort, Helen knew how to help Kent get out of their car and into his wheelchair. Despite the challenges he persisted, for he loved to travel and write and cherished history. He was especially talented in writing history in a manner that was appealing to the general public. While he was dedicated to accuracy, one Oklahoma historian proclaimed that Ruth's greatest gift was his ability to popularize history. He also served at various times on the boards of the Oklahoma Historical Society, the Oklahoma Heritage Association, and the Canadian County Historical Society, and he was a charter member of the Indian Territory Posse of the Oklahoma Westerners. All of these volunteer affiliations required travel, but Ruth was determined to participate in the historical community to the fullest extent possible.

Ruth received numerous honors through the years in addition to his induction into the Oklahoma and Oklahoma Historians halls of fame. In 1989 he received an award from the National Trust for Historic Preservation in recognition of his "inspiration and unending leadership in historic preservation in the State of Oklahoma." That same year, Helen and Kent, who still lived in the same house that their father had built, were honored by the citizens of Geary with a special dinner and program. Sponsored by the town of Geary, the Geary Chamber of Commerce, and Geary Alumni, this recognition was especially meaningful to Kent and Helen.

Many of Kent and Helen's friends worried about what Kent would do if Helen were to precede Kent in death, because she had devoted her life to taking care of him and to helping make his work possible. That concern was never realized, however, as Kent died of acute respiratory failure and Post-Polio Syndrome in January of 1991 at age 74. Helen, her life-long responsibility completed, died in May of 1992. Together they had made a remarkable team. Kent had risen above his physical disabilities and, with Helen's help, had led a productive and inspirational life.

In 1923, when the Scottish Rite Masons of Guthrie outgrew their original building, the citizens of the community voted to give them the 10.6 acres known as Capitol Park, which included the original legislative hall, where the State Legislature met until the capitol was moved to Oklahoma City in 1910. The Masons decided to construct a new temple and attached the legislative hall to their new building, giving them more than 400,000 square feet of space. The elegantly furnished building features a concert hall with outstanding acoustics. The Masons hope to restore the legislative hall to its 1907 appearance. Arrangements may be made to tour this remarkable building. (Courtesy State Historic Preservation Office, Oklahoma Historical Society)

A Two-Party State: Politics, 1982-2006

From 1982 to 2006, Oklahoma's political institutions and leaders faced serious challenges in the form of scandals, revenue shortfalls, and disasters, both natural and man made. These challenges were met, and the state and its people emerged from these situations strengthened for the future. The Republican Party continued to grow stronger during this period, leading to significant struggles between the two major parties over a variety of issues.

When George Nigh began his second term as governor in January of 1983, Oklahoma's economy was spiraling downward. Six months earlier, Penn Square Bank had collapsed, and yet another oil and gas boom was over. For the next four years Nigh and the State Legislature struggled to cope with dramatic declines in revenue to the state government as a severe recession blanketed Oklahoma. Economic stress was compounded for Oklahomans by embarrassment and outrage when corruption in county government was uncovered by the Federal Bureau of Investigation.

County government since statehood had been dominated by county commissioners. Oklahoma counties were divided into three districts, each with its own commissioner who oversaw the maintenance of roads and bridges. As a group they also controlled the budgets of their counties. The commissioners became powerful, establishing budgets and spending public funds with little or no oversight. Controlling many jobs, they became powerful politically, as it became difficult for individuals to win election to local offices or to the Legislature if

Busts of the governors of Oklahoma are displayed in the State Capitol. Among those who gathered for the dedication of the bust of Governor Frank Keating in January 2003 were, left to right, former Governor David L. Walters, Lieutenant Governor Mary Fallin, sculptor Jo Saylors, Governor Keating, former Governor George Nigh, former Governor Henry Bellmon, and Betty Price, Executive Director of the Oklahoma Arts Council. (Courtesy Oklahoma Arts Council)

opposed by commissioners. The FBI's "OKSCAM" probe revealed that commissioners statewide had been taking kickbacks from vendors who were paid inflated amounts for goods and services purchased by the commissioners. Moreover, the practice had been going on for decades. Ultimately, of the state's 231 county commissioners more than 200 of them were indicted in federal courts, and many of them were convicted. Among the reforms enacted was a requirement that commissioners must use the state's central purchasing office, a change that exposed their expenditures to outside scrutiny.

Former governor and United States Senator Henry Bellmon was elected governor in November of 1986, becoming the first governor to be elected to non-consecutive terms. In his second term as governor, he attempted to maximize the efficiency of state government during a period in which the state's economy had not recovered from recession. Bellmon had been replaced in the United States Senate in 1980 by Don Nickles of Ponca City, and when David Boren resigned from the Senate in 1994, he was replaced by Republican James Inhofe of Tulsa. When Nickles retired in 2005, he was replaced by Republican Tom Coburn of Muskogee. Citizens of the state have sent a strong majority of Republicans to Congress since 1980.

Bellmon chose not to seek reelection as governor in 1990 and was succeeded by Democrat David L. Walters of Canute. The first governor from the far western part of the state, Walters benefited from an improving state economy, was able to increase education funding by 30 percent, and secured a $350 million bond issue for higher education. He also promoted and secured passage of a Quality Jobs program to encourage companies to establish business operations in Oklahoma. He chose not to seek election to a second term.

Frank A. Keating of Tulsa followed Walters in the Governor's Mansion. Keating promoted the largest road building program in state history to date, pushed a significant cut in the state's income tax through the Legislature, and promoted policies that resulted in a decline in the number of welfare recipients in the state. He also served ably as the state's representative to the world following the devastating bombing of the Alfred P. Murrah Federal Building in Oklahoma City on April 19, 1995. During his second term, he secured passage in 2001 of a Right-to-Work law, which advocates believed would make Oklahoma more competitive with other states in the region in attracting new businesses.

Shawnee native Brad Henry won the gubernatorial race in 2002. A

Democrat, Henry presided over a government in which the Lieutenant Governor, Mary Fallin, was a Republican, and the Republicans controlled the House of Representatives while the Democrats clung to control of the Senate. Yet he managed to keep his campaign promise of establishing a state lottery with the bulk of proceeds being pledged to support education. As he neared the end of his term, the state began experiencing a new energy boom, primarily based on natural gas production, that enabled Henry and the Legislature in 2006 to enact significant tax cuts while increasing funding for teacher salaries and other state employees and for other aspects of state government.

As Oklahoma ended its first century of statehood, its politics had become intensely competitive. Throughout the previous 100 years, the balance of power between the two major parties in the state had continually shifted—a circumstance that likely will continue throughout Oklahoma's second century.

The bombing of the Alfred P. Murrah Federal Building in Oklahoma City on April 19, 1995 was a horrific event that required strong leadership from state and local officials to deal with the immediate emergency, the rescue and recovery operations, and the long-term rebuilding process. (Courtesy Oklahoma Publishing Company)

Paula Marshall: Quest for Quality

The failure of Penn Square Bank in Oklahoma City in 1982 dramatically signaled the end of the oil and gas boom that had fueled Oklahoma's economy in the late 1970s and early 1980s. The energy bust that followed, when combined with hard times in the state's agricultural sector, caused the state's economy to spiral downward and remain depressed for more than a decade. Yet, even during this difficult period, some Oklahoma companies thrived. Businesses that were not tied directly to oil and gas and did not depend primarily on the local economy had a chance to prosper, especially if they enjoyed dynamic leadership. One such business was Bama Pie, headquartered in Tulsa, Oklahoma, and led by Paula Marshall.

Marshall took the reins of a sound company in 1984 and soon began a quest to enhance the quality of products and service. Through the years, she proved to be an outstanding executive while also fulfilling the roles of wife and mother in a family that eventually grew to four children. Her efforts were recognized many times over the last 20 years, culminating in 2004 when The Bama Companies, Inc., received the Malcolm Baldrige National Quality Award in the manufacturing category. Marshall's company was the first Oklahoma business to receive the coveted award, and it was a tribute not only to Marshall's vision but also to the company's hardworking, dedicated workforce.

The company that had grown so remarkably under Marshall's leadership had its origins in the work of Marshall's grandmother, Cornelia Alabama Marshall. When her husband, H. C. Marshall, lost his job, Cornelia began making pies to be sold at a lunch counter. They proved to be so popular that she soon was making 75 pies per day. H. C. loaded her pies on a truck and drove a route through the city to sell them. Even though Cornelia was not fond of the nickname "Bama," H. C. suggested the name "The Bama Pie Company." Cornelia and H. C.'s children helped with the fledgling business, and their son Paul grew to love it. It was Paul and his young wife Lilah who moved to Tulsa in 1937 to make it big in the pie business. They

Paula Marshall

worked long hours as they slowly built their company, operating a retail store and selling to local businesses.

Paul achieved a major breakthrough in the development of their business in 1967 when, after two years of intensive effort, he reached an agreement to provide fried pies for the McDonald's chain nationwide. This required a dramatic expansion of production facilities, machinery, and staff, but it allowed economies of scale, along with an efficient labor force, to lower the unit cost of the pies.

Meanwhile, Paul and Lilah's children—John, Roger, and Paula—each were involved with various aspects of the company. The youngest child, Paula, began working at the plant on 11th Street when she was in high school. By the time she graduated in 1970, she was working full time. She first worked in the company's retail shop and then helped Lilah in the office, handling filing and bookkeeping among other chores.

As McDonald's continued to grow rapidly, so did Bama Pies. Soon Paul and Lilah realized that they needed to invest in new technology that had become available. Paula went to Chicago for training on the new computer system, and when she returned to Tulsa, she took charge of the computer room. Her father observed that Paula "was a natural. The financial reports she could generate for me on a moments notice were amazing." Paula also used the new system

to keep up with inventory and purchasing, thereby learning the details of the business. Over time, Paul and Lilah felt increasingly comfortable in going on business trips and even vacations, knowing that they had quality employees and Paula to keep the operation running smoothly in their absence.

Paula and her parents also valued education, so they decided that Paula should earn a college degree in business. She did that at Oklahoma City University, graduating in 1982. By this time her father realized that Paula had outstanding people skills. He moved her out of the computer room and placed her in charge of increasing sales by developing new accounts. In 1981

she demonstrated her capabilities while working with McDonald's to develop a frozen biscuit. The effort ultimately failed because of technical problems, but Paula emerged from the process as a strong leader, and the relationship with McDonald's preserved. When the plant foreman retired, Lilah informed Paul that Paula had anticipated the retirement and had been preparing. She had the knowledge and the "moxie" to keep things running efficiently. Paula became the plant foreman. In 1984 Paul and Lilah retired and Paula took over the operation. With both formal education and practical experience, she was determined to succeed.

Paula had her hands full, running an

(Facing page) Paula Marshall of Tulsa has emphasized quality in her company's products so effectively that her company became the first in Oklahoma to receive the Malcolm Baldrige National Quality Award in the manufacturing category. (Courtesy The Bama Companies)

One of Marshall's strengths as an executive has been her ability to motivate employees. Here she is speaking at an employee retirement party. (Courtesy The Bama Companies)

operation that employed 450 people, and making a million pies per day for McDonald's and nearly as many for other customers. Her father was so impressed by her performance that he bought her a personalized car tag that read "BAMA II". She reminded him of his mother, the original "Bama." Paula was determined to broaden the company's market and products, and in 1987 Bama began producing "Ready to Heat Biscuits," which became a staple in the fast food industry.

Paula also became known for her devotion to quality. When McDonald's suggested that she increase the number of inspectors at the end of the production process to enhance quality control, she determined that this approach would increase costs without significantly improving the quality of the product. Instead, she read a book by Phil Crosby that emphasized the principle of Total Quality Management. Paula adopted this approach, satisfied McDonald's, and then over time modified the program to create the Bama Quality Process. The primary goals of the process were to maximize customer satisfaction and foster continuous improvement in service and quality of products. This was accomplished by encouraging customer feedback, by responding to that feedback quickly, by encouraging employees to contribute their insights and practical suggestions to improve

efficiency and quality, and by engaging in comprehensive, long-term planning. As a result, Paula won the Philip Crosby Quality Fanatic of the Year Award in 1989.

These efforts quickly paid off as Bama's business continued to grow rapidly and awards for quality were received. In 1992 the company went international as Bama opened a production facility in Beijing, China, which was expanded in 1998. Marshall's accomplishments were recognized in 1993 when she was awarded a Doctor of Commercial Science degree by her alma mater. That same year, Pizza Hut became a new customer. In 1994 Bama won the Oklahoma Quality Award and in 1996 received the McDonald's Sweeney Excellence Award.

Meanwhile, the company's Tulsa facilities continued to expand. Ever mindful that people make the company, Marshall continuously looked for ways to reward employees for excellence. A generous profit sharing plan was inaugurated as was a tuition reimbursement plan to encourage employees to earn college degrees. This focus on people and the customer resulted in Bama receiving Pizza Hut's Supplier of the Year and Innovator of the Year awards in 2002 and 2003.

By the time Marshall's company received the Baldrige Award in 2004, it operated four production facilities in Tulsa and two in China. The company employed 1,100 people and generated more than $200 million

per year in revenues. Its three primary products—pies, pizza crust, and biscuits—accounted for 92 percent of revenues. The company was honored yet again in January 2006 when McDonald's presented its 2005 U. S. Quality Supplier Award to The Bama Companies, Inc.

By this time Paula Marshall had received numerous personal awards, but she was not prepared to rest on her laurels. Instead, she was focused on planning for the future. Marshall and her leadership team expected continued double digit growth and recognition for world-class quality, while remaining the supplier of choice in its target markets and providing employees and other stakeholders with "unparalleled personal and financial goals." For Marshall, the business climate and the people of Oklahoma were major positives. When asked in 2006 if she might consider moving her company's headquarters elsewhere, she responded, "Oklahoma has been good to my family—and me. The people here have always been so supportive and loyal. Leave Oklahoma? What on earth for?"

In the latter half of the twentieth century, companies like Bama had played an important role in diversifying Oklahoma's economy. Manufacturing, service industries, advanced technology, and tourism had joined energy and agriculture as economic pillars for the Sooner State in the twenty-first century.

The skyline of Tulsa is that of a modern prosperous city. With petroleum-related companies declining as a source of employment, companies in other fields, such as The Bama Companies, have contributed significantly to Tulsa's growth. (Courtesy Jim Argo)

Sports Heroes:
Tradition of Excellence

By 1982 Oklahoma had a well-deserved reputation in the world of sports for producing outstanding teams and dominant athletes. That reputation would be reinforced during the subsequent 25 years by many teams in a variety of sports and by a significant number of individuals. Prominent among the exceptional athletes were Steve Largent, Wayman Tisdale, John Smith, and Shannon Miller.

Largent was born in Tulsa in 1954, graduated from Putnam City High School in Oklahoma City in 1972, and starred at Tulsa University as a wide receiver, twice leading the nation in touchdown receptions. He was considered to have only average speed and size by National Football League standards, so he was the 117th player taken in the 1976 NFL draft. During his 14-year career with the Seattle Seahawks, he set six major NFL career pass receiving records, including most receptions (819), most yards on receptions (13,089), and most touchdowns on receptions (100). Largent proved to be amazingly durable, missing only four games during his entire NFL career.

Largent was recognized as NFL Man of the Year in 1988 for his commitment to community service, and he became the first Seahawk to be inducted into the Pro Football Hall of Fame in 1995. He returned to Tulsa in 1989, was elected to Congress in 1994, and served until leaving office

Olympic wrestler John Smith had the honor of lighting the flame to open the United States Olympic Festival before a packed house at Memorial Stadium on the campus of the University of Oklahoma on the evening of July 22, 1988. The 10-day festival was the culmination of months of intense work on the part of volunteers headed by Lee Allan Smith of OK Events in Oklahoma City. The world-class event helped lift the spirits of Oklahomans whose state had been mired in economic difficulties as a result of the oil and gas bust and agricultural recession of the 1980s. (Courtesy Oklahoma Publishing Company)

in 2002 to make what proved to be an unsuccessful run for the office of governor of Oklahoma.

A native Tulsan born in 1964, Tisdale was a star basketball player at Tulsa Washington High School before becoming one of the most outstanding players in college basketball history at the University of Oklahoma. A 6-foot, 9-inch power forward, Tisdale was the first freshman to be named first-team All-American by the Associated Press, and he was the first player to be named first-team All-American by the AP as a freshman, sophomore, and junior. He led the Big Eight Conference in scoring for three consecutive years and was named Big Eight Player of the Year three times. He set career school records for points (2,661), rebounds (1,048), field goals (1,077), field goal percentage (.578), free throws (507) and free throw attempts (767). He was the first athlete in any sport to have his jersey number retired at OU.

During Tisdale's 12-year NBA career with the Indiana Pacers, Sacramento Kings, and Phoenix Suns, he scored more than 12,000 points and snagged more than 5,000 rebounds. While playing pro basketball, Tisdale formed a jazz band and played bass guitar, a skill he had developed as a youth. His music career blossomed after he retired from basketball, and within eight years he had become a nationally known musician with six CDs in distribution.

Del City native John Smith became the most dominant amateur wrestler in the world, winning an unprecedented six world championships, including Olympic Gold Medals in 1988 and 1992. Relying on superior speed, technique, balance, and conditioning, Smith became a dominant wrestler at Oklahoma State University from 1984 to 1988. In 1987 he became the first individual to win a world championship in wrestling while still a college student. He became the first amateur wrestler to receive the James E. Sullivan Award as the nation's top amateur athlete in 1990, and the United States Olympic Committee named him Sportsman of the Year in 1990.

Smith began his coaching career as an assistant wrestling coach at OSU in 1989, three years before concluding his wrestling career in 1992. He took over as head wrestling coach at his alma mater after the 1991 season, when the program was hit with sanctions by the NCAA. The program remained on probation until 1994. Smith held the program together and then brought it back to prominence. Beginning in 2003, he led the team to four consecutive NCAA championships and had gained recognition as one of the best collegiate coaches in the nation.

While Smith was earning Olympic glory at Barcelona, Spain, in 1992, Shannon Miller also was there, establishing herself as a dominating international figure in gymnastics. Born in Missouri in 1977, Shannon Miller moved to Edmond, Oklahoma, with her parents when she was six months old. For awhile she had to wear corrective braces on her legs. Nonetheless, at age four she began her gymnastics training. She began serious training with renowned coach Steve Nunno at age eight, and at 11 she placed second all-around and won four medals at the Junior Pan American Games in Puerto Rico. By 1990 she had become the youngest gymnast ever on the senior national team. Miller finished second all-around at the 1992 Olympics. She won the all-around world championships in 1993 and 1994, becoming the first American to win two such championships.

Although Miller was six inches taller and 25 pounds heavier than she had been at Barcelona, at the 1996 Olympics she led the American women's team to the team gold medal, the first in United States gymnastics history. She won the gold medal in the balance beam event, becoming the first American to do so. Miller earned 42 international medals during her career, becoming the most decorated gymnast in U. S. history. After retiring from the sport, she graduated from the University of Oklahoma and entered law school in Boston, Massachusetts.

Oklahomans are proud of University of Oklahoma graduate Bart Connor, the most decorated male gymnast in the history of the sport. Connor married Olympic gymnast Nadia Comaneci and the couple settled in Oklahoma where they have pursued various business interests as well as work in television. He was inducted into the U. S. Olympics Hall of Fame in 1991 and into the International Gymnastics Hall of Fame in 1996. (Courtesy Oklahoma Historical Society)

Patricia Breilh Fennell: Coming to Oklahoma

Because of its relative youth and unique history, Oklahoma is populated by people who either are new arrivals or descendants of individuals who arrived here in the fairly recent past. Most of the Indian tribes now associated with Oklahoma were forced to move here from other parts of the United States. Virtually all of the non-Indian settlement of the state began after 1865. The lure of opportunity on the frontier—the possibility of obtaining land in land runs and even a land lottery, the prospect of working in the coal mines of Indian Territory, or the hope of prospering in oil fields throughout much of the state—attracted both native-born Americans and first-generation immigrants from foreign lands to Oklahoma. This trend continued in the twentieth century as various economic and political factors fueled an influx of Asian and Hispanic immigrants into the state. Like immigrants of other nationalities and different eras, they have contributed to the state's economic growth and cultural richness, and many have made outstanding personal contributions. One such individual is Patricia Breilh Fennell.

Pat Fennell was born in Quito, Ecuador, in 1941. Her mother, Germania Paz y Mino, was a renowned artist and her father, Eduardo Breilh, was a prominent banker. Both parents were well educated and believed that they had an obligation to help others, especially children. This commitment to social obligation ultimately influenced her choice of social work as a career.

Pat's first visit to the United States came as a result of her mother's friendship with a woman from Buffalo, New York, which was based on their mutual interest in contemporary Ecuadorian art. This friendship soon included members of both women's extended families and resulted in a family-to-family cultural exchange program. Pat thus was afforded the opportunity to live with members of her host family in Hamburg, New York. Although she had graduated from high school and had completed a year and a half of college work in Ecuador, she attended high school in New York, improved her English skills, and attended Bryant & Stratton Business Institute for a year. She returned home where she studied political science at the Central University of Ecuador from 1960 to 1962.

Her proficiency in English and experience in the United States helped Pat obtain a job at the United States Embassy in Quito while she was a student. After two years at the embassy,

Patricia Breilh Fennell

she met a young United States marine who was stationed at the embassy. An Oklahoma native, he had completed two years of college at Cameron University in Lawton. The couple was living in California when he left the Marine Corps, and Pat pushed him to complete his college education. To do that, the couple, who by now had two boys, moved from California to Lawton. Pat worked until her husband completed his degree and then enrolled at the University of Central Oklahoma at Edmond. She continued to work, eventually earning her Bachelor of Arts in Sociology and Psychology in 1975. Her family agreed that she should continue to work fulltime and pursue a graduate degree, with the understanding that the men of the house would have to handle household chores and cooking. At first, this led to some "hilarious meals" and white underwear turned pink in the laundry. During this time she began working at Children's Hospital in Oklahoma City and eventually earned a Master of Social Work degree from the University of Oklahoma in 1980.

At Children's Hospital, Pat was able to exercise her creativity in patient education, preparing children and their families for varied treatments and procedures. She obtained permission to use Hanna Barbera cartoon characters to produce a video on Bedrock Children's Hospital, featuring Fred Flintstone and his family and friends. The

approach proved to be highly successful and received national attention. She also observed that children with chronic illnesses often are overprotected by their families. This led her to suggest establishing a camp for children on dialysis. A cabin at Beaver's Bend was rewired and fitted with freezers to store special foods for the youngsters so their basic needs were met. Cooks, doctors, and nurses also accompanied the children who were allowed to have the same experiences of healthy children at camp. The program was so successful it made the national news. Later an entire camp was transformed to serve as a medical camp.

After 12 years at the hospital, Fennell was ready for new challenges. She accepted a job with the Central Oklahoma Community Council, led by William J. Bross, who proved to be a "tough boss but an incredible mentor." She worked two years there and the experience, she believed, was worth as much to her as all her years of formal education. In 1987 she was asked by the United Way of Oklahoma City to chair a task force to identify Hispanic men and women in the community who could be trained to serve on non-profit boards and commissions. She also became involved in founding the Oklahoma Hispanic Professional Association, serving as president. Pat enjoyed these activities as she began to reconnect with her Hispanic

Hispanic culture is vibrant in Oklahoma. Shannon Calderon, with Anything Goes Dance Studio in Oklahoma City, performs during Bricktown's Cinco de Mayo celebration on May 4, 2003. (Courtesy Oklahoma Publishing Company)

(Facing page) In building the Latino Community Development Agency, Pat Fennell often joined volunteers and employees in completing whatever task was at hand. Here she is working on a mailing at the agency's headquarters, ca. 1993. (Courtesy Latino Community Development Agency)

heritage and learn what was happening in the Latino community.

While chairing the task force, Pat accepted a job with Healthy Futures, an organization dedicated to reducing the mortality rate among infants. She served as the coordinator for a 16-county area in central Oklahoma. This job provided valuable administrative experience. She also found time to serve as president of the Oklahoma Chapter of the National Association of Social Workers. After about one year, Pat's task force was asked to facilitate the creation of an agency to serve the Latino community to replace one that had been disbanded. The United Way made $42,000 available to get the new agency started. The Oklahoma City Community Council and the Neighborhood Services Organization submitted a joint proposal to help sponsor and mentor a new organization and then, when it was ready, have it become an independent agency. Thus, the Latino Community Development Agency was born and Pat was named executive director in April 1991.

The agency began with a $42,000 annual budget and two employees—Pat and a secretary. She immediately began writing grant proposals and formulating programs to benefit the Hispanic community. An early challenge, because of her Ecuadorian heritage, involved gaining the trust of the larger

Latino community, which was dominated by Mexican-Americans. She accomplished this by demonstrating that the organization was dedicated to benefiting all elements of the Hispanic community. Her career to date was recognized in 1992 when she was named State Social Worker of the Year.

The rapidly growing agency soon needed more space in which to operate. Fennell and her board of directors quickly targeted the vacant Riverside Elementary School building at 421 Southwest 11th Street. After months of delays and "red tape," the persistent leader obtained the beautiful, 30,000-square-foot structure and began raising money and recruiting volunteers to renovate the building. Restoring and using this building, important to the heritage of the Hispanic neighborhood in which it was located, helped spark a new pride among area residents. Fennell and her agency moved into the building in November of 1995 and soon had the organization's tutoring program for students in operation. Other programs, often partnerships with other organizations, included English language courses, a General Educational Development high school equivalency program, literacy and computer classes, a gang prevention program, a health clinic, and a senior citizen's center. By 2006, with a staff of 50 and an amazing array of programs and activities headquartered in the community

center, Pat Fennell had become a widely-respected spokesperson for the Latino community.

In the late 1990s the Oklahoma Department of Transportation and community leaders announced plans to move the route of Interstate Highway 40 through downtown Oklahoma City to the south. As initially proposed, the new road would damage and perhaps destroy the Hispanic Riverside neighborhood. Fennell in 1999 voiced strong opposition and through legal action threatened to delay or even end the project. Strongly condemned in some quarters, Fennell observed, "I've always fought for justice, and this is not the first time I've fought for a cause that isn't particular popular." Fennell stood her ground and eventually won changes in the plans for the highway that ultimately made the relocation acceptable to the Hispanic community.

By 2006 Fennell had received numerous honors in recognition of her effective work, including serving as chair of the board of directors of the Oklahoma City Branch of the Federal Reserve Bank of Kansas City; being a director of the National Council of La Raza, a powerful national Latino organization; and serving as a member of the state's Human Rights Commission. She had honored the values of her family and her Hispanic culture and had given voice to the Latino community in Oklahoma City.

Reflecting the growing Asian community in Oklahoma, Mai Ly Do in January 2005 delivers her daily broadcast of local and international news in Vietnamese from a small office on North Classen Boulevard in Oklahoma City. (Courtesy Oklahoma Publishing Company)

Innovation and Determination: Creative Oklahomans

Creative Oklahomans during the latter part of the twentieth and early twenty-first centuries continued to demonstrate the innovative genius and determination characterized by their predecessors. Among many who could be cited were Greg Burns, Reba McEntire, Garth Brooks, and Edgar Cruz.

Burns was born in Fort Worth, Texas, in 1947 and moved with his family to Chickasha, Oklahoma, when he was five. He had been born with Arthrogryposis, a disorder that adversely impacted the joints of his arms and legs and made it difficult for him to grasp a pen. Nonetheless, his mother encouraged him to draw, and he soon realized that he had an eye for detail and a talent for art. He learned to paint holding a paint brush in his teeth, graduated from Bishop McGuinness High School in Oklahoma City, and in 1971 earned a degree in drawing and printmaking from the University of Oklahoma. By this time he already was recognized regionally and beyond.

Burns' career received a boost when he married Patricia Campbell in 1978. She provided both sound business management and a wonderful home life. In 1986 the couple opened Greg Burns Fine Art & Framing in Oklahoma City, a place where patrons could purchase Greg's critically-acclaimed original watercolors or prints and have them framed. The successful business was closed in 2006 when the couple decided that it was time for "more freedom and less responsibility." Burns' works, many of them featuring historic structures and sites in Oklahoma, remained available to collectors via his internet website and participation in various art shows. He continued to paint, feeling "like the most fortunate person in the world because I love what I do."

Edgar Cruz of Oklahoma City is internationally known for his virtuosity on the guitar. (Courtesy Oklahoma Publishing Company)

Doc Tate Nevaquaya was an outstanding Comanche artist and flute player. Here he was taking a break from his painting by playing his flute. Named a State Treasure in 1995 by the Oklahoma Arts Council, he died in 1996. (Courtesy Oklahoma Publishing Company).

Reba McEntire parlayed her love of rodeo and music into a remarkable career. Born near Kiowa, Oklahoma, in southern Pittsburg County, she grew up on a ranch in Atoka County in a prominent rodeo family infused with musical talent. For a while she was a barrel racer and sang with her two sisters and brother. In 1974 country music star Red Steagall heard her perform the National Anthem at the National Finals Rodeo in Oklahoma City. He helped her to launch a solo career. She signed a contract with Mercury Records in 1975, married Charley Battles, a professional rodeo cowboy, and completed her degree in education at Southeastern State University at Durant.

She had some initial success, but after signing with MCA Records in 1984, she quickly became a dominant country music star. Reba's remarkable vocal range and ability to convey emotion set her apart, as did her innovative use of videos to interpret her music. Her marriage to Battles ended in 1987, and in 1989 she married Narvel Blackstock. The pair took over the management of her career, and her record sales continued to soar. Between 1985 and 1992 she had 24 consecutive Top Ten hits, including 14 number one singles. She also launched what would become a successful acting career and performed on Broadway. She set new standards for concert performances and proved that female country performers could "match the boys" in concert ticket and record sales. More than 30 years after she initiated her career, she remained one of the most prominent and honored stars in country music.

Singer and songwriter Garth Brooks was encouraged by the success of McEntire, Vince Gill, and other Oklahomans to pursue his dream. Born in Tulsa in 1962, Brooks was raised in Yukon and graduated from Oklahoma State University in 1984. He had become a successful artist on the local scene and decided in 1985 to go to Nashville to secure a record contract. This effort failed. He returned to Oklahoma, married Sandy Mahl, and the couple moved to Nashville in 1987. By 1988 he had a contract with Capitol Records. His self-titled, first album in 1989 was a hit on both the country and pop album charts, foreshadowing his future success as a "crossover" artist.

In 1990 Brooks' album *No Fences* became his greatest selling album, with more than 20 million copies sold internationally. Influenced by rock musicians Billy Joel and Bruce Springsteen, he routinely sold out huge stadiums for his visually stunning and musically memorable performances. He went on to dominate the 1990s with more than 70 hit singles, 15 charted albums, and more than 115 million albums sold in the

Blues legend D. C. Minner and his wife Shelby are shown in their home in Rentiesville. The Minners perform regularly at their Down Home Blues Club where the stated hours of operation are "dusk to dawn." The Minners also organize the Annual Dusk to Dawn Blues Festival in Rentiesville each September. (Courtesy Oklahoma Publishing Company)

United States alone. Brooks retired from touring and recording in 1999 to spend more time with his children. His marriage ended in 2001, and he married country music star Trisha Yearwood in 2005.

While Brooks returned to Oklahoma, Edgar Cruz never departed his home state. Born in Oklahoma City in 1962 to Manuel and Joann Cruz, Edgar at age 14 began playing the Mexican bass in Mexican restaurants with his talented father, who played guitar. By the time he graduated from Northwest Classen High School in 1980, he had learned to play rock music by ear. He studied classical guitar at Oklahoma City University but noted that his father played a wide range of music to please his audiences. Edgar resolved to learn to do that as well.

After graduation, Cruz continued to expand his repertoire. Audiences were mesmerized by his virtuosity on acoustic guitar, which he would amplify for large audiences. A fingerstyle guitarist, he plucked the strings with his fingernails rather than using a pick. He also developed an ability to play multiple parts of a song—bass, rhythm, and melody—and began to write transcriptions of various songs for solo guitar. His performance of Queen's "Bohemian Rhapsody" brought him international attention. One critic described him as a "wizard" for his ability to capture the sound of an entire band and produce it on solo guitar. By 2006 Cruz had released 15 CDs and two DVDs and was performing approximately 250 times a year in Oklahoma, the United States, and in Europe. But he continued to live in Oklahoma City, because for Edgar "it is home," a good place to enjoy life with his wife and daughter.

A significant cultural activity in Oklahoma is the Oklahoma Summer Arts Institute at Quartz Mountain State Park. Students from all parts of the state study the visual and performing arts under the direction of internationally

Oklahoma's Reba McEntire has enjoyed a remarkable career as one of the most popular female recording artists in the history of country music. (Courtesy Oklahoma Heritage Association)

Larry W. Brummett and David L. Kyle: Best Friends

During the 1980s the oil and natural gas industry in Oklahoma enjoyed a spectacular boom and a disastrous bust, caused in large part by the federal government's clumsy attempt to deregulate the natural gas industry over a two-decade period. At the depths of the crisis, executives at ONEOK, Inc., the parent company of Oklahoma Natural Gas Company, did not know how they were going to make the payroll that was due in less than one week. Yet, under the capable leadership of J. D. Scott, ONEOK managed to survive, regain financial stability, and resume its growth. Scott was aided in this successful effort by a strong board of directors and a capable group of executives, including two younger men who were being groomed and evaluated for possible elevation to the chief executive officer position upon Scott's retirement.

Scott knew that the deregulation of the natural gas industry would accelerate in the 1990s, so he began his search for his successor almost as soon as he became CEO in 1986. He knew that the next leader of the corporation would have to make major changes in the corporate structure and culture to prosper in the increasingly competitive natural gas industry. Two men eventually emerged as Scott and his management team evaluated individuals who had been through the company's engineer trainee program. They were David L. Kyle and Larry W. Brummett.

During the latter half of the 1980s both men were placed in various positions of increasing responsibility, which gave them broad experience in the company's operations and allowed Scott to evaluate their performance. Impressed with both Brummett and Kyle, Scott arranged for both of them to complete Harvard Business School's Advanced Management Program.

Larry W. Brummett and David L. Kyle

When Kyle and Brummett were appointed to executive vice president positions, it was clear that the two were being put into direct competition for the top leadership position. Some believed this would create an intense rivalry that could only harm the company, but those individuals did not understand the relationship that developed between Kyle and Brummett.

Brummett and Kyle had started to work for ONG in 1974 on the same day at the same location. They were even dressed similarly that day. They maintained a good relationship as each moved through various assignments within the company. Even as it became apparent that they were being scrutinized for future leadership, they became close friends. One evening in the late 1980s they met for dinner and candidly discussed the future. They agreed that they could accomplish more "working together" than they could "bumping heads." They made a "pact" that neither of them would do anything to harm the other. "We would always try to do what was best for the company and help the other," Kyle later recalled, and that is what they did. From that point forward, as Kyle said, "it was a team effort."

Scott faced a difficult decision. He knew that both of them were highly intelligent and had outstanding leadership skills. He believed that he could not go wrong in selecting either of them. Scott did

(Facing page) David Kyle, left, and Larry Brummett were "best friends" even while both were being considered for the chief executive officer position at ONEOK. Their determination to work together and to put the interests of the company above their individual goals was a significant factor in the dramatic growth of ONEOK from 1994 to the present. (Courtesy ONEOK Inc.)

The natural gas industry in Oklahoma was booming as Oklahoma neared its centennial celebration. Among the companies leading the way in exploration in Oklahoma was Chesapeake Energy. Here a crew is working on a gas well near Marlow, Oklahoma. (Courtesy Oklahoma Publishing Company)

observe that Brummett was an extrovert who enjoyed public appearances, giving speeches, and interacting with large or small groups of people. Kyle was more of an introvert. Brummett was comfortable with the public relations role that the CEO position demanded, and in the end that is what inclined Scott to select him to be the next CEO, beginning in February 1994.

Born in Tulsa, Brummett had spent much of his life in Oklahoma City and graduated from U. S. Grant High School in 1968 before earning bachelor's and master's degrees in civil engineering from the University of Oklahoma, where he became a serious Sooner fan, husband, and father. Yet Brummett indicated that what he had learned from his father, an Assembly of God minister, and his mother had "infinitely more application than what I learned in engineering school. I am talking about dealing with people. Values. Ethics. Doing what is right. Having a work ethic." By 1994 by virtue of his values, education, and training at ONEOK, he was prepared to lead the company. When a vacancy occurred due to a retirement, he lost little time in asking the board of directors to add Kyle to the board and to make him president of Oklahoma Natural Gas Company. Kyle later would be named president and chief operating officer of ONEOK.

Brummett believed that ONEOK had

to become "leaner, flatter, more efficient, better able to respond, an organization that reduces process bureaucracy to free up time and make people more productive. We have to reduce our red tape." Change would be dramatic and continuous, Brummett observed, because this would be required to compete in the increasingly competitive natural gas industry. The company would be in a "constant state of becoming."

Under their leadership, ONEOK began to grow dramatically, expanding the activities of various subsidiary companies in storage, processing, marketing, and transportation of natural gas for other companies through an ever expanding network of gas pipelines. Brummett was a popular CEO both within the company and the community. He was active in a wide range of industry and civic organizations. Both Brummett and ONEOK were on a major roll when in May of 1998 came stunning news; Brummett was diagnosed with cancer of the small intestine. As Brummett began his battle with cancer, Kyle was there to work closely with Larry in running the company. During the summer, Brummett had surgery followed by an aggressive chemotherapy program. By the fall, it was believed that that the surgery was successful and that Brummett would return to complete health, although the possibility of a recurrence of the disease was understood.

Unfortunately, Brummett's cancer returned and he underwent aggressive chemotherapy. He worked as much as he could and relied on Kyle's friendship and strong leadership capabilities. The company continued to prosper. In November of 1999, when Brummett was to be inducted into the Oklahoma Hall of Fame, his scheduled presenter, Congressman J. C. Watts, was detained in Washington, D. C. Brummett turned to his best friend, Kyle, to present him for induction. When Brummett came forward to acknowledge his induction, the physical toll that cancer and aggressive chemotherapy treatments had taken was obvious. Bald and thin, Brummett's upbeat remarks, his humility, and his recognition of the many people who had made his successes possible left many in the room with tear-streaked faces. It was, as Kyle later recalled, "a special evening."

Brummett fought his disease valiantly, but he died on August 24, 2000, just one week short of his 50th birthday. Under his leadership, ONEOK had grown in assets from $1 billion to $5 billion. Four days later, Kyle was elevated to the chairman of the board, president, and chief executive officer, positions that Brummett had occupied.

Kyle had grown up in Oklahoma City, was a John Marshall High School graduate, and had graduated with an engineering degree from Oklahoma State University in

1974. In addition to his Harvard Business School training, he had earned an MBA degree from Tulsa University in 1987. By the time he assumed the leadership of ONEOK, he was well prepared through intellect and experience. He had learned to overcome his inherent shyness and was confident in himself and in his management team. He continued on the course that he and Brummett had plotted for ONEOK. Constantly evaluating the corporation's structure, strategy, and mix of assets, he was always on the outlook for strategic acquisitions that would add value to the company. By 2006, under Kyle's stewardship, ONEOK had more than doubled in size, controlled a pipeline network that extended from the Canadian border to the coast of the Gulf of Mexico, and, as an industry analyst observed, was "as broadly integrated an energy company as there is in America today."

ONEOK's withdrawal from the production of natural gas left that role to companies such as Chesapeake Energy and Devon Energy, both headquartered in Oklahoma City. Instead, the company become a major force in storing, processing, transporting, and marketing natural gas under the dynamic leadership of Larry Brummett and David Kyle, best friends who had put the interests of their company and its stockholders above their own.

In the early 1990s Tulsa's Gilcrease Museum underwent a $12.5 million expansion. The sculpture in front of the entrance is Allan Houser's *Sacred Rain Arrow*. (Courtesy Oklahoma Publishing Company)

Oklahoma's Miss Americas

Since 1921 the Miss America Pageant annually has sought to identify the ideal American woman. When the competition began in 1921, it reflected the changing views of women in the United States, as it continued to do into the twenty-first century. In the two decades preceding the first pageant, the role of women expanded socially, culturally, and politically. By the "Roaring Twenties" the ideal woman was expected to be physically fit and vigorous, rather than delicate or fragile. The Miss American Pageant in the 1920s began as a beauty pageant. Over the years, the pageant continued to evolve, reflecting the ever changing role of women in society, so that intelligence, talent, speaking ability, and poise became primary considerations along with physical fitness and beauty in selecting Miss Americas.

By 2006, 79 women had been crowned Miss America and five of them were Oklahomans, a remarkable number considering Oklahoma is one of 50 states and is relatively small in terms of population. The state's first

Three of Oklahoma's five Miss Americas were united during the program that accompanied the dedication of the Oklahoma State Capitol Dome on the evening of Saturday, November 16, 2002. They were, left to right, Shawntel Smith Wuerch, Jane Jayroe Gamble, and Susan Powell. (Courtesy Oklahoma Publishing Company)

Miss America was Norma Smallwood of Tulsa. At age 18 the Bristow native entered the pageant held at Atlantic City, New Jersey, as Miss Tulsa. There was no Miss Oklahoma Pageant at that time. The young Cherokee woman became the first Native American to hold the Miss America title. She made the most of her reign, earning an estimated $100,000 for public appearances and advertising endorsements. After her year as Miss America, she returned to Oklahoma and in 1928 married Tulsa oilman Thomas Gilcrease. The couple divorced in 1933, and she later married another oilman, George H. Bruce of Wichita, Kansas. She lived quietly thereafter, becoming heavily involved with charity work until her death in 1966.

Forty-one years would pass before another Oklahoman would be crowned Miss America. By 1967 the pageant had changed, with more emphasis being placed on talent, intelligence, and scholarships. The pageant had first been televised nationally in 1954, and by 1967, the first year it was telecast in color, it was attracting large audiences. Jane Jayroe, described as a green-eyed beauty from Laverne, was a music student at Oklahoma City University when she won the Miss America Pageant. During her reign, she went to Vietnam to entertain the troops and traveled an estimated 250,000 miles in meeting her obligations as Miss America. After her year as Miss America, she completed her education and embarked on a successful career in public relations, television news and production, and public service as director of the Oklahoma Department of Tourism and Recreation. She married Gerald Gamble of Oklahoma City in 1994.

Susan Powell of Elk City claimed the Miss America title in 1981. A vocal music major at Oklahoma City University, she impressed judges with her performance of "Lucy's Aria" from the opera The Telephone. In the ensuing years she enjoyed a highly successful career in opera, musical theater, and as a soloist with symphonic orchestras. In 2006 she performed with the Utah Symphony in Salt Lake and with the New Japan Philharmonic in Tokyo, Japan. She also hosted Home Matters, a one-hour series on the Discovery Channel, for nine years.

Yet another talented student from Oklahoma City University, Shawntel Smith of Muldrow, Oklahoma, was crowned Miss America in 1996. Emphasis in the judging by this time had shifted toward more toward interviews and the contestants' ability to articulate their platform—a statement that outlined their commitment to a particular cause or social issue relevant to society. Smith stressed "School to Work" education to help students plan and prepare for careers and emphasized the need for education and training to continue throughout adulthood. Following her year as Miss America, Smith returned to Oklahoma, pursued a public relations career, married Ryan K. Wuerch, and in 2006 was executive vice president of administration of PBH Holdings, a corporation involved in "handheld technology solutions."

Just ten years later, Jennifer Berry, a graduate of Jenks High School and a senior at the University of Oklahoma, was named Miss America for 2006. A talented ballerina, her platform issue was "Building Intolerance to Drunk Driving and Underage Drinking." During her reign Berry teamed with MADD, (Mothers Against Drunk Driving), to promote her message. Following her year as Miss America, she planned to return to OU to earn a master's degree in education and enter the teaching profession.

On the evening of November 16, 2002, Oklahoma's Miss Americas Jane Jayroe Gamble, Susan Powell, and Shawntel Smith Wuerch sang together for the first time to open the gala celebration marking the dedication of the newly constructed dome on the Oklahoma State Capitol in Oklahoma City. Each of them expressed their pride in Oklahoma, and the Oklahomans present for that historic occasion clearly were proud of their Miss Americas.

Wanda L. Bass: Giving Back to Oklahoma

Women always have played prominent roles in Oklahoma's history. Temperance crusader Carrie Nation, prison reformer Kate Barnard, and educator and United States Representative Alice M. Robertson are but three outstanding examples. Yet, only in the latter part of the twentieth century did opportunities for women in certain fields of endeavor, such as business and politics, began to expand significantly. Wanda Bass of McAlester was among those who led the way in business, and in so doing she enhanced the quality of life for present and future generations of Oklahomans.

A native of the East Texas sawmill town of Ewing, Wanda Jones was born in 1927. Although she grew up in Texas, she spent her summers in Oklahoma with her aunts, uncles, and cousins in the Broken Bow area. They taught her "the pride of being an Oklahoman . . . the pride of being what a person could be . . . to be a woman who is self-sufficient, a woman who is secure of her own identity." She also embraced the basic values of hard work and religious faith. The confident young woman graduated from the University of Texas in 1947, ready to face the world with a bachelor's degree in institutional management and nutrition.

Her first job was as a dietitian with the Humble Oil Company at Baytown, Texas in 1948. In 1950 she became a division director in the home service department for the Lone Star Gas Company, helping to develop retail markets for the company. This position took her to Sulphur, Oklahoma, before relocating to Wichita Falls, Texas, to serve as division director. Meanwhile, she had met Clark Bass and the couple fell in love. Clark, who lived in Durant, said that Wichita Falls was too far to travel regularly so they should get married. Wanda had promised her aunts that she would get to know Clark at least a year before marrying him. When the waiting period ended in 1951, they were married, beginning a partnership that lasted 48 years.

Born in Caddo, Oklahoma, in 1912, Clark Bass had graduated from the University of Oklahoma in 1934 with a degree in business administration. His banking career in Durant, Oklahoma, was interrupted by World War II, during which he served in the United States Army Air Corps, reaching the rank of captain. In 1947 he returned to Durant and purchased the

Wanda L. Bass

controlling interest in the Durant National Bank. Wanda moved to Durant to begin her new life as a wife and as an Oklahoman. Over the next 14 years, Clark built his banking business and helped build the economy of the community and region. During that time, Wanda became the mother of three children, Boyd, Louise, and Carlton. Ultimately the boys would follow in their parents' footsteps and become bankers, while Louise would reflect her mother's love of music and become a concert organist.

In 1961 Clark and Wanda moved to Dallas, Texas, where Clark organized a new bank. The couple quickly determined that they missed Oklahoma. When the opportunity came to purchase controlling interest in the First National Bank of McAlester, they made the investment and moved to that Pittsburg County community in 1963. It was to be their last move. For a time, Bass operated his banks in Durant and in Dallas in addition to his new bank in McAlester, but he eventually sold the Durant and Dallas banks to focus on developing his McAlester operation. A compassionate but conservative banker, Bass built the bank's asset base from $15 million in 1963 to more than $400 million by the end of the century. His remarkable success, with Wanda's able assistance, enabled Clark to be named Oklahoma Independent Banker of the Year in 1980. Wanda spent her first 10 years in McAlester completing her duties as a mother

and becoming involved in community affairs.

By 1973 Wanda was ready to restart her own business career and became vice president of the bank. In that capacity, she opened new accounts, worked in public relations, and helped in purchasing. If she saw a "niche that needed to be filled," she did it. Her role in the bank continued to grow. In 1985 she was elected to the institution's board of directors, and in 1992 she was named vice chairman of the board. As Clark's health began to decline in the 1990s Wanda took an ever increasing role in running the bank until Clark's death in 1999, when she became chairman of the board.

As conservative bankers, Clark and Wanda could not help everybody, so they looked for other ways to benefit their community. As the bank prospered, they started giving back in many ways, including an all-weather track at McAlester High School, a $1 million contribution toward what became the Wanda L. Bass Fine Arts Center at the school, and a $2 million contribution toward the establishment of a McAlester campus of Eastern Oklahoma State College, which was completed in 1998. They played a major role in the construction of a new regional hospital in McAlester, and they sponsored a project to preserve the coal mining heritage of the area. This project included the creation of an impressive memorial in a McAlester park to the

(Facing page) Wanda Bass, a prominent banker, civic leader, and philanthropist from McAlester, believed strongly that financially successful businesses and individuals should give back to their communities and state to enhance the quality of life for present and future generations. (Courtesy M. J. Alexander)

Wanda Bass was joined at the dedication of the Wanda Bass School of Music at Oklahoma City University by members of her family. Seated next to her was grandson Noah Bass. Standing, left to right, were her daughter, Louise, and her sons Boyd and Carlton. (Courtesy M. J. Anderson)

pioneer coal miners of the McAlester region, including a black granite memory wall listing the names of more than 1,700 men who died in mining accidents in the area and a bronze sculpture of a coal miner. A bronze sculpture of Carl B. Albert, a member of a local coal mining family who became Speaker of the United States House of Representatives, also was placed in the park.

Wanda's love of classical music convinced her to fund a "repeater station" established at McAlester for the University of Central Oklahoma's classical music station KCSC. The station's manager called Wanda a "fireball" and observed that "If she wants something to happen, she'll stick with it until it happens." Many other facilities at the community's high school and elsewhere in the McAlester owed their existence to the vision of Clark and Wanda Bass.

Wanda donated her own time as well as treasure. She was a founder of the McAlester Arts and Humanities Council and served on the State Arts Council from 1976 to 1982. She served multiple terms on the board of the Oklahoma Heritage Association and worked with the staff of that organization to provide large numbers of books on Oklahoma history to libraries in southeastern Oklahoma. She also served as one of the original board members of the Summer Arts Institute at Quartz Mountain, was a board member of the Tulsa Philharmonic, and was an

organizer and treasurer of McAlester's Main Street program. She found time to serve on the board of the Oklahoma Foundation for Excellence and the Oklahoma Educational Television Authority.

By the late 1990s, Wanda had received numerous awards, including the Governor's Arts Award. In 1998 she joined Clark as a member of the Oklahoma Hall of Fame. But her greatest philanthropic contributions were yet to come. Wanda's daughter, Louise, had graduated from Oklahoma City University in 1978 with a degree in music. Wanda had been impressed with the institution, and in 1996 she and Clark donated two nine-foot Steinway concert grand pianos to the school in Louise's honor. In May of 2005, Wanda donated $2.5 million to provide for the purchase and maintenance of an additional 105 Steinway pianos, which included three nine-foot grand pianos and 23 six-foot and seven-foot grand pianos. The gift would allow OCU to join the elite ranks of all-Steinway schools, such as New York's Julliard School of Music. The OCU order was the largest single order in the 148-year history of the Steinway Company. At this time it was noted by university officials that a planned expansion of the School of Music at the university would provide sufficient space to accommodate the new pianos.

Wanda received a great deal of satis-faction from the enthusiastic response of

the students, faculty, staff, and trustees of the university to her piano donation. Soon thereafter it was announced that the new expansion of the School of Music would cost $16 million and that Wanda had donated $8 million to the project. The new Wanda L. Bass Music Center would provide state-of-the-art facilities in 69,000 square feet of space. By the time the project was completed in 2006, the project had been enhanced and cost $36 million, $26 million of which had been donated by Wanda Bass. The facility was meant to move the music program at OCU to "world class status." For Wanda, the prospect of impacting positively the education of students and perpetuating the creation and performance of quality music was exhilarating.

Asked to comment on her generous gift, Wanda observed, "The rewards are to know you're helping others. We're put on this earth for a reason, and sometimes you spend a lifetime figuring out what that reason is." Wanda had solved the mystery of her purpose in life. A dedicated wife, a devoted mother, a wise banker, a civic volunteer, and a remarkable supporter of education and the arts, she had generously given back to the state in which she had enjoyed so much joy and prosperity.

The Dewey Hotel, located in Dewey, Oklahoma, is a three-story, Victorian style building that was completed in 1900 by Jacob Bartles, a pioneer for whom the nearby city of Bartlesville is named. The hotel is open to the public from April through October. (Courtesy State Historic Preservation Office, Oklahoma Historical Society)

A Generous People:
Philanthropy
in Oklahoma

Americans generally are regarded as a generous people. As a group, Oklahomans are among the most generous Americans. The Catalogue for Philanthropy reported in November 2005 that Oklahoma ranked fourth in its "Generosity Index" among the 50 states, based on 2003 tax data. The index was calculated by comparing average gross income with average itemized charitable deductions. From frontier times to the present, Oklahomans have been willing, even eager, to give time, labor, and money to help others.

The wealth generated by Oklahoma's oil and gas industry during the twentieth century was shared with Oklahoma by many of the oilmen who "struck it rich." Institutions such as the University of Tulsa benefited tremendously from huge donations by many of the oilmen who lived in the "Oil Capitol of the World." Campus buildings such as the McFarlin Library and the Mabee Legal Information Center reflect the contributions of Robert M. McFarlin and John E. Mabee and the foundations they created. The Samuel Roberts Noble Foundation, headquartered in Ardmore, Oklahoma, was created by oilman Lloyd Noble in 1945 with a major emphasis on agricultural research. The foundation also has donated millions of dollars for capital projects at educational institutions statewide. Other family names synonymous with the oil industry and

The McFarlin Library as it appeared on the campus of the University of Tulsa in 1931. The library and many other facilities on the campus were made possible through the generosity of Tulsa-area philanthropists. (Courtesy Beryl Ford Collection, Tulsa City-County Library)

The headquarters of the Tulsa Historical Society is the former mansion of Samuel Travis. Private philanthropy made possible the acquisition and renovation of the home and grounds, as well as the construction of a large,

The Chisholm Trail Monument in Duncan, along with the nearby Chisholm Trail Museum, was funded by the McCasland Foundation of Duncan. Outstanding

Broadway producer Max Weitzenhofer have shared their fortunes with Oklahoma institutions.

Many Oklahomans with estates of various sizes have made contributions to the Oklahoma City Community Foundation, Tulsa Community Foundation, and the Communities Foundation of Oklahoma, which invest donated funds in perpetuity and use the earnings to benefit institutions and causes designated by donors. As of 2005 the Oklahoma City and Tulsa community foundations were among the top five grant-making foundations in Oklahoma.

The generous spirit of Oklahomans in the aftermath of disasters has been impressive. In 1995 rescue personnel from around the nation who rushed to Oklahoma City in response to the bombing of the Alfred P. Murrah Federal Building were amazed by the gratitude exhibited by Oklahomans. Noting that during previous rescue operations in other parts of the nation they had been forced to sleep on the tarmac at airports and pay inflated prices for food and even water, rescue workers found that in Oklahoma City sleeping quarters, meals, and laundry service were provided by Oklahoma volunteers who could not imagine doing anything less. The professionalism of paid personnel and the generosity of the state's people in response to the bombing became known internationally as "the Oklahoma Standard."

As Oklahoma entered its second century of statehood, its citizens enjoyed a significantly higher quality of life than would have been possible without the philanthropy of its citizens, foundations, and companies. If history is indeed prologue, the generous spirit of Oklahomans will persist throughout the state's next 100 years—and Oklahoma will continue to benefit from philanthropic contributions both large and small.

philanthropy in Oklahoma include Warren, Schusterman, Zarrow, Helmerich, Sarkeys, Chapman, McCasland, Kirkpatrick, Viersen, Phillips, and Kerr. One individual, Holdenville native Boone Pickens, in 2005 made the largest single gift to a university athletic department, Oklahoma State University, in United States history. Many Oklahoma-based energy companies, such as ONEOK, Inc., Chesapeake Energy Corporation, Devon Energy Corporation, generously support worthy causes in the state.

Some of Oklahoma's charitable foundations, such as the McMahon Foundation of Lawton, focus their generosity on the region of the state in which they are located, while others spread their contributions statewide. As the state's economy matured during the twentieth century, individuals who made fortunes in endeavors other than energy became outstanding philanthropists. In journalism, the Gaylord and Lorton families have supported a wide range of educational and charitable institutions in the state. In banking, families such as Kaiser, Rainbolt, and Bass are among many who have made a major impact. Other entrepreneurs, such as Herman Meinders, founder of American Floral Services, Inc., and

The magnificent Electric Park Pavilion in Blackwell has been a centerpiece of civic and social activity in the community since it was opened in 1913 as a tribute to the advent of electricity in the town. Funded by a bond issue of the Blackwell Parks Department, its more than 500 lights could be seen for miles across the prairie. The building was designed by W. L. McAtee after styles exhibited at the great "White City" exhibit at the Chicago World's Fair of 1893. After the building was acquired by the Top of Oklahoma Historical Society, the citizens of the community approved a $300,000 bond issue to restore the "Prairie Palace." It now serves a museum with exhibits reflecting the heritage of the area. (Courtesy State Historic Preservation Office, Oklahoma Heritage Association)

At Tsa-La-Gi, a replica of a sixteenth century Cherokee village, craftspeople in traditional dress enact the daily activities of their ancestors. In this scene a girl sits by a spring while weaving a basket, while a boy practices with his blow gun. The Cherokee Heritage Center and village is located three miles south of Tahlequah.

The Centennial Memorial Plaza of the Oklahomans, located near the south steps of the State Capitol, was a joint project of the Oklahoma Department of Transportation and the Department of Central Services. These agencies provided both planning and funding to replace the original gray concrete with red, pink, and black granite. The design also incorporated 28 granite "rosettes" which commemorate various events in Oklahoma history. The Centennial Plaza was designed by Meyer Architects, Paul B. Meyer, Principal architect. (Courtesy Oklahoma Arts Council)

Oklahoma City's Bricktown Canal, shown here at night, is an important element in the success of the downtown entertainment district. (Courtesy Jim Argo)

Oklahoma City has recovered from the widespread devastation caused by the Alfred P. Murrah Federal Building bombing. With a new art museum, a new library, a renovated Civic Center Music Hall, the new Ford Center arena, new hotels, and continuously developing Bricktown entertainment district, many buildings were being converted to condominiums or loft apartments while others are being constructed. (Courtesy Jim Argo)

Lawrence Hart: The Search for Balance

When historians are asked to define the Oklahoma experience, their most frequent response is diversity. Indians and cowboys. Oil booms and homesteads. Land runs and skyscrapers. By examining these dramatic contrasts, the history of the territory and state unfold, one chapter after another, each overlapping the others. The one constant thread weaving in and out of this frontier story is balance, a juggling act that has pitted individuals and communities against the forces tugging and pushing them in all directions. One man who has spent a lifetime dealing with these winds of change is Cheyenne Peace Chief Lawrence Hart.

Hart was born in 1933 on the family farm about five miles south of Hammon in far western Oklahoma. His father, Homer Hart, was a full-blood Cheyenne who had attended Indian boarding schools, learned English, and dedicated his life as a "native helper" at the Red Moon Mennonite Church. His mother, Jennie Howling Water, had attended Chilocco Boarding School and was known for her church work and skills on the farm. One year during the Great Depression she won a local best garden contest. The first place prize was a pig.

For the first six years of his life, Lawrence was raised in the traditional Cheyenne home of his grandparents. John Peak Hart, his grandfather, was born in 1871, the son of Afraid of Beavers, who had survived Custer's attack on Black Kettle's village in 1868. By the time of his grandson's birth, John was one of 42 Cheyenne Peace Chiefs and a respected leader in the Native American Church. Lawrence's grandmother was the community matriarch and mid-wife, Anna Reynolds Hart, who carried the Cheyenne name Corn Stalk.

As a child, Lawrence was surrounded by family and the extended village of the Red Moon community, known as one of the more conservative Cheyenne camps that had resisted the early influences of the Indian agents. To the west of the family farm was the allotment of his great-uncle, Magpie, the Keeper of the Sacred Arrows. On the outskirts of Hammon was the community campground where the Cheyenne gathered for feasts, dancing, and ceremonies. By the time he was old enough for grade school, Lawrence spoke only Cheyenne.

Unlike his three older siblings, who left home for boarding schools, Lawrence attended local schools where he learned to walk in two worlds, one the road of the white man, the other the road of his ancestors. He excelled in sports, especially track and basketball,

Lawrence Hart

and was elected senior class president. At church, he absorbed the sermons of the Mennonite preacher, who said a few sentences in English, followed by Lawrence's father, who translated the message in Cheyenne.

One hot fall day, Lawrence was picking cotton when he took a break, laid back on his cotton sack, and saw two Navy airplanes flying low to the ground. At that moment he knew he wanted to be a pilot. When he learned he needed two years of college to get into flight school, he talked to his minister, who recommended either Bacone Indian College in Muskogee or his own alma mater, Bethel College in Kansas, a well-known school affiliated with the Mennonite Church. Lawrence knew he would have to live in the white man's world, so he chose the latter.

At Bethel, Lawrence ran track, completed his two years of study, and met his future wife, Betty, whose Mennonite ancestors had migrated from Germany to the western plains of Kansas in the late nineteenth century. In 1953 he enlisted in the Navy and started flight school in Florida. Eighteen months later he earned his wings as a jet fighter pilot in the Marine Corps, the first full-blood American Indian to earn that honor.

In the fall of 1957, as he was nearing the end of his enlistment, Lawrence received notice that his grandfather John P. Hart was dying and that the Peace Chiefs had chosen

him to take his place as a traditional leader. Lawrence knew what that meant. As a Peace Chief, he would have to give up his life as a warrior and take up the responsibilities to be a man of peace, to be brave, and to be of generous heart. He took it as a calling.

His family chose June 18, 1958, as the date when Lawrence would be accepted as a Peace Chief. The teepee was set up, food was prepared, and Lawrence had permission to fly an F-9 Cougar fighter jet to a nearby base at Altus on a two-day pass. On a day that he would never forget, Lawrence rode a horse into the circle of family, friends, and Peace Chiefs to take his sacred vows. That night, on the return to his home base, he flew his jet out over the Gulf and broke the sound barrier. It was a symbolic conversion experience from warrior to a man of peace.

The young Peace Chief, now with a growing family, finished college and attended the Mennonite Seminary in Elkhart, Indiana. In 1963 he received a call to serve the Koinonia Mennonite Church congregation east of Clinton, not far from where he grew up. For the next 40 years, he and his wife, Betty, would serve their community, preaching, conducting weddings and funerals, and reaching out to help others. Among their contributions would be a youth shelter in Clinton, an early effort to confront alcoholism among Indians, and taking care of 21 foster children.

In 1969 Lawrence was elected chairman of the 15th Business Committee of the Cheyenne and Arapaho tribes, the secular governing body that dealt with the federal government to provide services to tribal members. It was a critical time for the tribes, with new streams of federal funds available for housing, health care, and economic development. During Lawrence's tenure, the Cheyenne-Arapaho Housing Authority was created and the Special Indian Claims Commission ruled that the tribes

(Facing page) Lawrence Hart as a young Marine fighter pilot in the early 1950s. (Courtesy Lawrence Hart)

John P. Hart, a traditional Cheyenne peace chief born soon after George Armstrong Custer's attack on Black Kettle's Village, helped raise Lawrence Hart. (Courtesy Lawrence Hart)

would receive $15 million in reparations for injustices committed by the federal government in the past. When Lawrence surveyed tribal members across the country, he determined that a vast majority wanted per capita payments. He and his fellow Business Committee members also set aside funds for an education endowment.

A greater test for Lawrence was a lesson learned as a young Peace Chief. In 1968, to commemorate the 100th anniversary of the Battle of the Washita, the Chamber of Commerce in the county seat town of Cheyenne organized a reenactment of the massacre and asked Lawrence and other Cheyenne leaders to help. They had two conditions. One was that the event had to be factual, depicting the slaughter on that cold November morning. The other was to rebury the skeletal remains of a Cheyenne victim that had been on display at the local museum.

On the day of the reenactment, Lawrence, his small children, family, and friends were in the camp along the Washita as planned. Spectators, including the governor of Oklahoma, lined the ridge above. What they did not know was that chamber officials had invited a reenactment group from California called the "Grandsons of the 7th Cavalry." In the distance, as the Cheyenne waited for the ceremonies to begin, Lawrence heard a bugler playing "Garry Owen," the battle song favored by

George Armstrong Custer as he went on the attack. Then came the blue-coated soldiers, armed with Spencer carbines and carrying real sabers, riding at a full gallop firing blanks at the men, women, and children scattered throughout the camp. The panic and screams only slowly gave way to anger and a feeling of betrayal.

That afternoon, still feeling the anger of a warrior, Lawrence joined the other Peace Chiefs to rebury their ancestor's bones. During the solemn procession, a Cheyenne woman tenderly placed a blanket on the coffin, a humble gesture that made the blanket an item for a giveaway later in the day. When the time for the giveaway came, the older Peace Chiefs decided they would give the blanket not to the governor, but to the captain of the reenactment group that had attacked them earlier in the day. At that point, Lawrence knew what it meant to be a Peace Chief, a point made through a traditional Cheyenne act of reconciliation and restoration.

Lawrence, while serving his congregation at the church, found other ways to serve his tribe, his state, and his nation. In 1990 he was asked to serve on the Review Committee for the Native American Graves Protection and Repatriation Act, which was an attempt to return sacred objects and funerary remains to the tribes. Acting as a liaison for his own tribe, Lawrence negotiated the return of human remains

from the Smithsonian to Oklahoma where they were buried with the appropriate ceremonies. A decade later he would expand his service to all tribes through the "Return to the Earth Project," an attempt to establish regional burial sites where native peoples could return the unburied to the earth.

In 1994, in yet another act of reconciliation and restoration, Lawrence provided insight and counsel to the Oklahoma Historical Society to secure political authorization, funding, and tribal support for the designation of Black Kettle's village as a unit of the National Park Service. Two years later, after numerous visits to the site and testimony before Congress on two separate occasions, the Battle of the Washita National Historic Monument was established as sacred ground to both the tribe and the nation.

Today, Lawrence and Betty Hart run the Cheyenne Cultural Center located on the former allotment of Red Wheat, a Cheyenne woman who had long ago donated 20 acres to establish a church on the site. Scattered about the river bottom are several buildings, markers, and places to gather. It is a community center. It is a museum and place to gather information important to the Cheyenne. Most of all, it is a place that helps people understand who they are and where they belong in the world. To Lawrence Hart, it is sacred ground, a place where people can search for balance in life.

Lawrence Hart, founder of the Cheyenne Cultural Center near Clinton, has spent a lifetime serving others as a Marine pilot, Mennonite minister, and peace chief. (Courtesy Lawrence Hart)

Preserving a Sense of Place

Capturing the essence of Oklahoma history has long challenged the best scholars and keenest observers. Angie Debo described the diversity of Oklahoma as "footloose and fancy free," a telling phrase that largely admits there is no one identity. Arrell M. Gibson, coming to the same conclusion, said that the most common thread running through the state's history was mobility.

In large part, both historians were correct. Most Oklahomans, if you dig only a generation or two into the past, have come from someplace else. First came more than 40 American Indian tribes, removed from their homelands to a colonization zone set aside from the westward march of the young American nation. Then came the land openings, each with its own unique personality, and the twin booms of oil and agriculture that swelled the population of the 46th state. Interlaced with this unfolding saga were subplots such as the all-black towns, Italian coal miners, Mennonites from the Steppes of Russia, and Vietnamese searching for freedom and opportunity.

To create a common sense of place within this constantly swirling mixture of cultural heritage, someone had to collect the stories, documents, and artifacts that trace these various paths, then make those materials accessible for study and reflection. Fortunately, efforts to collect that story began early in our history and gained momentum throughout the twentieth century.

The first concerted effort to collect, preserve, and share Oklahoma history began in 1893 when the Oklahoma Territory Press Association created the Oklahoma Historical Society. The first task was to collect newspapers, which essentially recorded the first draft of history as seen by a small army of reporters and editors scattered throughout the Twin Territories. Following moves to the University of Oklahoma in 1895, the basement of the Carnegie Library in Oklahoma City in 1902, and the basement of the State Capitol in 1918, the Society's collection grew to include books, manuscripts, photographs, and artifacts. In 1930 these priceless collections were moved into the Oklahoma Historical Building, located at Northeast 21st and Lincoln Boulevard southeast of the Oklahoma State Capitol. There, concerned citizens collected more than 4 million Indian records when the Indian agencies were closed in the 1930s, gathered materials in partnership with the WPA Writers Project, and continued to amass a mountain of newspapers and family histories from every community in the state.

Others joined the crusade to save the cultural legacy of the state and its people. Private individuals such as Frank Phillips and Thomas Gilcrease collected art, artifacts, and records beginning in the 1930s. These collections would ultimately form the foundations for institutions such as Woolaroc Museum near Bartlesville, Gilcrease Museum in Tulsa, and the Western History Collections in Norman. In 1955 the National Cowboy Hall of Fame, later renamed the National Cowboy and Western Heritage Museum, was opened to the public.

In the 1960s and 1970s, spurred by a growing awareness of history and historic preservation, a generation of regional facilities emerged to collect the story of the state in towns such as Lawton, Woodward, Goodwell, Enid, Muskogee, Duncan, Ponca City, Pawnee, Perry, Ardmore, Idabel, Seminole, and Guthrie. Others, more aware of their own heritage, came together to form local historical and genealogical societies as well as historic preservation districts in hundreds of communities.

At the statewide level, the non-profit Oklahoma Heritage Association, founded in 1927, has become the leader in publishing Oklahoma's history, offers more than $400,000 annually in college scholarships, and recognizes citizens and organizations for preserving and promoting Oklahoma's unique heritage. The Association also hosts the Oklahoma

Hall of Fame, induction into which is the highest honor an Oklahoman can receive from their native state.

The Oklahoma Historical Society capped six years of construction with the opening of the Oklahoma History Center on November 5, 2005. From its offices in the History Center, the Society administers more than 30 historical sites and museums throughout Oklahoma and conducts numerous outreach programs and historical reenactments. It also publishes a quarterly journal on Oklahoma history, operates a Smithsonian-affiliated museum, and manages a Research Center meeting National Archives standards within the confines of the History Center.

Today, the images and documents of Oklahoma history are being collected on a daily basis. As researchers plow through those materials and as professional educators create exhibits and write books on the various themes of that story, the picture of our past comes into better focus. With time, this greater understanding of who we are and where we have been will lead to a better sense of place called Oklahoma.

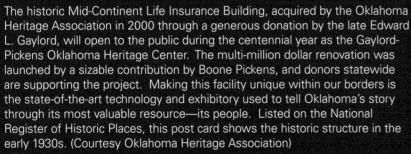

The historic Mid-Continent Life Insurance Building, acquired by the Oklahoma Heritage Association in 2000 through a generous donation by the late Edward L. Gaylord, will open to the public during the centennial year as the Gaylord-Pickens Oklahoma Heritage Center. The multi-million dollar renovation was launched by a sizable contribution by Boone Pickens, and donors statewide are supporting the project. Making this facility unique within our borders is the state-of-the-art technology and exhibitory used to tell Oklahoma's story through its most valuable resource—its people. Listed on the National Register of Historic Places, this post card shows the historic structure in the early 1930s. (Courtesy Oklahoma Heritage Association)

The Oklahoma History Center was opened to the public on November 16, 2005. The 215,000-square-foot, 18-acre facility is affiliated with the Smithsonian Institution. The History Center houses a world-class museum, a research library and archives, and the staff of the Oklahoma Historical Society. Located immediately northeast of the State Capitol, the History Center, opened to great fanfare on November 16, 2005, represents more than 10 years of dedicated effort and was made possible by the State of Oklahoma with many enhancements funded by private donations. (Courtesy Oklahoma Historical Society)

The beautiful interior of the State Capitol Dome is surrounded by Charles Banks Wilson's magnificent murals depicting the state's history. The impressive interior of the State Capitol dome features the Great Seal of the State of Oklahoma. (Courtesy Jim Argo)

Oklahoma Centennial Projects, Publications and Activities

CENTENNIAL CAPITAL PROJECTS

Ode to Byrd's Mill Springs	Ada
Wintersmith Amphitheatre Restoration	Ada
Allen Historical Society Heritage Center Restoration	Allen
Air Refueling Memorial Park, Altus AFB	Altus
Altus Centennial Grove, Honoring Veterans, Tree Project	Altus
Altus Centennial Memorial Center	Altus
Altus Museum of the Western Prairie (OHS)	Altus
Runnymeade Restoration Project	Alva
Anadarko - Centennial Clock	Anadarko
Antlers' Wildlife Heritage Center Museum	Antlers
Wildlife Heritage Center Museum in Antlers	Antlers
Arapaho - Centennial Clock	Arapaho
Ardmore Centennial Center	Ardmore
Ardmore's Centennial Sculpture Garden	Ardmore
Ardmore's Pioneer Memorial Center	Ardmore
Atoka Centennial Clock	Atoka
Atoka Confederate Museum	Atoka
Barndall's Friendship - Memory Wall of Honor	Barnsdall
Nellie Johnstone No. 1 Oil Well Restoration	Bartlesville
Phillips Company Museum	Bartlesville
USS *Oklahoma* - Pearl Harbor Memorial Mural	Bartlesville
Beaver - Centennial Clock	Beaver
Douglas A-26 Aircraft Restoration Project	Bethany
Southern Nazarene University Centennial Gate	Bethany
Henry and Shirley Bellmon Museum	Billings
Boise City - Centennial Clock	Boise City
Bristow Auditorium	Bristow
Broken Arrow Walking to Rooster Days Centennial Statue	Broken Arrow
Broken Arrow Women's War Memorial	Broken Arrow
Broken Bow Centennial Clock	Broken Bow
Forrest Heritage Center	Broken Bow
Buffalo Museum Project	Buffalo
Capitol Hill Centennial Clock	Capitol Hill
Stockyards "Headin' to Market" Sculpture	Capitol Hill
Kiowa Cultural Center and Museum	Carnegie
Cement, Oklahoma Centennial Plus Five	Cement
Chandler's Quilt of the Official Oklahoma 46th Flag	Chandler
Route 66 Visitor's Center Restoration (Chandler Armory)	Chandler
Checotah's The Heartland Heritage Center	Checotah
Jefferson Highway Signage	Checotah
Alfalfa Co. Courthouse Preservation & Restoration	Cherokee
Cheyenne, Centennial Community Museum	Cheyenne
Chickasha Centennial Park	Chickasha
Chickasha Community Theatre Washita Theatre Project	Chickasha
Grady County African American Museum and One Room School	Chickasha
Te Ata World Premiere/Renovation of Historic Troutt Hall Auditorium	Chickasha
Choctaw Centennial Main Street Clock Project	Choctaw
Historical Shadow Art Gardens	Choctaw
Veteran's Memorial at Choctaw	Choctaw
Claremore - Centennial Clock	Claremore
Claremore Historical Banner Program	Claremore
Claremore's Historical Tour of Claremore (Walking or Driving)	Claremore
Clayton Lake Centennial Center	Clayton
Coalgate - Centennial Clock	Coalgate
Colcord's Springtown School Renovation	Colcord
Collinsville's Centennial Plaza Project	Collinsville
Mickey Mantle Museum	Commerce
Washita County Courthouse Restoration	Cordell
Cushing Centennial Park, Downtown	Cushing
Custer City Centennial Park	Custer City
Del City's Centennial Memorial Trail	Del City
W.T. Foreman House Restoration	Duncan
Ft. Washita (OHS)	Durant
Market Square Project	Durant
Centennial Grove - Santa Fe High School	Edmond
Edmond Centennial Clock	Edmond
Edmond's Classen's Grove	Edmond
First Public Schoolhouse in Oklahoma Territory Restoration	Edmond
Kentucky Daisy Statue	Edmond
Rodkey Mill Signage	Edmond
Shannon Miller Bronze Statue	Edmond
Donald W. Reynolds Caring Center	El Reno
Fort Reno Restoration	El Reno
Jesse Reno Monument	El Reno
Trolley on Track	El Reno
Elk City Centennial Soccer Park	Elk City
Elk City's Centennial Lighthouse	Elk City
"Elmore City, Centennial Civic Center"	Elmore City
"Aviators Statue, Vance AFB"	Enid
Museum of the Cherokee Strip (OHS)	Enid
City of Erick Community Project	Erick
Fairview - Centennial Clock	Fairview
Fairview Auditorium	Fairview
Fargo's Oklahoma Centennial Covered Foot Bridge and Working Windmill	Fargo
Camp Radziminski and Laing School Centennial Project	Frederick
Frederick Centennial Square	Frederick
Frederick Pioneer Village (OHS)	Frederick
Freedom Museum	Freedom
National Army Museum of the Southwest- US Field Artillery Museum	Ft. Sill
Ft. Towson Restoration (OHS)	Ft. Towson
Glenpool - Centennial Clock	Glenpool
Ida E. Glenn Well Site and Exhibit	Glenpool
Har-Ber Village Transportation Museum and Welcome Center	Grove
46-Star Sculpture	Guthrie
First State Capitol Legislative Hall Restoration Project	Guthrie
Guthrie's Oklahoma Frontier Drug Store Museum Apothecary Garden	Guthrie
Oklahoma Territorial Railroad	Guthrie
Warren Spahn Statue	Guthrie
Guymon - Centennial Clock	Guymon
Guymon Centennial Park	Guymon
Hammon's "Local Heroes" Monument	Hammon
Harrah Historical Main Street	Harrah
Peter Conser House (OHS)	Heavener
Hennessey Community / Shelter / Concession Room	Hennessey
Hennessey Walking Trail	Hennessey
Oklahoma Labor and Mining Museum	Henryetta
Heritage Hills Centennial Clock	Heritage Hills
Kiowa County Mosaic Map and Memorial on Courthouse Lawn	Hobart
Holdenville Centennial Fountain	Holdenville
Hollis - Centennial Clock	Hollis
Hugo Frisco Depot Museum - Choctaw County Historical Society	Hugo
Idabel Centennial Clock	Idabel
Idabel's 1st Bank & Trust Bronze Buffalo	Idabel
Idabel's 1st Bank & Trust Centennial Grove	Idabel
McCurtain County Heritage Center	Idabel
Jay Centennial Project	Jay
Oklahoma Aquarium	Jenks
Kingfisher Centennial Grove - Middle School Campus	Kingfisher
Kingfisher Trails	Kingfisher
South Grand Lake Visitor Center and Community Center	Langley
Lawton High School, Restoration of the Original Building	Lawton
Lawton's Birthday Rodeo Facility Renovation	Lawton
Mattie Beal House	Lawton
Murray-Lindsay Mansion	Lindsay
Madill - Centennial Clock and Benches	Madill
Mangum - Centennial Clock	Mangum
Marietta - Centennial Pavilion	Marietta
First Presbyterian Church Restoration (now a Community Center)	McAlester
McAlester Army Ammunition Depot	McAlester
OKLA Theatre Restoration	McAlester
Pittsburg County Health Department Facility	McAlester
Medford - Centennial Clock	Medford
Cascading Waters Fountain	Midwest City
Midwest City Millennium: Launching our Legacy	Midwest City
Studio Mid-Del	Midwest City
Tinker Air Park, TAFB	Midwest City
Muskogee River Center	Muskogee
Oklahoma Music Hall of Fame	Muskogee
Newalla Memorial Pavilion	Newalla
Newkirk Heritage Center	Newkirk
Nichols Hills Centennial Clock	Nichols Hills
Nicoma Park, City of - Central Park Renovation	Nicoma Park
Centennial Grove - City of Norman	Norman
Cleveland County Veterans Memorial	Norman
Heisman Trophy Winner Statues (4)	Norman
Jacobson House Renovation	Norman
James Garner Commemorative Plaza	Norman
Legacy Trail Historic Plazas	Norman
Nowata - Centennial Clock	Nowata
Nowata Park Project	Nowata
Excelsior Rural School Monument	Okemah
Okemah Centennial Park Benches and Landscaping	Okemah
Oklahoma! Mural	Oklahoma City
American Indian Cultural Center	Oklahoma City
Beacon of Hope, Founders' Plaza at Stiles Park	Oklahoma City
Boy Scout Redbud Tree Project	Oklahoma City
Boys and Girls Club Memorial Park	Oklahoma City
Bricktown Ballpark Busts	Oklahoma City
Bricktown Ballpark Centennial Clock	Oklahoma City
Bricktown Ballpark Warren Spahn Statue	Oklahoma City
Bricktown Historic Oklahoma Cityscape Mural	Oklahoma City
Carillon, Leadership Square	Oklahoma City
Centennial Choo Choo at the OKC Zoo	Oklahoma City
Centennial Clock at INTEGRIS Baptist Medical Center	Oklahoma City
Centennial Excursion Train	Oklahoma City
Centennial Fountain at the United Way Plaza	Oklahoma City
Centennial Grove - Oklahoma River	Oklahoma City
Centennial Grove North Classen Boulevard	Oklahoma City
Centennial Grove North MacArthur and Memorial Road	Oklahoma City
Centennial Grove Oklahoma City Zoological and Botanical Park	Oklahoma City
Chesapeake Centennial Boathouse	Oklahoma City
Donation to Oklahoma City Museum of Art for Chihuly Collection	Oklahoma City
Infant Crisis Center	Oklahoma City
Jungle Gym at the Oklahoma City Zoo	Oklahoma City
Kerr-McGee Bell Tower	Oklahoma City
Kerr-McGee Trails	Oklahoma City
Leaping Waters Fountain	Oklahoma City
Lyric Theatre's Restoration of the Plaza Theatre	Oklahoma City
Mosaic Mural in Bricktown, Oklahoma Centennial	Oklahoma City
Museum of the Telephone Industry in Oklahoma	Oklahoma City
Oklahoma Centennial Rodeo Opry	Oklahoma City
Oklahoma City Centennial Clock at City Hall	Oklahoma City
Oklahoma City Centennial Mural on OKC Rocks Grain Elevator	Oklahoma City
Oklahoma City National Memorial and Museum Centennial Educational Program	Oklahoma City
Oklahoma Heritage Association Museum Complex (Mid Continent Building)	Oklahoma City
Oklahoma Land Run Monument	Oklahoma City
Oklahoma Railway Museum: Murals and Statue	Oklahoma City
Oklahoma Sports Hall of Fame - Jim Thorpe Musuem	Oklahoma City
Oklahoma State Fair Park Centennial Fence and Entrance Way	Oklahoma City
Oklahoma State Fair Park Quarter Horse Statue	Oklahoma City
Omniplex Science Museum - Champion Oak Centennial Tree House	Oklahoma City
Spirit of the Buffalo: Over 100 Buffalo Statues	Oklahoma City
Wiley Post Hangar Restoration	Oklahoma City
Okmulgee Black Hospital Cultural Center	Okmulgee
Centennial Grove at Southern Oklahoma Resource Center	Pauls Valley
Ben Johnson Memorial Gateway	Pawhuska
Boy Scout Sculpture (What It's All About)	Pawhuska
Pawnee Bill Ranch (OHS)	Pawnee
USS *Oklahoma* at Pearl Harbor	Pearl Harbor, HI
Perkins Centennial Clock	Perkins
Perry - Centennial Clock	Perry
Conoco Company Museum	Ponca City
Marland Mansion Ceilings Restoration	Ponca City
Pioneer Woman Statue Restoration Landscaping	Ponca City

POW-MIA Monument	Ponca City
Standing Bear Park Project	Ponca City
Carl Albert Museum	Poteau
Pryor Centennial Park	Pryor
Purcell Veteran's Memorial	Purcell
Rainy Mountain Archive Media Center and Camp	Rainy Mountain
Otoe Veterans Memorial Wall	Red Rock
Honey Springs Battlefield Park	Rentiesville
Sallisaw High School Centennial Park and Pavilion	Sallisaw
Sapulpa Centennial Buffalo	Sapulpa
Sapulpa's Downtown Sapulpa Historic Miniature	Sapulpa
Sayre - Centennial Clock	Sayre
Sayre Fire Truck Restoration	Sayre
Sayre's "Spirits of the West" - Horse Sculptures	Sayre
Jasmine Moran Children's Museum:	
Maze and History Street Projects	Seminole
Seminole Centennial Recreational Complex	Seminole
Shattuck's Northwest Oklahoma Veteran's Centennial Memorial	Shattuck
Centennial Grove at I-40 - City of Shawnee	Shawnee
Shawnee - Centennial Clock	Shawnee
The Ritz Theatre, Shawnee	Shawnee
Spencer, City of - Kringlen Centennial Park	Spencer
Capitol Welcoming Center	State Capitol
Centennial Memorial Plaza of the Oklahomans	State Capitol
Constitutional Display	State Capitol
Kate Barnard: Oklahoma's Voice for Social Justice Statue	State Capitol
Landscapes in State Capitol Rotunda:	
"Oklahoma Centennial Suite"	State Capitol
Oklahoma Supreme Court and Judicial Center	State Capitol
Restoration and Decoration of the Oklahoma State Senate	State Capitol
State Capitol Dome	State Capitol
Te Ata Garden for Oklahoma Cultural Treasures	State Capitol
We Belong to the Land: State Capitol Mural	State Capitol
African American History Plaza	State Capitol Complex
Buffalo Soldier Monument	State Capitol Complex
Fountain Pool: Oklahoma History Center	State Capitol Complex
Harn Homestead Entrance off Lincoln Boulevard	State Capitol Complex
Korean War Memorial	State Capitol Complex
Lincoln Renaissance	State Capitol Complex
Oil Well Renovation/Restoration	State Capitol Complex
Oklahoma Attorney General's Office Building	State Capitol Complex
Oklahoma Attorney General's Office	
Centennial Art Project	State Capitol Complex
Oklahoma History Center Grand Opening	State Capitol Complex
Red River Journey Park	State Capitol Complex
State Capitol Centennial Clocks (2)	State Capitol Complex
State Capitol Park Welcoming Signs (2)	State Capitol Complex
Weyerhaeuser's State Capitol Park:	
100 Holiday Trees	State Capitol Complex
95th Infantry Division Display	Statewide
Centennial Bells Project	Statewide
Centennial Clocks	Statewide
Centennial Groves	Statewide
Centennial Park Benches	Statewide

County Courthouses Restoration	Statewide
Stigler - Centennial Clock	Stigler
Stigler Historical Murals	Stigler
Stillwater's African-American School Site	Stillwater
Stilwell - Centennial Clock	Stilwell
Stilwell Kansas City Railroad Depot Restoration	Stilwell
Jim Thorpe Birthplace: Road Improvements	Stroud
Sulphur - Centennial Clock	Sulphur
Chisholm Trail Historical Corridor and Centennial Cattle Drive	SW / NW
Cherokee National Historical Society Renovation	Tahlequah
Tahlequah - Centennial Clock	Tahlequah
Taloga - Centennial Clock	Taloga
Tecumseh Centennial Clock	Tecumseh
Tecumseh Memorial Monument	Tecumseh
Tishomingo - Centennial Clock	Tishomingo
5 Moons - Sculpture of Oklahoma's Indian American Ballarina	Tulsa
Centennial Green	Tulsa
Centennial Mosaic	Tulsa
Centennial Walk - River Extension	Tulsa
Courage and Compassion - Tulsa Firefighters Sculpture	Tulsa
Oklahoma Centennial Botanical Garden	Tulsa
Renovation of the Travis Mansion (Tulsa Historical Society)	Tulsa
The Art of Tulsa (Book) by John Brooks Walton	Tulsa
Up With Trees at Tulsa's Centennial Grove	Tulsa
Choctaw Nation Capital Museum Windows	Tuskahoma
Dwight Mission Restoration	Vian
Vinita - Centennial Clock	Vinita
Wagoner Centennial Hall	Wagoner
Walters Centennial Clock	Walters
Warr Acres Centennial Planting	Warr Acres
Watonga Main Street Centennial Park	Watonga
Waurika - Centennial Clock	Waurika
Waynoka Transportation Museum Restoration	Waynoka
Wilburton - Centennial Clock	Wilburton
Wilburton Park: The Goldberg and Joseph Heritage Park	Wilburton
Southern Plains Conference Center	Woodward
Wynnewood Confederate Veterans Monument	Wynnewood
Wynnewood's Oklahoma Centennial Street Clock Project	Wynnewood

PUBLICATIONS

A Century of Art Renaissance	
A Directory of Oklahoma Artists	
Alice & J.F.B.: 100 Year Saga of Two Seminole Chiefs	
Bloodmoon at Cabin Creek	
Book Series: OU Press	
Brochure of the Capitol	
Oklahoma Centennial Commission Brochure, The	
Buffalo Train Ride, The	
Building Traditions, Educating Generations: A History of the University of Central Oklahoma	
Buildings of Oklahoma Publication	
Celebrate 100: An Architectural Guide to Central Oklahoma	
Celebrating Oklahoma - Photography by Mike Klemme	
Centennial Writing Project - Oklahoma Arts Institute	
Cheyenne's Roger Mills Stories From the First Hundred Years	
Chihuly Oklahoma City Museum of Art	
Dreams to Dust: A Tale of the Oklahoma Land Rush	
Duncan's 100 Years of Notable Women of Stephens County, Oklahoma	
Friday Night in the Big Town: The Life of Gary England	
General Federation of Women's Club (GFWC) Delphian Review Club	
Great Oklahomans, OK Centennial Publications	
Guide to Oklahoma Historical Markers	
Heart Land - Essays by Oklahoma Women	
Heavenly Patchwork II - Quilt Stories to Warm Your Heart	
Heavenly Patchwork: Quilt Stories Stitched with Love	
High Plains Rural Conservation & Development Cookbook	
Historic Oklahoma County	
Historical Atlas of Oklahoma - Centennial Edition	
History of Elk City	
Hobart's Volume 7 Pioneering in Kiowa County	
Lee Allan Smith: Oklahoma's Best Friend	
Mama Grace	
More Grace than Glamour: My Life as Miss America and Beyond	
Oklahoma III - Photography by David Fitzgerald	
Oklahoma City Zoo: 1902-1959	
Oklahoma Greats - Sante Fe High School Class Project	
Oklahoma Land Tract Book Index	
Oklahoma Women: Creators of Destiny	
Oklahoma Women's Almanac	
Oklahoma: A Rich Heritage	
Oklahoma's Historical Centennial Cookbook	
Palace on the Prairie: The Marland Family Story	
Robert S. Kerr, Jr.: Mr. Water	
Small Towns, Ghost Memories of Oklahoma	
Southwestern Oklahoma State University - The First 100 Years	
Spirit of the Buffalo: Oklahoma's Past and Future	
Story of Byrds Mill Spring - Ada's Fountainhead	
This Paradise on the Prairie	
Tushka-Atoka Centennial Books	
War Chief, The	
Will Rogers Papers of Oklahoma Centennial Scholars Collection	
Willie of the Valley: The Life of William G. Paul	
You Know We Belong to the Land: The Centennial History of Oklahoma	

DOCUMENTARY/FILM/VIDEO/RADIO

100 Voices: The Story of Oklahoma	Statewide
100 Years of Oklahoma - Documentary Film	Norman
En Pointe: The Lives & Legacies of Ballet's Native Americans	Statewide
Get Your Kicks on Route 66 (Film)	Route 66
Historical Documentary on Archaeological Investigations	Statewide
Horseshoe Road International Tour Documentary	Statewide
Lincoln County Oral History Project	Chandler

ART AND CULTURE

Oklahoma Centennial Suite For Band	Ada
Broken Bow's Salute to University Greats Photo Portraits	Broken Bow
Broken Bow's Where Hochatown Was - Painting	Broken Bow
Enid's Centennial Symphony "Where the West Remains"	Enid
Pioneer Family Sculpture	Enid
Brothers Gone But Not Forgotten - Painting	Ft. Sill
Guthrie's "Oklahoma's' Greatest Athletes of the Century, 1907 - 2007" -Painting"	Guthrie
Idabel's Surveying the Red - Painting	Idabel
Muskogee's Guitar Public Art Project	Muskogee
"Oklahoma Rising" State Anthem Jimmy Webb and Vince Gill	Statewide
Centennial Poem "The Land", "Settlement", and "Statehood" by N. Scott Momaday"	Statewide

HERITAGE ACTIVITIES

Centennial Calliope	Statewide
Centennial Collage Project	Statewide
Centennial Hot Air Balloon	Statewide
Centennial Quilt Project	Hobart
Centoonials (Four State Symbol Mascots)	Statewide
Chautauqua Series/OK Themes	Statewide
Ladies of the Mayo/Women in Oklahoma History	Statewide
Literary Landmarks, Oklahoma	Statewide
Museum Grants Program	Statewide
Okii Taiko	Oklahoma City
Oklahoma All*Star Centennial Band	Statewide
Oklahoma Heritage	Statewide
Oklahoma Historical Theatre, Inc.	Statewide
Oklahoma Reads Oklahoma	Statewide
Oklahoma Tartan Educational Project	Checotah
Ponca City's Oklahoma Centennial Quilt Challenge	Statewide
Stillwater's Partners of the Prairie	Statewide
Sweet Biscuits / Ebony Voices	Statewide
Tahlequah's City Flag Contest	Tahlequah
The Oklahoman and *Tulsa World* Centennial Student Essay and Poster Contest	Statewide
TRACKS - Traveling Humanities Exhibit	Statewide
Uncrowned Queens	Statewide
Wings of the Centennial: Promoting Oklahoma Aviation with the FAA's last DC-3, N34	Statewide
Witness Tree	Statewide
World Neighbors Student Essay Competition & Hunger Banquet	Statewide

Bibliography

BOOKS

Agnew, Brad. *Fort Gibson, Terminal on the Trail of Tears*. Norman: University of Oklahoma Press, 1980.

Alexander, Mabel Hovdahl. *Via Oklahoma: And Still the Music Flows*. Oklahoma City: Oklahoma Heritage Association, 2004.

Allen, Gene. *Voices on the Wind: Early Radio in Oklahoma*. Oklahoma City: Oklahoma Heritage Association, 1993.

Bearss, Edwin C., and Arrell M. Gibson. *Fort Smith, Little Gibraltar on the Arkansas*. 2d ed. Norman: University of Oklahoma Press, 1979.

Bischoff, John Paul. *Mr. Iba: Basketball's Aggie Iron Duke*. Oklahoma City: Oklahoma Heritage Association, 1980.

Blackburn, Bob. *Heart of the Promised Land: Oklahoma County, An Illustrated History*. Woodland Hills: Windsor Publications, 1982.

Blackburn, Bob. *Heritage Hills: Preservation of a Historic Neighborhood*. Oklahoma City: Western Heritage Books, 1990.

Bonnifield, Paul. *The Dust Bowl: Men, Dirt, and Depression*. Albuquerque: University of New Mexico Press, 1979.

Bryant, Keith L. *Alfalfa Bill Murray*. Norman: University of Oklahoma Press, 1979.

Burke, Bob and Tom Butler. *Flowers to Philanthropy: The Life of Herman Meinders*. Oklahoma City: Oklahoma Heritage Association, 2004.

Burke, Bob and Reba Neighbors Collins. *Alice Robertson: Congresswoman from Oklahoma*. Oklahoma City: Oklahoma Heritage Association and University of Central Oklahoma, 2001.

Burke, Bob, and Angela Monson. *Roscoe Dunjee: Champion of Civil Rights*. Oklahoma City: Oklahoma Heritage Association, 1998.

Burke, Bob, and Betty Crow. *The House Oklahoma Built: A History of the Oklahoma Governors Mansion*. Oklahoma City: Oklahoma Heritage Association, 2001.

Burke, Bob, and Gini Moore Campbell. *Lee Allan Smith: Oklahoma's Best Friend*. Oklahoma City: Oklahoma Heritage Association, 2005.

Burke, Bob, Betty Crow, and Sandy Meyers. *Art Treasures of the Oklahoma State Capitol*. Oklahoma City: Oklahoma State Senate Historical Preservation Fund, Inc., 2003.

Burke, Bob, Kenny A. Franks, and Royce Parr. *Glory Days of Summer: The History of Baseball in Oklahoma*. Oklahoma City: Oklahoma Heritage Association, 1999.

Burke, Bob. *From Oklahoma to Eternity: The Life of Wiley Post and the Winnie Mae*. Oklahoma City: Oklahoma Heritage Association, 1998.

Carter, L. Edward. *The Story of Oklahoma Newspapers—1844 to 1984*. Oklahoma City: Oklahoma Heritage Association, 1984.

Carter, L. Edward. *The Story of Oklahoma's Newspapers, 1884-1984*. Oklahoma City: Oklahoma Heritage Association, 1984

Colcord, Charles. *The Autobiography of Charles Colcord*. Tulsa: Privately Printed, 1970.

Crockett, Norman. *The Black Towns*. Lawrence: Regents Press of Kansas, 1979.

Cross, George Lynn. *Blacks in White Colleges: Oklahoma's Landmark Cases*. Norman: University of Oklahoma Press, 1975.

Cross, George Lynn. *President's Can't Punt: The OU Football Tradition*. Norman: University of Oklahoma Press, 1977.

Dale, Edward Everett, Gene Aldrich. *History of Oklahoma*. Edmond: Thompson Book and Supply Company, 1972.

Debo, Angie. *And Still the Waters Run: The Betrayal of the Five Civilized Tribes*. Princeton: Princeton University Press, 1940, 1990.

Debo, Angie. *Oklahoma, Foot-loose and Fancy-free*. Norman: University of Oklahoma Press, 1949, 1987.

Debo, Angie. *Prairie City: The Story of an American Community*. 1944. Reprint. Tulsa: Council Oaks Publishing Company, 1992.

Debo, Angie. *Rise and Fall of the Choctaw Republic*. Norman: University of Oklahoma Press, 1972.

Debo, Angie. The Road to Disappearance: A History of the Creek Indians. Norman: University of Oklahoma Press, 1941.

Egan, Timothy. *The Worst Hard Time: The Untold Story of Those Who Survived the Great American Dust Bowl*. Boston: Houghton Mifflin Company, 2006.

Faulk, Odie B. and Bill Welge. *Oklahoma: A Rich Heritage*. Sun Valley: American Heritage Press, 2004.

Faulk, Odie B., Kenny A. Franks, and Paul F. Lambert, eds. *Early Military Forts and Posts in Oklahoma*. Oklahoma City: Oklahoma Historical Society, 1978.

Faulk, Odie B., Laura E. Faulk, and Sally Gray. *Imagination and Ability: The Life of Lloyd Noble*. Oklahoma City: Oklahoma Heritage Association, 1995.

Fischer, LeRoy H., ed. *Oklahoma's Governors, 1907-1929: Turbulent Politics*. Oklahoma City: Oklahoma Historical Society, 1981.

Fischer, LeRoy H., ed. *Oklahoma's Governors, 1929-1955: Depression to Prosperity*. Oklahoma City: Oklahoma Historical Society, 1983.

Fischer, LeRoy H., ed. *Oklahoma's Governors, 1955-1979: Growth and Reform*. Oklahoma City: Oklahoma Historical Society, 1985.

Fischer, LeRoy H., ed. *The Territorial Governors of Oklahoma*. Oklahoma City: Oklahoma Historical Society, 1975.

Foreman, Grant. Indian Removal: *The Emigration of the Five Civilized Tribes of Indians*. Norman: University of Oklahoma Press, 1932.

Foreman, Grant. *Indians and Pioneers*. Norman: University of Oklahoma Press, 1936.

Foreman, Grant. *Pioneer Days in the Early Southwest*. Cleveland: Arthur H. Clark, 1926.

Foreman, Grant. *The Five Civilized Tribes*. Norman: University of Oklahoma Press, 1934, 1966.

Franklin, Jimmie Lewis. *Journey Toward Hope: A History of Blacks in Oklahoma*. Norman: University of Oklahoma Press, 1982.

Franklin, John Hope and John Whittington Franklin, eds. *My Life and an Era: The Autobiography of John Hope Franklin*. Baton Rouge: Louisiana State University Press, 1997

Franks, Kenny A. *Citizen Soldier: Oklahoma's National Guard*. Norman: University of Oklahoma Press, 1984.

Franks, Kenny A. The Oklahoma Petroleum Industry. Norman: University of Oklahoma Press, 1980.

Franks, Kenny A., Paul F. Lambert, and Carl N. Tyson. *Early Oklahoma Oil: A Photographic History, 1859-1939*. College Station: Texas A&M University Press, 1981.

Garrison, Denzil. *Remembrances of a Redleg: The Story of a Korean War Artilleryman of the 45th Thunderbird Division*. Oklahoma City: Oklahoma Heritage Association, 2003.

Gibson, Arrell M. *America's Exiles: Indian Colonization in Oklahoma*. Oklahoma City: Oklahoma Historical Society, 1976.

Gibson, Arrell M. *Oklahoma: A History of Five Centuries*. 2d ed. Norman: University of Oklahoma Press, 1981.

Gibson, Arrell M. *The Chickasaws*. Norman: University of Oklahoma Press, 1971.

Goble, Danney. *Progressive Oklahoma: The Making of a New Kind of State*. Norman: University of Oklahoma Press, 1980.

Goble, Danney, and W. David Baird. *The Story of Oklahoma*. Norman: University of Oklahoma Press, 1981.

Goins, Charles R., and John W. Morris. *Oklahoma Homes, Past and Present*. Norman: University of Oklahoma Press, 1980.

Green, Donald E. *Panhandle Pioneer: Henry C. Hitch, His Ranch, and His Family*. Oklahoma City: Oklahoma Heritage Association, 1979.

Green, Donald E., ed. *Rural Oklahoma*. Oklahoma City: Oklahoma Historical Society, 1977.

Green, Richard. *Te Ata: Chickasaw Storyteller, American Treasure*. Norman: University of Oklahoma Press, 2002.

Greenberg, Jonathan D. *Staking a Claim: Jake Simmons and the Making of an African-American Oil Dynasty*. New York: McMillan Publishing Company, 1990.

Gregory, James N. *American Exodus: The Dust Bowl Migration and Okie Culture in California*. New York: Oxford University Press, 1989.

Guthrie, Woody. *Bound for Glory*. New York: E. P. Dutton, 1943.

Hendrickson, Kenneth D., Jr., ed. *Hard Times in Oklahoma: The Depression Years*. Oklahoma City: Oklahoma Historical Society, 1983.

Hoig, Stan. *Tribal Wars of the Southern Plains*. Norman: University of Oklahoma Press, 1992.

Hurst, Irvin. *The Forty-sixth Star: A History of Oklahoma's Constitutional Convention and Early Statehood*. Oklahoma City: Semco Color Press, 1957.

Irving, Washington. *A Tour on the Prairies*. Edited with an introductory essay by John Francis McDermott. Norman: University of Oklahoma Press, 1956.

Jayroe, Jane, with Bob Burke. *More Grace than Glamour: My Life as Miss America and Beyond*. Oklahoma City: Oklahoma Heritage Association, 2006.

Jones, Kim, and Carl Gregory, Keith Tolman, and Bill Moore. *The Oklahoma Aviation Story*. Oklahoma City: Oklahoma Heritage Association, 2004.

Klein, Joe. *Woody Guthrie: A Life*. New York: Alfred A. Knopf, 1980.

Lambert, Paul F. *Never Give Up! The Life of Pearl Carter Scott*. Ada: Chickasaw Press, 2007.

Lambert, Paul F., Kenny A. Franks, and Bob Burke. *Historic Oklahoma: An Illustrated History*. Oklahoma City: Oklahoma Heritage Association, 2000.

Littlefield, Daniel F., Jr. *Alex Posey: Creek Poet, Journalist, and Humorist*. Lincoln: University of Nebraska Press, 1992.

Loughlin, Patti. *Hidden Treasures of the American West*. Albuquerque: University of New Mexico Press, 2005.

Luper, Clara. *Behold the Walls*. Oklahoma City: Jim Wire, 1979.

Marshall, Paul, with Brian Miller and Sandy Miller. A Piece of the Pie. Tulsa: Privately Printed, 1987.

Masterson, V. V., *The Katy Railroad and the Last Frontier.* Norman: University of Oklahoma Press, 1952.

McReynolds, Edwin C. *Oklahoma: A History of the Sooner State*. Norman: University of Oklahoma Press, 1954, 1964.

Meredith, Howard, and Mary Ellen Meredith. *Mr. Oklahoma History: The Life of George H. Shirk.* Oklahoma City: Oklahoma Heritage Association, 1982.

Milsten, David R. *Thomas Gilcrease*. San Antonio: Naylor, 1969.

Morris, John W., Charles R. Goins, and Edwin C. McReynolds. *Historical Atlas of Oklahoma*. Norman: University of Oklahoma Press, 1986.

Morris, John W., ed. *Drill Bits, Picks, and Shovels: A History of Mineral Resources in Oklahoma*. Oklahoma City: Oklahoma Historical Society, 1982.

Morris, John W., ed. *Geography of Oklahoma*. Oklahoma City: Oklahoma Historical Society, 1977.

Myers, Fred A. *Art Treasures of the Gilcrease Museum*. Tulsa: Thomas Gilcrease Museum Association, 1984

Ormsby, Waterman L. *The Butterfield Overland Mail*. San Marino: Huntington Library, 1942.

Rabb, Penn. *Tomahawk and Peace Pipe: The 179th Infantry Regiment*. Oklahoma City: Oklahoma Heritage Association, 2000.

Ruth, Kent, and Jim Argo. *Window on the Past: Historic Places in Oklahoma*. Oklahoma City: Oklahoma Historical Society. 1984.

Ruth, Kent. *Oklahoma Travel Handbook*. Norman: University of Oklahoma Press, 1977.

Scales, James R., and Danney Goble. *Oklahoma Politics: A History*. Norman: University of Oklahoma Press, 1981.

Shirley, Glenn. *Law West of Fort Smith*. Lincoln: University of Nebraska Press, 1957, 1968.

Skaggs, Jimmy M., ed. *Ranch and Range in Oklahoma.* Oklahoma City: Oklahoma Historical Society, 1978.

Stafford, Thomas P., with Michael Cassutt. *We Have Capture: Tom Stafford and the Space Race*. Washington, D. C.: Smithsonian Institution Press, 2002.

Stout, Joseph A., Jr., ed. *Frontier Adventurers: American Exploration in Oklahoma*. Oklahoma City: Oklahoma Historical Society, 1976.

Strickland, Rennard. *The Indians in Oklahoma*. Norman: University of Oklahoma Press, 1980.

Turner, John S., and Michael J. Brodhead. *A Naturalist in Indian Territory: The Journals of S. W. Woodhouse, 1849-50.* Norman: University of Oklahoma Press, 1981.

Utley, Robert M. Frontiersmen in Blue: *The United States Army and the Indian, 1848-1864*. Lincoln: University of Nebraska Press, 1981.

Wright, Peggy Quinn, and Odie B. Faulk. *Coletta: A Sister of Mercy*. Oklahoma City: Oklahoma Heritage Association, 1981.

ARTICLES

Avery, Ruth Sigler. "Cyrus Stevens Avery." *The Chronicles of Oklahoma*. 45(1967) 84-91.

Boggs, Frank. "Geary Writer Unfolds Travel Lore." *The Daily Oklahoman*, May 18, 1986, 23.

Bruce, Michael. "Our Best Men are Fast Leaving Us: The Life and Times of Robert M. Jones." *The Chronicles of Oklahoma*. 66 (Fall 1988) 294-305.

Campbell, Gini Moore. "Attention to Detail: Oklahoma's Own Greg Burns." *Oklahoma: Magazine of the Oklahoma Heritage Association.* 8 (Fall/Winter 2003-2004): 3-7, 32.

Challacombe, Doris. "Alexander Lawrence Posey." *The Chronicles of Oklahoma*. 11(1933): 1011-1018.

Daily Oklahoman, The. "NCO Association Chapter to Honor War Hero's Folks." April 1, 1967, 5.

Daily Oklahoman, The. "Sooner Wins Korean War's Second Congressional Medal of Honor." January 1, 1951, 31.

Daily Oklahoman,The. "State GI Wins Top Medal for Korea Bravery." July 13, 1952, 119.

DeFrange, Ann. "Ruth's Old House Becomes Geary Museum Site." *The Daily Oklahoman*, April 23, 1994, 108.

Gilliland, Pat. "McAlester Bankers Decide to Give Back." *Daily Oklahoman*. April 18, 1999, 112.

Harris, Rodger, Bob Blackburn, "Whatever Happened to 3D Danny? The Golden Age of Oklahoma Television, 1949-1974," *The Chronicles of Oklahoma*. 69(1991): 228-255.

Hutchison, Mark A. "Hero's Bravery Remembered." *Daily Oklahoman*, November 11, 1999, 1.

Kroeker, Marvin E. "Mennonites in the Oklahoma Land Rushes." *The Chronicles of Oklahoma.* 67(Spring 1989): 76-95.

LeFebvre, Irene. "Painter of the Prairies." *The Daily Oklahoman. Orbit Magazine*, November 14, 1965, 6, 12.

Love, Bernice. "Three State Beauties Bring Home Miss America Crown." *The Daily Oklahoman*, November 15, 1987, 160.

Maddox, Cynthia. "The Art of the Old West*.*"*Southern Living.* (July, 1989), 20-21.

Mazumdar, Maitreyi. "Alice's Restaurant: Expanding a Woman's Sphere." *The Chronicles of Oklahoma*. 70(1992): 302-325.

McDonnell, Brandy. "Philanthropist's Efforts Reflect Community Spirit." *The Daily Oklahoman*, January 19, 2003, 72.

Mellinger, Phillip. "Discrimination and Statehood in Oklahoma." *The Chronicles of Oklahoma* 49(1971): 43-78.

Miles, Ray. "King of the Wildcatters: Tom Slick and the Cushing Oil Field." *The Chronicles of Oklahoma*. 65(Summer 1987): 173.

Morrison, Daryl, "Twin Territories: The Indian Magazine and its editor, Ora Eddleman Reed," *The Chronicles of Oklahoma*. 60(1982): 136-166.

Nesbitt, Paul. "J. J. McAlester." *The Chronicles of Oklahoma*. 11(1933):758-64.

Pemberton, Tricia. "Artist Shuts Shop, But Still Sells." *The Daily Oklahoman*, October 15, 2005, 4B.

Peters, Edmund. "Joseph Danne: Oklahoma Plant Geneticist and His Triumph Wheat." *The Chronicles of Oklahoma*. 59(1981): 54-72.

Shirk, George H. "Oklahomans in Space." *The Chronicles of Oklahoma.* 52(1974): 139-148.

OTHER SOURCES

Vertical files, Oklahoma History Center Library
Oklahoma Hall of Fame Archive Files, Oklahoma Heritage Association

INTERNET WEBSITES

www.45thdivisionmuseum.com
www.bama.com
www.baseballhalloffame.com
www.bioguide.congress.gov
www.edgarcruz.com
www.gilcrease.com
www.heisman.com
www.hoophall.com
www.hq.nasa.gov
www.jsc.nasa.gov
www.koreanwar.org
www.medalofhonor.com
www.metcalfemuseum.com
www.missamerica.org
www.nationalcowboymuseum.com
www.ok-history.mus.ok.us
www.profootballhall.com
www.womenshistory.about.com
www.woodyguthrie.org

Index